القُرآنُ الكَريمُ

ترجمة ودراسة

THE QUR'AN
Translation and Study

JUZ 30

عَمَّ يَتَسَآءَلُونَ

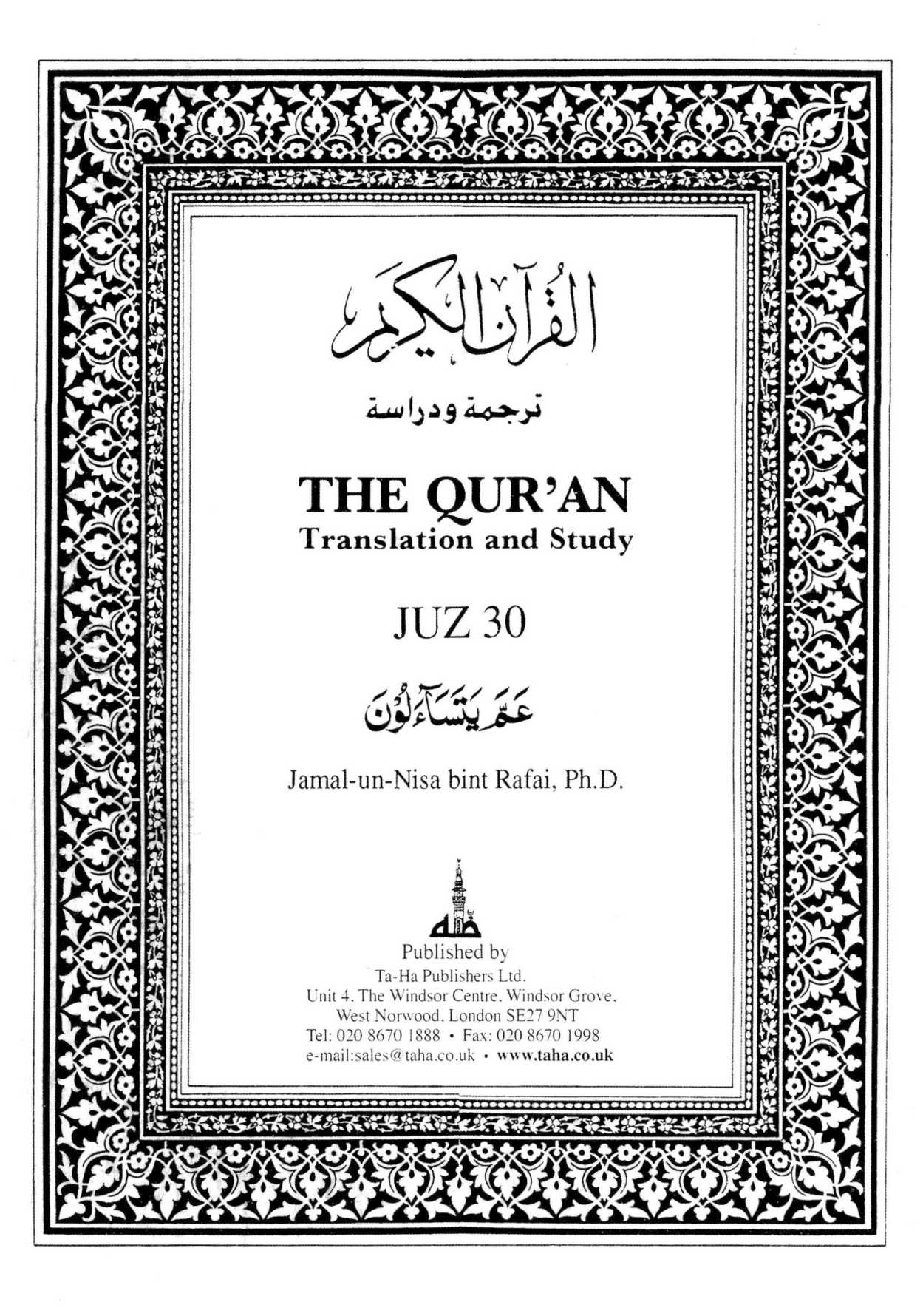

Jamal-un-Nisa bint Rafai, Ph.D.

Published by
Ta-Ha Publishers Ltd.
Unit 4, The Windsor Centre, Windsor Grove,
West Norwood, London SE27 9NT
Tel: 020 8670 1888 • Fax: 020 8670 1998
e-mail:sales@taha.co.uk • www.taha.co.uk

© 1416 AH/1995 CE Ta-Ha Publishers Ltd.
First Published in February 1995
Reprinted 1999, 2013

Ta-Ha Publishers Ltd.
Unit 4, The Windsor Centre
Windsor Grove, West Norwood
London, SE27 9NT, UK
www.tahapublishers.com
support@tahapublishers.com

All rights reserved. No part of this publication may be
reproduced, stored in any retrieval system, or transmitted in
any form or by any means, electronic, mechanical, photocopying,
recording or otherwise, without the prior written permission
of the publishers.

by: Jamal-un-Nisa bint Rafai
Edited by: Abdassamad Clarke

A catalogue record of this book is available from the British Library

ISBN: 978 1 89794 035 8

Printed and bound by:
Mega Basim, Turkey

بسم الله الرحمن الرحيم

Acknowledgements

I firstly thank Allah (SWT), all praise is for Him, the All-Kind and Merciful. Then my cordial thanks to ʿAbdassamad Clarke and Ridwan Mohammed for their generously lavished help in the grammatical analysis of the Qur'anic text; I acknowledge my deep gratitude for all the pains they took in going through this work and giving me the help I needed to carry it out. I thank ʿAbdassamad Clarke for the laborious work of typesetting. I deeply thank the artist Brother Muhammad Ishaq for the difficult job of beautifully pasting up the Qur'anic text in a very short time in spite of his ill-health (may Allah grant him good health). In grateful appreciation I thank my parents and teachers who taught me the Qur'an (may Allah grant them the *Jannah*). Last but not least I acknowledge with apprecation and deeply thank my daughter Abia and my husband Afsar Siddiqui for their help, patience and encouragement, and my husband who cheerfully carried out the thankless but difficult job of converting the scattered typeset material into book form. Again I thank Allah (SWT) the All-Knowing and Wise.

Jamal-un-Nisa bint Rafai,

Merton Park,

London,

1 Rabiʿ al-Awwal 1416AH/28th July 1995CE.

بِسْمِ اللَّهِ الرَّحْمَٰنِ الرَّحِيمِ

In the name of Allah
The Merciful the Compassionate

DEDICATION

With genuine humility, I acknowledge YOUR Aid, O' ALLAH. Without Your Guidance and Help this work would not have been possible. I thank YOU O' ALLAH. It is dedicated to YOU, O' ALLAH. Please bless it with YOUR Acceptance.

Contents

Surah 78	An-Naba'	النَّبَإِ	8
Surah 79	An-Nazi'at	النَّازِعَات	17
Surah 80	'Abasa	عَبَسَ	26
Surah 81	At-Takwir	التَّكْوِير	33
Surah 82	Al-Infitar	الانْفِطَار	38
Surah 83	Al-Mutaffifin or At-Tatfif	المطففين	42
Surah 84	Al-Inshiqaq	الانْشِقَاق	49
Surah 85	Al-Buruj	البُرُوج	54
Surah 86	At-Tariq	الطَّارِق	59
Surah 87	Al-A'la	الأعْلَى	62
Surah 88	Al-Ghashiyah	الغَاشِيَة	66
Surah 89	Al-Fajr	الفَجْر	70
Surah 90	Al-Balad	البَلَد	77
Surah 91	Ash-Shams	الشَّمْس	81
Surah 92	Al-Layl	اللَّيْل	85
Surah 93	Ad-Duha	الضُّحَى	89
Surah 94	Ash-Sharh	الشَّرْح	92
Surah 95	At-Tin	التِّين	94
Surah 96	Al-'Alaq	العَلَق	97
Surah 97	Al-Qadr	القَدْر	101
Surah 98	Al-Bayyinah	البَيِّنَة	104
Surah 99	Az-Zilzal	الزِّلْزَلَة	108
Surah 100	Al-'Adiyat	العَادِيَات	111
Surah 101	Al-Qari'ah	القَارِعَة	114
Surah 102	At-Takathur	التَّكَاثُر	116
Surah 103	Al-'Asr	العَصْر	118
Surah 104	Al-Humazah	الهُمَزَة	120
Surah 105	Al-Fil	الفِيل	123
Surah 106	Quraysh	قُرَيش	126
Surah 107	Al-Ma'un	المَاعُون	128
Surah 108	Al-Kawthar	الكَوْثَر	131
Surah 109	Al-Kafirun	الكَافِرُون	133
Surah 110	An-Nasr	النَّصْر	135
Surah 111	Al-Lahab or Al-Masad	المَسَد	137
Surah 112	Al-Ikhlas	الإخْلاص	139
Surah 113	Al-Falaq	الفَلَق	141
Surah 114	An-Nas	النَّاس	144
Prayer	To be read after reciting the Glorious Qur'an		146

Abbreviations

(For fuller explanation of grammar see the appropriate sections of Juz 1, 2&3, and 4, or the companion volume to be published to accompany this volume when purchased alone.)

I., II., III.,	First, Second and Third Persons respectively
acc.	Accusative
act. prtc.	Active participle (*Fa‘ilun*)
adj.	Adjective
adj. pat.	Adjectival Pattern
adj. sup. dg.	Adjective, superlative degree
adv.	Adverb or adverbially used
amr	Imperative mood of the verb denoting an order
att.	Attached
br. pl.	Broken plural
card. no.	Cardinal number
class.	Classification
coll. noun	Collective noun
cond. ptcl.	Conditioned particle
conj.	Conjunction
def.	Definite
dem pro.	Demonstrative pronoun
dipt.	Diptote/second declension
dr. vrb. II to X	Derived Verbal Forms, frequently mentioned in the Root Words
elat.	Elative
emph.	Emphasis
exc.	Exception
exh.	Exhortation, an indirect imperative (i.e. G with jussive mood of *mudari‘* e.g. 'let him...')
fem.	Feminine gender
fut.	Future
gen.	Genitive
gh.	*Ghair munsarif* (does not show by its endings nom., acc., and gen.)

VI

imp.	Imperative
indecl.	Indeclinable
inter.	Interrogative
interj.	Interjective
juss. md.	Jussive mood of the verb
maj.	*Majhool*, the passive form of the verb
mdf.	*Mudaf* (that which is annexed)
mdfi	*Mudaf Ilayh* (that to which it is annexed)
msc.	Masculine gender
nahy	Prohibition, a negative command
negn.	Negation
nom.	Nominative
obj.	Object
ord. no.	Ordinal Number (i.e. first, second., etc.)
past cont.	Past Continuous
per.	Personal
pass. prtc.	Passive participle (*Maf^coolun*)
past cont.	Past continuous
pl.	Plural number
prec.	Preceding
pred.	Predicate
prep.	Preposition (note that many of the particles are prepositions, and that this term will be gradually introduced during the book in place of the more general particle).
pro.	Pronoun
prop.	Proper (i.e. nouns)
ptcl(s).	Particle(s) (some of which are prepositions; see note above).
quad.	Quadriliteral
rel. adj.	Relative adjective
rel. pro.	Relative Pronoun
rep.	Repetition (e.g. فَعَّال a doer repeatedly)
rt. w.	Root word
sing.	Singular number
snd. pl.	Sound plural
subj.	Subject
subj. md.	Subjunctive mood of the verb
subst.	Substantive
tetra.	Tetraliteral – a four lettered root
voc.	Vocative
vrb. n.	Verbal noun or noun of action

Makki Surah

Surah 78 An-Naba'

40 *Ayat*

Meaning	Words	Meaning	Words
They shall soon know (Future III. msc. pl.)	سَيَعْلَمُونَ	About what[1] Concerning what (ptcls.)	عَمَّ
Again, by no means (they can escape it) (ptcls.)	ثُمَّ كَلَّا	Do they ask one another? They ask each other? (dr. vrb. VI *mudari*ᶜ III. msc. pl.)	يَتَسَاءَلُونَ
They shall soon know (Future III. msc. pl.)	سَيَعْلَمُونَ	About (ptcl.)	عَنِ
Did We not make? (*Alif* ptcl. inter., *mudari*ᶜ with لَمْ[3] I. pl.)	أَلَمْ نَجْعَلِ	The news[2] (def. noun gen.)	النَّبَإِ
The earth (def. noun acc.)	الْأَرْضَ	The great[2] (adj. gen.)	الْعَظِيمِ
A resting place A place of wide extent (noun acc.)	مِهَادًا	The one (rel. pro.)	الَّذِي
And the mountains (def. noun br. pl. acc.)	وَالْجِبَالَ	They in it (i.e. the great news) (pro., ptcl., pro.)	هُمْ فِيهِ
Stakes or pegs[4] (to fix the earth) (noun br. pl. acc.)	أَوْتَادًا	Differing with one another (act. prtc. dr. vrb VIII pl. nom.)	مُخْتَلِفُونَ
And We created you (ptcl., *madi* I. pl., pro.)	وَخَلَقْنَاكُمْ	Nay, verily By no means, (they can escape it) (ptcl.)	كَلَّا

[1] عَمَّ is originally عَنْ + مَا the الف being elided in the interrogation after the preposition عَنْ. مَا when used interrogatively after a prefixed preposition, the *Alif* is generally omitted and both prepositions united in writing. Therefore عَنْ + مَا becomes عَمَّ.

[2] the news of the Resurrection and the Hereafter.

[3] لَمْ always precedes *mudari*ᶜ to denote the negative meaning of a *madi* with emphasis on it.

[4] Refer *Surah* 16 *ayah* 15 which explains the purpose of mountains acting as pegs.

Surah 78 An-Naba'

Meaning	Words	Meaning	Words
A lamp (the sun) (noun acc.)	سِرَاجًا	In pairs (as two different sexes, as msc. and fem.) (noun br. pl. acc.)	أَزْوَاجًا
Brightly burning (adj. acc.)	وَهَّاجًا	And We made (ptcl., *madi* I. pl.)	وَجَعَلْنَا
And We sent down (ptcl., dr. vrb. IV *madi* I. pl.)	وَأَنزَلْنَا	Your sleep (vrb. n. acc., pro. pl.)	نَوْمَكُمْ
From the wind-driven clouds/rainfilled (ptcl., act. part. dr. vrb. IV fem. pl. gen.)	مِنَ الْمُعْصِرَاتِ	(as) A rest (noun acc.)	سُبَاتًا
Water pouring in abundance (noun acc., adj. acc.)	مَاءً ثَجَّاجًا	And We made (ptcl., *madi* I. pl.)	وَجَعَلْنَا
That We bring forth thereby (ptcl., dr. vrb. IV *mudari* I. pl., ptcl., rel. pro.)	لِنُخْرِجَ بِهِ	The night (def. noun acc.)	الَّيْلَ
Grains and vegetation (noun, acc., ptcl., noun acc.)	حَبًّا وَنَبَاتًا	A covering (noun acc.)	لِبَاسًا
And gardens (ptcl., noun br. pl. acc.)	وَجَنَّاتٍ	And We made (ptcl., *madi* I. pl.)	وَجَعَلْنَا
Dense with foliage with thick trees (adj. br. pl. acc.)	أَلْفَافًا	The day (def. noun acc.)	النَّهَارَ
Indeed, the Day of Distinction (between good and evil) (ptcl., noun acc. *mdf.*, noun *mdfi.*)	إِنَّ يَوْمَ الْفَصْلِ	To seek livelihood to do the necessary to support life (noun acc.)	مَعَاشًا
Is certainly an appointed time (كَانَ emph., noun acc.)	كَانَ مِيقَاتًا	And We built (ptcl., *madi* I. pl.)	وَبَنَيْنَا
		Above you (فَوْقَ noun used as ptcl., pro. pl.)	فَوْقَكُمْ
		Seven strong, firm (Heavens) (card. no. acc., adj. pl.)	سَبْعًا شِدَادًا
A day (in which) shall be blown in (noun adv., *mudari* maj. III. msc. sing., ptcl.)	يَوْمَ يُنفَخُ فِي	And We made (ptcl., *madi* I. pl.)	وَجَعَلْنَا

Meaning	Words	Meaning	Words
Is lying in wait, a place of ambush (*madi* III. fem. sing., noun acc.)	كَانَتْ مِرْصَادًا	The Trumpet (def. noun gen.)	الصُّورِ
For the transgressors (ptcl., def. noun pl. gen.)	لِلطَّاغِينَ	Then you all shall come (ptcl., *mudari'* II. msc. pl.)	فَتَأْتُونَ
A place of return, fixed abode, dwelling place (noun acc.)	مَآبًا	In multitudes (noun br. pl. acc.)	أَفْوَاجًا
(They) continuing to remain or dwell (act. part. pl. acc.)	لَّابِثِينَ	And shall be opened (ptcl., *madi* maj. III. fem. sing.)	وَفُتِحَتِ
In her (Hell) (ptcl., pro. fem.)	فِيهَآ	The sky, the heaven (def. noun nom.)	السَّمَآءُ
For a long time, for ages (noun br. pl. acc.)	أَحْقَابًا	So[5] (there) will be doors (in it) So[5] it will come to be (have) doors (ptcl., *madi* III. fem. sing., noun br. pl. acc.)	فَكَانَتْ أَبْوَابًا
They shall not taste (ptcl. negn., *mudari'* III. msc. pl.)	لَا يَذُوقُونَ	And will be moved uprooted, made to vanish (ptcl., dr. vrb. II *madi* maj. III. fem. sing.)	وَسُيِّرَتِ
In her (Hell) (ptcl., pro.)	فِيهَا	The mountains (def. noun br. pl. nom.)	الْجِبَالُ
Coolness (noun acc.)	بَرْدًا	So[5] they were (as if) a mirage (ptcl., *madi* III. fem. sing., noun acc.)	فَكَانَتْ سَرَابًا
Nor any drink (ptcls., noun acc.)	وَلَا شَرَابًا	Indeed, Hell (ptcl., noun dipt. acc.)	إِنَّ جَهَنَّمَ
Except hot water (ptcl. exc., noun acc.)	إِلَّا حَمِيمًا		
And the washing from wounds (ptcl., noun acc.)	وَغَسَّاقًا		
A recompense or reward (noun adv. acc.)	جَزَآءً	[5] فَ is a particle of classification or gradation which sometimes unites simple words but more usually connects two clauses.	

Surah 78 An-Naba'

Words	Meaning	Words	Meaning
وِفَاقًا	Suitable, fitting (vrb. n. dr. vrb. III acc.)	فَلَنْ نَزِيدَكُمْ	So We will never increase you (ptcl., *mudari* with لَنْ [6] subjunctive mood I. pl., pro.)
إِنَّهُمْ	Indeed they (ptcl., pro. pl.)	إِلَّا عَذَابًا	Except (in) punishment. (ptcl. exc., noun acc.)
كَانُوا لَا يَرْجُونَ	Were not expecting, not hoping (past cont. III. msc. pl.)	إِنَّ لِلْمُتَّقِينَ	Indeed, for the Allah-conscious ones (ptcls., act. part. dr. vrb. VIII msc. pl. gen.)
حِسَابًا	(to be called to give) an account (noun acc.)	مَفَازًا	Real victory, supreme achievement (noun acc.)
وَكَذَّبُوا	And they belied, denied, called a lie (ptcl., dr. vrb. II *madi* III. msc. pl.)	حَدَائِقَ	Gardens (noun fem. pl. acc.)
بِآيَاتِنَا	(With) Our signs (ptcl., noun pl. gen. *mdf*, rel. pro. *mdfi*.)	وَأَعْنَابًا	And grapes (vineyards) (ptcl., noun br. pl. acc.)
كِذَّابًا	(With) a denial (vrb. n. dr. vrb. II acc.)	وَكَوَاعِبَ	And full-breasted maidens (act. part. fem br. pl. acc.)
وَكُلَّ شَيْءٍ	And every thing (ptcl., noun *mdf.* acc., noun *mdfi*.)	أَتْرَابًا	Of same age (noun br. pl. acc.)
أَحْصَيْنَاهُ	We numbered it (dr. vrb. IV *madi* I. pl., pro.)	وَكَأْسًا	And a cup (ptcl., noun acc.)
كِتَابًا	(in writing, on record) (in)a book (vrb. n. acc.)	دِهَاقًا	Full, overflowing (vrb. n. acc.)
فَذُوقُوا	So taste (ptcl., *amr* II. msc. pl.)	لَا يَسْمَعُونَ	They shall not hear (ptcl. negn., *mudari* III. msc. pl.)
		فِيهَا	In her (the Gardens) (ptcl., pro. fem.)

[6] the particle لَنْ (a construction of لَا and أَنْ) which precedes the subjunctive mood of *mudari* denotes very strong negation of the future (consult Juz 1 p.102 old ed., p.106 new ed., Juz 2&3 p.129)

Words	Meaning	Words	Meaning
لَغْوًا	(Neither) empty talk, vain discourse (noun acc.)	يَقُومُ	Shall stand (*mudari'* III. msc. sing.)
وَلَا كِذَّابًا	nor any lie (ptcls., negn., vrb. n. dr. vrb. II acc.)	الرُّوحُ	The Spirit (the angel Jibril {AS}) (def. noun nom.)
جَزَاءً مِّن رَّبِّكَ	A reward from your Lord (noun acc., ptcl., noun gen. *mdf.*, pro. *mdfi*.)	وَالْمَلَٰٓئِكَةُ	And the angels (ptcl., noun br. pl. nom.)
عَطَاءً	A gift (in accordance with) (noun acc.)	صَفًّا	In rows, in a line, rank (vrb. n. adv. acc.)
حِسَابًا	(His) account or reckoning (noun acc.)	لَّا يَتَكَلَّمُونَ	They shall not speak (ptcl. negn., dr. vrb. V *mudari'* III. msc. pl.)
رَّبِّ السَّمَٰوَٰتِ	The Lord of the heavens (noun gen. *mdf.*, noun fem. pl. *mdfi*.)	إِلَّا مَنْ	Except whomever (ptcl. exc., pro.)
وَالْأَرْضِ	And the earth (ptcl., def. noun *mdfi*.)	أَذِنَ لَهُ	He has given permission to him (*madi* III. msc. sing., prtc., pro.)
وَمَا بَيْنَهُمَا	And what is between the two (ptcl., ptcl. *mdfi.*, ptcl., pro. dual)	الرَّحْمَٰنُ	The Most Gracious (All-Merciful) (def. noun nom.)
الرَّحْمَٰنِ	The Most Gracious (All-Merciful) (def. noun gen.)		
لَا يَمْلِكُونَ	They shall not have (the power) (ptcl. negn., *mudari'* III. msc. pl.)	وَقَالَ	And he said (ptcl., *madi* III. msc. sing.)
مِنْهُ	Before Him (ptcl., pro.)	صَوَابًا	That which is right (noun acc.)
خِطَابًا	To speak, (vrb. n. acc.)	ذَٰلِكَ الْيَوْمُ	That is the day (dem. pro. msc. sing., def. noun)
يَوْمَ	(On the) day (noun adv. acc.)	الْحَقُّ	The True (def. noun adj.)
		فَمَن شَآءَ	So whoever wished (prtcl., pro., *madi* III. msc. sing.)

Surah 78 An-Naba'

Words	Meaning	Words	Meaning
اتَّخَذَ	Took (himself), has taken (dr. vrb. VIII *madi* III. msc. sing.)	الْمَرْءُ	The man (def. noun nom.)
إِلَى رَبِّهِ	Towards his Lord (ptcl., noun gen. *mdf.*, pro. *mdfi.*)	مَا قَدَّمَتْ	What (she) advanced (dr. vrb. II *madi* III. fem. sing.)
مَآبًا	A place of return fixed abode, dwelling place (noun acc.)	يَدَاهُ	His hands (noun dual nom. *mdf.*, pro. *mdfi.*)
إِنَّا أَنذَرْنَاكُمْ	Indeed We, We warned you (ptcl., pro., dr. vrb. IV *madi* I. pl., pro. pl.)	وَيَقُولُ	And shall say (ptcl., *mudari* III. msc. sing.)
عَذَابًا قَرِيبًا	Suffering near at hand (noun acc., adj. acc.)	الْكَافِرُ	The disbeliever (def. noun nom.)
يَوْمَ	(On) a day (when) (adv. noun)	يَالَيْتَنِي	O, would that[7] I, (ptcl. voc.., ptcl. of desire, pro.)
يَنظُرُ	Shall look at, see (*mudari* III. msc. sing.)	كُنتُ تُرَابًا	I were dust. (*madi* I. msc. sing., noun acc.)

[7] لَيْتَ (Would that) + نِي (I) = لَيْتَنِي

Root Words for Surah 78

التَّبَأ The news, نَبَأَ * he was exalted, he announced, نَبَأ pl. أَنْبَاء news, نَبِيّ prophet, pl. أَنْبِيَاء and نَبِيُّونَ (dipt.) نَبَّأَ dr. vrb. II he made acquainted with.

مِهَادًا A couch, resting place, a place of wide extent, مَهَدَ * he spread open a bed.

أَوْتَادًا Stakes, وَتِدٌ a stake (sing.) يَتِدُ وَتَدَ * he drove in a stake.

أَزْوَاجًا Spouses, husbands or wives, kinds, pairs, species, زَوْج (sing.), زَاجَ * he stirred up strife.

سُبَاتًا Rest, سَبَتَ * he rested, he celebrated the sabbath.

لِبَاسًا Covering, garment, clothing, dress, لَبَسَ * he covered, لَبِسَ he wore, put on, was clothed in.

مَعَاشًا Whatever is necessary to support life, عَاشَ * he lived.

بَنَيْنَا We built, بَنَى * he built, constructed, اِبْن for بَنُو a son, اِبْنَة a daughter, بُنْيَان a building.

شِدَادًا	Strong, violent, severe, شَدِيدٌ (sing.), شَدَّ	* he bound firmly, established, strengthened.
سِرَاجًا	A lamp or candle, سَرَجَ	* he shone.
وَهَّاجًا	Brightly burning, glowing, يَهِجُ وَهَجَ	* he burned.
مُعْصِرَاتٍ	Clouds emitting or pressing out rain, عَصَرَ * he pressed (grapes), عَصْرٌ age, afternoon, time.	
ثَجَّاجًا	Pouring forth abundantly, ثَجَّ he flowed.	
حَبًّا	Grain, corn, حَبَّ * he loved.	
نَبَاتًا	Plants, that which is produced from the ground, نَبَتَ * it germinated, it grew, it sprouted. (a plant).	
أَلْفَافًا	Densely growing trees, thick foliage, trees thickly planted with interlacing boughs, لَفَّ * it was thick and tangled (trees).	
الْفَصْلِ	Distinction, separation, distinguishing good from evil, فَصَلَ * he judged between, he made a distinction	
مِيقَاتًا	A fixed time or place of appointment, وَقَّتَ * he appointed a fixed time.	
يُنْفَخُ	Will be blown, نَفَخَ * he blew with the mouth, breathed, نَفْخَةٌ a single blast.	
الصُّورِ	The trumpet, صَارَ * he inclined, صُورَةٌ a form, مُصَوِّرٌ one who forms.	
أَفْوَاجًا	Troops, crowd, hosts, groups, فَوْجٌ (sing.) فَاجَ * it (he) diffused a fragrant odour.	
سُيِّرَتْ	Moved, uprooted, سَارَ * he journeyed, travelled, went, سَيَّرَ II, he made to go, caused to pass away.	
سَرَابًا	A mirage, deceitful appearance as of water in the desert, سَرَبَ * it enjoyed free pasture (a camel).	
مِرْصَادًا	A place of observation, or of ambush, رَصَدَ * he lay in wait, he observed.	
الطَّاغِينَ	Transgressors, insolent, طَغَى * he transgressed, he exceeded all bounds (in wickedness).	
مَآبًا	A place of return, أَوَّبَ for أَابَ * he returned.	
لَابِثِينَ	Those who are staying, لَبِثَ * he stayed.	
أَحْقَابًا	Long spaces of time, long years, حُقْبٌ (sing.), حَقِبَ * it was withheld, he suffered from a retention of urine.	
بَرْدًا	Coolness, cool, cold, بَرَدَ * he was cold.	
شَرَابًا	Drink, a beverage, شَرِبَ * he drank.	
حَمِيمًا	Boiling hot water, a near relative or friend, حَمَّ * he heated.	
غَسَّاقًا	Corruption which flows from the bodies of the damned, غَسَقَ * it was very dark (the night).	
وِفَاقًا	The act of suiting or becoming fit, وَفِقَ * يَفِقُ he found a thing to be fitting.	

أَحْصَيْنَٰهُ	We counted, calculated it, أَحْصَىٰ clever in calculating, أَحْصَىٰ he calculated, computed, حَصَىٰ * he struck with a pebble.	
مَفَازًا	A place of safety or felicity, فَازَ * he got possession of, he obtained his desire.	
حَدَائِقَ	Gardens, حَدِيقَة (sing.) حَدَقَ * he surrounded.	
أَعْنَابًا	Grapes, عِنَبٌ * (sing.) a grape.	
كَوَاعِب	Full breasted girls, كَاعِبٌ (sing.), كَعَبَتْ * she had swelling breasts (a girl).	
أَتْرَابًا	Of the same age, تِرْبٌ (sing.) تَرِبَ * he had much earth, he held earth in the hand, تُرَابًا dust, earth.	
كَأْسًا	A cup (fem.), no verbal root.	
دِهَاقًا	Overflowing, full (a cup), دَهَقَ * he filled a cup, he cut in pieces.	
لَغْوًا	Nonsense speech, idle talk, لَغِيَ * he used vain words.	
عَطَاءً	A gift, عَطَا * he took anything in the hand, أَعْطَىٰ IV he gave.	
حِسَابًا	A reckoning, computation, account, حُسْبَانٌ (plur.), حَسَبَ * he reckoned.	
خِطَابًا	A discourse, declaration, speech, address, خَطَبَ * he gave speech, addressed.	
الرُّوحُ	Angel Jibril (AS), رُوحٌ soul, a spirit, رَاحَ * he did anything in the evening or at sunset.	
صَفًّا	Rank, a row, in order, صَفَّ * he set, arranged in row or rank.	
يَتَكَلَّمُونَ	They speak, كَلَمَ * he wounded, كَلَّمَ II he spoke, كَلِمٌ كَلِمَةٌ كَلَامٌ a word, a decree.	
صَوَابًا	That which is right, صَابَ * he hit the mark, he poured forth.	
الْحَقُّ	The truth, حَقَّ * he (it) was right, just or fitting, worthy of, it was justly due to.	
أَنْذَرَ	He admonished, warned, نَذَرَ * he devoted, he vowed.	
الْمَرْءُ	A man, اِمْرَأَةٌ a woman, مَرُؤَ * he was possessed of virtue or manliness.	
قَدَّمَتْ	She sent on before, قَدَمَ * he proceeded, قَدَّمَ he brought upon, he prepared beforehand.	
يَٰلَيْتَنِي	Would that, I wish, لَاتَ * he hindered, يَا لَيْتَ would that or would to God (a particle of desire).	

* Root words are marked with an asterisk.

Translation of Surah 78 An-Naba' (The Great News)

(1) About what do they question one another? (2) About the Great News, (3) About which they are in disagreement. (4) Nay, they will come to know! (5) Again, nay, they will come to know! (6) Have We not made the earth as a bed, (7) And the mountains as pegs? (8) And We have created you in pairs. (9) And We have made your sleep for rest. (10) And We have made the night as a covering (through its darkness). (11) And We have made the day for livelihood. (12) And We have built above you seven strong (heavens). (13) And We have made (therein) a shining lamp (the sun). (14) And We have sent down from the rainy clouds abundant water, (15) That We may produce therewith corn and plants (16) And gardens of thick growth. (17) Verily the Day of Decision is a fixed time. (18) The Day when the Trumpet will be blown and you shall come forth in crowds. (19) And heaven shall be opened and it will become as gates (20) And the mountains shall vanish, as if they were a mirage. (21) Truly

Hell is a place of ambush, (22) For the transgressors a place of destination. (23) They will abide therein for ages. (24) Nothing cool shall they taste therein, nor any drink, (25) Except boiling water and an intense cold, (26) A fitting recompense (for them). (27) For verily, they used not to hope for (fear) any account (for their deeds) (28) But they belied Our Signs completely, (29) And all things We have recorded in a Book (30) So taste (the results of your evil actions); no increase shall We give you except in torment. (31) Verily for the pious who fear Allah and avoid evil theirs will be a success (Paradise). (32) Gardens and vineyards. (33) And young full-breasted maids of equal age. (34) And a full cup (of wine). (35) No Falsehood shall they hear therein, and no lying - (36) Recompense from your Lord, a gift (amply) sufficient. (37) (From) the Lord of the heavens and the earth and all between them, the Most Beneficent. None can dare to argue with Him. (38) The Day that the Spirit (Jibril) and the angels will stand forth in rows, none shall speak except he whom the Beneficent (Allah) allows and he will speak what is right. (39) That is the true day. So who-so-ever wills, let him take a return to his Lord (by obeying Him in this worldly life). (40) Verily, We have warned you of a near torment, the Day when man will see (the deeds) which his hands have sent forth and the disbeliever will say; "Woe to me! Would that I were dust!"

Explanatory Notes for Surah 78

The Qur'anic view of the life to come is that there is an undiminished survival of the individual person and consciousness. It regards death and resurrection as the twin stages of a positive act of re-creation of the entire human person, in whatever form this may necessarily involve.

The *surah* opens by shunning the enquirers and the enquiry, it wonders that anyone should raise any doubts about resurrection and judgement. We see in the universe a multitude of scenes, creatures and phenomena, contemplation of which would strongly shake any human heart. With the advance in knowledge human beings should be able to appreciate more fully Allah's elaborate planning of the universe and the careful design of this existence.

Allah (SWT) has made two different sexes, each playing its role in life fully: this Qur'anic statement needs to be appreciated by every society in every age according to that society's abilities and knowledge.

Sleep is one of the secrets of the constitution of man and all living creatures unknown except to the Creator Who has made sleep essential for life. There is the hand of the Designer, who has assigned to everything in the universe its respective qualities. The consonance in the design of the universe could not have been achieved without the careful Designer and wise Planner.

A great horror is apparent in the upheaval which envelops the universe as well as in men's resurrection after the blowing in the trumpet. Such is the Day of Decision carefully and wisely fixed.

The *surah* describes the fate of the tyrant disbelievers and that of the righteous. The former group who raise doubts about the fateful tiding, will receive a "fitting recompense" as the Qur'an comments, and it is in keeping with what they have done in their lives. Allah (SWT) keeps a meticulous record which does not leave out anything they do or say. The righteous shall be in complete bliss, the luxuries provided to them are given a physical description so that they may be appreciated by human beings.

On the Day of Judgement Jibril (AS) and all the angels shall stand in ranks before Allah (SWT); they stand in awe of Him; no one dares utter a word without prior permission from the Merciful. The reward He assigned to each group is the manifestation of His mercy. For it is indeed part of the mercy that evil should be punished and that it should not have the same end as good.

There is time for mending one's erring ways before Hell becomes a permanent home.

Surah 79 An-Nazi'at

Makki Surah *Surah 79 An-Nazi'at* 46 *Ayat*

Meaning	Words	Meaning	Words
A command, an affair (of their Lord) (vrb. n. acc.)	أَمْرًا	By[1] those[2] who tear out or pluck out (ptcl., act. part. fem. pl.)	وَالنَّازِعَاتِ
A day (in which everything) (noun adv.)	يَوْمَ	Violently, from the depths, at a single draught (vrb. n. acc.)	غَرْقًا
Shall tremble, shake violently (mudari' III. fem. sing.)	تَرْجُفُ	By[1] those[2] who draw out, move, go out (ptcl., act. part. fem. pl.)	وَالنَّاشِطَاتِ
The first blast[3] (def. noun fem. sing.)	الرَّاجِفَةُ	Quickly and easily, gently (vrb. n. acc.)	نَشْطًا
There shall follow her (the first blast) (mudari' III. fem. sing., with att. pro. هَا)	تَتْبَعُهَا	By[1] those[2] who glide out, float through space (ptcl., act. part. fem. pl.)	وَالسَّابِحَاتِ
Another (blast) (act. part. def. fem. sing.)	الرَّادِفَةُ	Swimmingly, floating serenely (vrb. n. acc.)	سَبْحًا
Hearts on that day (noun br. pl., يَوْمَ day, إِذْ = then, يَوْمَئِذٍ)	قُلُوبٌ يَوْمَئِذٍ	Then those[2] who precede (ptcl., act. part. fem. pl.)	فَالسَّابِقَاتِ
Palpitating (with fear) (act. part. fem.)	وَاجِفَةٌ	Racing, hurrying (vrb. n. acc.)	سَبْقًا
Eyes of them[4] (noun br. pl. mdf., pro. mdfi.)	أَبْصَارُهَا	Then those[2] who manage, conduct (ptcl., act. part. fem. pl.)	فَالْمُدَبِّرَاتِ
Downcast, humbled (with humiliation) (act. part. fem. sing.)	خَاشِعَةٌ		

---

[3] name of the first blast of the trumpet which is to precede the general Resurrection.

[4] هَا is for hearts (palpitating with fear), their owners' eyes will be downcast.

[1] وَ is for swearing an oath, the object sworn by being in the genitive.

[2] there are differing views as to the meaning 1) Angels 2) Stars 3) Death or dying souls 4) Strong winds.

Words	Meaning	Words	Meaning
يَقُولُونَ	They shall say (*mudari*ʿ III. msc. pl.)	فَإِذَاهُم	Then (behold) when they (will be) (ptcls., pro.)
أَإِنَّا	Is it that we (shall be)? (أ ptcl. inter., ptcl., pro.)	بِالسَّاهِرَةِ	On the surface (of the earth) awakened, (place of last judgement) (ptcl., def. noun)
لَمَرْدُودُونَ	Restored, made to return (ptcl. ل emph., pass. part. pl.)	هَلْ أَتَاكَ	Has (there) come to you? (ptcl. inter., *madi* III. msc. sing., pro.)
فِي الْحَافِرَةِ	To (our) former state (ptcl., act. part. fem. sing. gen.)	حَدِيثُ مُوسَى	Story or narration of Musa (act. part. msc. sing. *mdf.*, proper noun *gh. mdfi.*)
أَإِذَا كُنَّا	Is it that when we are (أ ptcl. inter., ptcl., *madi* I. pl.)	إِذْ نَادَاهُ	When (there) called him (ptcl., *madi* III. msc. sing., pro.)
عِظَامًا	Skeletons, bones (Vrb. n. acc.)	رَبُّهُ	His Lord (noun *mdf.*, pro. *mdfi.*)
نَخِرَةً	Rotten and decayed (shall we be restored?) (noun sing.)	بِالْوَادِ	In the valley (ptcl., def. noun gen.)
قَالُوا	They said (*madi* III. msc. pl.)	الْمُقَدَّسِ طُوًى	The sacred, Tuwa[5] (Pass. part. dr. vrb. II msc. sing. gen., proper noun *gh.*)
تِلْكَ إِذًا	It would then be (dem. pro. fem. sing., ptcl.)	اذْهَبْ إِلَى فِرْعَوْنَ	'Go to Firʿaun (Pharaoh) (*amr* II. msc. sing., ptcl., proper noun dipt.)
كَرَّةٌ	A return (noun)	إِنَّهُ طَغَى	Indeed he transgressed, exceeded all bounds (of wickedness) (ptcl., pro., *madi* III. msc. sing.)
خَاسِرَةٌ	(as) a loser, (with) a loss (act. part. fem. sing.)	فَقُلْ	(and) then say (to him) (ptcl., *amr* II. msc. sing.)
فَإِنَّمَا هِيَ	Then only it (will be) (ptcls., pro.)		
زَجْرَةٌ	A cry (noun fem.)		
وَاحِدَةٌ	One only (card. no. adj.)		

[5] a valley just below Mount Sinai (Qur'an 20: 12)

Surah 79 An-Naziʿat

Meaning	Words	Meaning	Words
Then he gathered (ptcl., *madi* III. msc. sing.)	فَحَشَرَ	"Would you (like) to (become)? Are you desirous of attaining? Would you mind to adopt? (ptcl. inter., ptcl. لَ , pro. كَ , ptcl. إِلَى)	هَلْ لَكَ إِلَى
And called (to his people) (ptcl., dr. vrb III *madi* III. msc. sing.)	فَنَادَىٰ	That you purify yourself, You adopt purity (ptcl., drv. vrb V تَتَزَكَّىٰ for تَزَكَّىٰ *mudariʿ* II. msc. sing.)	أَن تَزَكَّىٰ
Then he said, 'I (am) (ptcl., *madi* III. msc. sing., pro.)	فَقَالَ أَنَا	And I shall guide you (ptcl., *mudariʿ* I. sing., pro. كَ)	وَأَهْدِيَكَ
Your Lord, the highest' (noun *mdf.*, pro. كُم *mdfi.*, adj. elat. msc. sing.)	رَبُّكُمُ الْأَعْلَىٰ	To your Lord (ptcl., noun gen. *mdf.*, pro. *mdfi.*)	إِلَىٰ رَبِّكَ
So Allah took him to task Allah seized him (ptcl., *madi* III. msc. sing., pro., def. noun nom.)	فَأَخَذَهُ اللَّهُ	So you (may) fear (Him)'" (ptcl., *mudariʿ* II. msc. sing.)	فَتَخْشَىٰ
(and made him) a warning example, a punishment (noun acc. *mdf.*)	نَكَالَ	So he showed him (ptcl., dr. vrb. IV *madi* III. msc. sing., pro.)	فَأَرَاهُ
Of the Hereafter (def. noun fem. *mdfi.*)	الْآخِرَةِ	The greatest sign[6] (def. noun acc., adj. elat. fem. acc.)	الْآيَةَ الْكُبْرَىٰ
And of the first (life of this world) (ptcl., ord. no. def. noun elat. fem. *mdfi.*)	وَالْأُولَىٰ	But he belied (it), denied, charged (it) with falsehood (ptcl., dr. vrb. II *madi* III. msc. sing.)	فَكَذَّبَ
Indeed, in this (ptcls., dem. pro. msc. sing.)	إِنَّ فِي ذَٰلِكَ	And disobeyed, rebelled (ptcl., *madi* III. msc. sing.)	وَعَصَىٰ
(there) certainly is a lesson (ptcl. لَ emph., noun fem. acc.)	لَعِبْرَةً	Then he (Firaʿun) turned back (ثُمَّ ptcl. class., dr. vrb. IV *madi* III. msc. sing)	ثُمَّ أَدْبَرَ
For (all) who fear (ptcl., pro., *mudariʿ* III. msc. sing.)	لِمَن يَخْشَىٰ	Striving, endeavouring (against Allah) (*mudariʿ* III. msc. sing.)	يَسْعَىٰ
Are you harder more difficult (ptcl. inter., per. pro. msc. pl., adj. elat. nom.)	أَأَنتُمْ أَشَدُّ		

[6] the turning of the staff into a serpent

Words	Meaning	Words	Meaning
خَلْقًا	A creation (to create) (vrb. n. acc.)	أَخْرَجَ مِنْهَا	He brought forth from it (dr. vrb. IV *madi* III. msc. sing., ptcl., pro. هَا for earth)
أَمِ السَّمَاءُ	or the heaven (ptcl., def. noun)	مَاءَهَا	Its water (noun *mdf.*, pro. هَا for earth *mdfi.*)
بَنَاهَا	He built it (*madi* III. msc. sing., pro. هَا for heaven)	وَمَرْعَاهَا	And its pasture (ptcl., noun *mdf.*, pro. هَا for earth *mdfi.*)
رَفَعَ	He raised (*madi* III. msc. sing.)	وَالْجِبَالَ	And the mountains (ptcl., noun br. pl. acc.)
سَمْكَهَا	It (as) a roof (noun acc. *mdf.*, pro. هَا for heaven *mdfi.*)	أَرْسَاهَا	He fixed them firmly (dr. vrb. IV *madi* III. msc. sing., pro. هَا for mountains)
فَسَوَّاهَا	Then He perfected, levelled, fashioned, proportioned it (ptcl., dr. vrb. II *madi* III. msc. sing., pro. هَا for heaven)	مَتَاعًا لَكُمْ	A benefit for you (noun acc., ptcl. لَ, pro. msc. pl.)
وَأَغْطَشَ	And He made dark (ptcl., dr. vrb. IV *madi* III. msc. sing.)	وَلِأَنْعَامِكُمْ	And for your animals (ptcls., noun br. pl., pro. كُمْ)
لَيْلَهَا	Its night (noun *mdf.*, pro. هَا for heaven *mdfi.*)	فَإِذَا جَاءَتِ	So, when (there) came (ptcls., *madi* III. fem. sing.)
وَأَخْرَجَ	And took out, brought forth (ptcl., dr. vrb. IV *madi* III. msc. sing.)	الطَّامَّةُ الْكُبْرَى	The great Calamity[8] (def. noun, adj. elat. fem.)
ضُحَاهَا	Its light of day its (the sun's) full brightness (noun acc. *mdf.*, pro. هَا for heaven *mdfi.*)	يَوْمَ	(on) A day (the Day of Judgement) (noun adv.)
وَالْأَرْضَ	And the earth (ptcl., def. noun acc.)	يَتَذَكَّرُ الْإِنْسَانُ	Man shall remember (dr. vrb. V *mudari* III. msc. sing., def. noun)
بَعْدَ ذَلِكَ	After that[7] (prep. noun بَعْدَ, dem. pro. msc. sing.)		
دَحَاهَا	He expanded it, spread it out (*madi* III. msc. sing., pro. هَا for earth)	مَا سَعَى	What he strived (for) (ptcl., *madi* III. msc. sing.)

[7] بَعْدَ noun used as a preposition in accusative.

[8] The Day of Judgement

Surah 79 An-Naziʿat

Meaning	Words	Meaning	Words
And shall be laid open (dr. vrb. II *maj. madi* III. fem. sing.)	وَبُرِّزَتِ	And restrained his self/soul (his inner self) (ptcl., *madi* III. msc. sing., def. noun acc.)	وَنَهَى النَّفْسَ
Hell (def. noun nom.)	الْجَحِيمُ	From (base, evil) desires (ptcl., def. noun *gh.* gen.)	عَنِ الْهَوَىٰ
For whoever shall see (ptcl., pro., *mudariʿ* III. msc. sing.)	لِمَن يَرَىٰ	So indeed Paradise (ptcls., def. noun acc.)	فَإِنَّ الْجَنَّةَ
So, as for (ptcls.)	فَأَمَّا	She is the (eternal) home, place of abode (for him) (pro. fem., def. noun)	هِيَ الْمَأْوَىٰ
Whoever transgressed (pro., *madi* III. msc. sing.)	مَن طَغَىٰ	They ask you (*mudariʿ* III. msc. pl., pro. ك)	يَسْأَلُونَكَ
And chose, preferred (ptcl., dr. vrb. IV *madi* III. msc. sing.)	وَآثَرَ	About the Hour (ptcl., def. noun gen.)	عَنِ السَّاعَةِ
The lower, nearer life (the life of the world) (def. noun fem., adj. elat. fem.)	الْحَيَاةَ الدُّنْيَا	When will it come to pass, When is its arrival, its fixed time (ptcl., noun *mdf.*, pro. *mdfi.*)	أَيَّانَ مُرْسَاهَا
So, indeed Hell (ptcls., def. noun acc.)	فَإِنَّ الْجَحِيمَ	Wherein are you (how can you) (ptcls., per. pro. msc. sing.)	فِيمَ أَنتَ
She is the (eternal) home the place of abode (for him) (pro. fem., def. noun *gh.*)	هِيَ الْمَأْوَىٰ	With regard to stating it? (telling about it) (ptcl., noun *gh. mdf.*, pro. *mdfi.*)	مِن ذِكْرَاهَا
And as for (ptcls.)	وَأَمَّا	To your Lord (your Lord alone) is (ptcl., noun gen. *mdf.*, pro. *mdfi.*)	إِلَىٰ رَبِّكَ
Whoever feared (pro., *madi* III. msc. sing.)	مَنْ خَافَ	Its utmost limit (Its knowledge) (noun *mdf.*, pro. *mdfi.*)	مُنتَهَاهَا
(the) Time and place of standing (noun *mdf.*)	مَقَامَ	Only, you (are) (ptcls., per. pro.)	إِنَّمَا أَنتَ
(before) his Lord (noun *mdfi. mdf.*, att. pro. *mdfi.*)	رَبِّهِ		

Meaning	Words	Meaning	Words
They had not remained (in this world) (ptcl. negn.⁸, *mudari* juss. md. III. msc. pl.)	لَمْ يَلْبَثُوا	**The warner (of)** (act. part. dr. vrb. IV msc. sing. *mdf*.)	مُنذِرُ
Except a night (an evening) (ptcl. exc., noun fem. acc.)	إِلَّا عَشِيَّةً	**Whoever fears it (her)** (pro. mdfi., *mudari* III. msc. sing., pro. هَا for the Last Hour)	مَن يَخْشَاهَا
Or its morning . (ptcl., noun gh. *mdf*., pro. هَا for the Last Hour *mdfi*.)	أَوْ ضُحَاهَا	**As if (it were) that they** (ptcls., pro.)	كَأَنَّهُمْ
		(on the) day (noun adv. acc.)	يَوْمَ
⁸ لَمْ preceding *mudari* denotes an emphatic negative meaning of *madi*.		**When they see it** (*mudari* III. msc. pl., pro. هَا for the Last Hour)	يَرَوْنَهَا

Root Words of Surah 79

الثَّازِعَاتِ Who tear out, pluck out (souls) (i.e. angels), نَزَعَ * he plucked out, brought out, snatched away, dragged forth.

غَرْقًا Violently, suddenly, at a single draught, غَرِقَ * he was submerged, غَرْق a draught.

النَّاشِطَاتِ Those who draw up easily (i.e. angels) نَشَطَ * he went out from a place, drew up a bucket at one pull, نَشْط the act of drawing up quickly and easily.

السَّابِحَاتِ Those who move with swimming or floating motion, (applied to angels who come down from heaven with their Lord's command), سَبَحَ * he swam or floated.

السَّابِقَاتِ Those who strive to excel or reach before another (i.e. angels), سَبَقَ *he was in advance of, he went before.

الْمُدَبِّرَاتِ Those who manage the affairs (i.e. angels), دَبَرَ * he was behind, دَبَّرَ II he governed, managed, he disposed, أَدْبَرَ IV he turned the back, retreated.

تَرْجُفُ Shall quake or tremble, رَجَفَ * he (it) shook violently, رَجْفَة an earthquake.

الرَّادِفَةُ Follower, one that comes after another without break, رَدِفَ * he came behind, that which follows.

وَاجِفَةٌ Palpitating, throbbing, يَجِفُ * وَجَفَ he was agitated.

خَاشِعَةٌ (In a state of) humility, خَشَعَ * he humbled himself, خُشُوعٌ humility.

مَرْدُودُونَ Made to return, restored, رَدَّ * he restored, he drove back, averted.

الْحَافِرَةِ Former condition, the original state, حَفَرَ * he dug, حُفْرَة a pit.

عِظَامًا Skeleton, bones عَظَمَ * he gave a dog a bone, عَظُمَ he was great.

Surah 78 An-Naba'

نَخِرَةٌ	Decayed (bone), crumbled, rotten, worn, نَخِرَ * it was worn full of holes.
كَرَّةٌ	A return, كَرَّتَيْنِ twice again, كَرَّ * he returned.
خَاسِرَةٌ	A loser (fem.) خَاسِرٌ a loser (msc.), خَسِرَ * he suffered loss, he wandered from the right way.
زَجْرَةٌ	A single cry, a shout, زَجَرَ * he drove away, he prohibited.
السَّاهِرَةُ	The surface of the earth, awakened, سَهِرَ * he was watchful.
حَدِيثٌ	Story, narrative, discourse, أَحَادِيثُ (pl.) حَدَثَ * he happened, it was new.
نَادَى	III he called upon, نَدَا * he called, نَادِيٌّ نَدِيٌّ a council.
طُوًى	Name of a valley near Mount Sinai, طَوَى * he rolled up.
طَغَوْا	they transgressed, طَغَى * he transgressed, exceeded the limit, exceeded all bounds (in wickedness), طَاغِيَةٌ a storm of thunder and lightning of extreme severity.
تَزَكَّنْ	V he purified, cleansed, زَكَى * he was pure, he was purified, زَكَّى he purified, تَزَكَّى and ازَّكَّى he endured, he was pure, زَكَوةٌ alms, purity, portion of one's substance given in order to purify the rest.
أَهْدِيَكَ	I shall lead you in the right way, * هَدَى he led in the right way.
فَحَشَرَ	So He gathered together and hence: He raised from the dead, حَشَرَ * he gathered together.
نَكَالَ	A punishment, an example, نَكَلَ * he made an example of.
الْآخِرَةِ	Hereafter, the last, (no verbal root of form I), أَخَّرَ he put behind, delayed.
الْأُولَى	The beginning, former, the first, أَوَّلَ * he returned, he was before.
عِبْرَةٌ	An instructive warning, عَبَرَ * he interpreted, he passed over.
بَنَاهَا	He built it, بَنَى * he built, constructed.
سَمْكَهَا	Its roof, سَمْكٌ a roof, or height, سَمَكَ * he raised on high.
فَسَوَّاهَا	Then proportioned, perfected, fashioned it or made it level, سَوَى * he intended, سَوَّى II he proportioned, fashioned, perfected.
أَغْطَشَ	IV he made dark, * غَطَشَ it was dark.
ضُحَاهَا	Its bright day, ضَحَا * it appeared conspicuously, ضَحِيَ * he suffered from the heat of the sun.
دَحَاهَا	He stretched it out, دَحَا * he spread out, expanded.
مَرْعَاهَا	Its pasture, رَعَى * he pastured, fed (cattle).
أَرْسَاهَا	He established it firm, أَرْسَى IV he fixed firmly, مُرْسَاهَا its fixed time and place, رَسَا * he was or he stood firm.
مَتَاعًا	Provision, convenience, comfort, ease, household stuff, مَتَعَ * it was advanced (the day).
الطَّامَّةُ	The calamity, طَمَّ * it was much.
يَتَذَكَّرُ	He receives admonition, remembers, تَذَكَّرَ he was admonished, remembered, ذَكَرَ * he remembered, ذَكَّرَ II he reminded, ذِكْرَى a remembering, admonition.

بُرِّزَت	II it was made manifest, brought up, بَرَزَ * he went forth.	
الجَحِيمُ	Any fiercely burning fire (fem.), hell-fire, Hell, جَحَمَ * he lit a fire.	
المَأْوَى	Home, abode, the shelter, أَوَى * he betook himself for rest or shelter.	
نَهَى	* He hindered, prohibited, he forbade, مُنْتَهَهَا its fixed term, its terminus or limit.	
هَوَى	* He (it) inclined, set, rose, loved, disappeared, was destroyed.	
عَشِيَّةً	An evening, "عِشَاء commencement of darkness, عَشَا * he was purblind, he withdrew from.	

Translation of Surah 79 An-Naziᶜat (Those who pull out)

(1) By those (Angels) who pull out (the souls of the wicked) with great violence. (2) By those (Angels) who gently take out (the souls of the believers). (3) And by those who swim along (e.g. planets in their orbits, etc.) (4) And by those who press forward as in a race (e.g. horses). (5) And by those who arrange to do the commands of their Lord (angels) (so verily you disbelievers will be called to account).

(6) On the Day (when the first trumpet is blown) the earth and the mountains will shake violently (and everybody will die), (7) The second follows it (and everybody will be raise up), (8) (Some) hearts that Day will beat with fear. (9) their eyes cast down. (10) They say, "Shall we indeed be returned to (our) former state of life? (11) Even after we are crumbled bones?" (12) They say: "It would in that case, be a return with loss!" (13) But only, it will be a single cry, (14) When behold, they find themselves awakened.

(15) Has there come to you the story of Musa? (16) When his Lord called him in the sacred valley of Tuwa, (17) (He said to him): "Go to Firᶜawn, verily he has transgressed all bounds. (18) And say to him: 'Would you purify yourself (from sin)? (19) And that I guide you to your Lord, so you should fear Him?'"

(20) Then (Musa) he showed him the greatest Sign. (21) But (Firᶜawn) he denied and disobeyed (22) Then he turned his back striving hard (against Allah). (23) Then he collected (his men) and made a proclamation, (24) Saying: "I am your lord, the most high." (25) So Allah seized him with punishment for the last [verse (24) (i.e. 79:24)] and first [verse (28:38)] (transgression). (26) Verily in this is an instructive admonition for whosoever fears Allah.

(27) Are you the more difficult to create or is the heaven that He constructed? (28) On high has He raised its building and He has equally ordered it. (29) Its night He covers with darkness and its forenoon He brings out (with light). (30) And after that He spread the earth, (31) And produced therefrom its water and its pasture. (32) And the mountains He has fixed firmly; (33) for enjoyment and convenience to you and your cattle.

(34) But when there comes the greatest Event - (35) The Day when man shall remember what he strove for, (36) And Hell-Fire shall be placed in full view for him who sees.

(37) Then as for him who transgressed all bounds, (disbelieved), (38) And preferred the life of this world, (39) The Abode will be Hell-Fire.

(40) But as for him who feared to stand before his Lord and restrained his soul from impure desires, (41) Verily, Paradise will be his Abode.

(42) They ask you (O Muhammad [SAAS]) about the Hour - when will be its appointed time? (43) You have no knowledge to say anything about it, (44) To your Lord belongs (the knowledge of) the term thereof. (45) You (O Muhammad [SAAS]) are only a warner for those who fear it. (46) The Day they see it (it will be) as if they had but tarried a single evening or the following morning.

Explanatory Notes for Surah 79 An-Nazi'at

The Surah begins with an oath to affirm that the Resurrection is a certainty. The account of the Day of Judgement given in the above verses makes men's hearts feel the quake and shake of the earth with fear and worry. The Surah goes on to speak of their surprise and wonder when they are resurrected. Then they realise that their awakening does not take them back to their life on earth, but to their second life. At this point they feel their great loss. They have not banked on such a return, and have not prepared for it. The story of Musa (AS) helps to make the message of the Surah clearer. Only those who know their true Lord and fear Him will benefit from the lessons of Fir'awn's history. Those who do not fear Allah will continue in their erring ways until they reach their appointed end, when they shall suffer the scourge of both this life and the life to come. Allah (SWT) elaborately planned the grand universe and gave man a special place in it. If the origins of the universe and man are so, then the cycle must be completed and everyone must have his reward and punishment according to his deeds. The reality of the Hereafter is the main theme of the Surah.

Surah 80 ʿAbasa

Makki Surah — بِسْمِ اللَّهِ الرَّحْمَٰنِ الرَّحِيمِ — *42 Ayat*

Words	Meaning	Words	Meaning
عَبَسَ	He looked angry, frowned (*madi* III. msc. sing.)	فَتَنفَعَهُ	So (thus) might profit him, prove useful to him (ptcl., *mudariʿ* III. fem. sing., pro.)
وَتَوَلَّىٰ	And turned away (dr. vrb. V *madi* III. msc. sing.)	الذِّكْرَىٰ	The reminder, the admonition (def. noun fem. مَزِيدٌ فِيهِ dipt.)
أَن جَاءَهُ	That (there) came to him (ptcl., *madi* III. msc. sing., pro. ه)	أَمَّا مَنِ	As for him who (ptcls., pro.)
الْأَعْمَىٰ	The blind (man) (def. noun msc. sing.)	اسْتَغْنَىٰ	(believes) he is without need (of guidance), (is indifferent to guidance) (dr. vrb. X *madi* III. msc. sing.)
وَمَا	And what (would) (could) (ptcls.)	فَأَنتَ لَهُ	So you, to him (ptcl., per. pro. msc sing., ptcl., pro.)
يُدْرِيكَ	Make you know? (tell you?) (dr. vrb. IV *mudariʿ* III. msc. sing. att. pro. ك)[1]	تَصَدَّىٰ	You receive with honour Direct your full attention (تَتَصَدَّدُ for تَتَصَدَّىٰ or even تَصَدَّىٰ dr. vrb. V *mudariʿ* II. msc. sing.)
لَعَلَّهُ	Perhaps he (would) O that he might (ptcl., pro.)	وَمَا عَلَيْكَ	And it is not on you (you are not accountable) (ptcls., att. pro. ك)
يَزَّكَّىٰ	Grow in purity, reform himself cleanse himself (from wrong) (dr. vrb. V يَتَزَكَّىٰ for يَزَّكَّىٰ *mudariʿ* III. msc. sing.)	أَلَّا يَزَّكَّىٰ	That he does not grow in purity, is not reformed, not cleansed from wrong (ptcl. negn., dr. vrb. V يَتَزَكَّىٰ for يَزَّكَّىٰ *mudariʿ* III. msc. sing.)
أَوْ يَذَّكَّرُ	Or (bring himself) to remember, admonish himself (ptcl., dr. vrb. V يَتَذَكَّرُ for يَذَّكَّرُ *mudariʿ* III. msc. sing.)	وَأَمَّا مَن	And as for him who (ptcls., pro.)
		جَاءَكَ	Came to you (*madi* III. msc. sing., att. pro. ك)

---

[1] See Juz 1 pps.115-116 old ed., pps. 119-120 new ed.

Surah 80 ʿAbasa

Meaning	Words	Meaning	Words
Striving, endeavouring (*mudariʿ* III. msc. sing.)	يَسْعَىٰ	(written) by hands (ptcl., noun br. pl.)	بِأَيْدِى
And he fears (Allah) (ptcl., pro., *mudariʿ* III. msc. sing.)	وَهُوَ يَخْشَىٰ	of scribes (noun br. pl. gen.)	سَفَرَةٍ
(then) so you, from him (ptcl., per. pro. msc. sing., ptcl., pro.)	فَأَنتَ عَنْهُ	(who are) Honourable, noble (noun br. pl. of كَرِيم gen.)	كِرَامٍ
(are) unmindful, careless (dr.vrb. V تَتَلَهَّىٰ is for تَلَهَّىٰ *mudariʿ* II. msc. sing.)	تَلَهَّىٰ	Innocent, pious, right-acting (act. prtc. br. pl. of بَارّ gen.)	بَرَرَةٍ
Nay, verily, it is By no means, it (the reminder الذِّكْرَىٰ) is (ptcls., pro. fem.)	كَلَّآ إِنَّهَا	May man be killed! cursed (madi maj. III. msc. sing, noun msc. sing. nom.²)	قُتِلَ الْإِنسَانُ
A reminder, warning, an admonition (noun)	تَذْكِرَةٌ	How (stubbornly) he denies it (the truth)! or (what made him a disbeliever?) (verb of surprise and wonder. Juz 2 & 3, p.134., pro.)	مَآ أَكْفَرَهُ
So whoever wished (is willing) (ptcl., pro., madi III. msc. sing.)	فَمَن شَآءَ	Out of what thing (or substance) (ptcl., noun *mdf*., noun *mdfi*.)	مِنْ أَىِّ شَىْءٍ
(should) bear it (the Qur'an) in mind, made a mention of it (madi III. msc. sing., pro.)	ذَكَرَهُ	He created him? (madi III. msc. sing., pro.)	خَلَقَهُ
(it is) in scrolls, or pages, records (ptcl., noun br. pl. gen.)	فِى صُحُفٍ	From a drop (of sperm) (ptcl., noun gen.)	مِن نُّطْفَةٍ
Honoured (pass. part. fem. dr. vrb. II. gen.)	مُّكَرَّمَةٍ	He created him (madi III. msc. sing., pro.)	خَلَقَهُ
Exalted, lofty (pass. part. fem. gen.)	مَّرْفُوعَةٍ	Then He planned his destiny, He formed him in due proportion, He determined his nature (ptcl., dr. vrb. II madi III. msc. sing., pro.)	فَقَدَّرَهُ
Purified (pass. part. fem. dr. vrb. II gen.)	مُّطَهَّرَةٍ	² In the passive form قُتِلَ is sometimes used as an imprecation, i.e. 'may he be killed (cursed)'.	

Meaning	Words	Meaning	Words
We poured the water (ptcl., att. pro., *madi* I. pl., noun acc.)	أَنَّا صَبَبْنَا ٱلْمَآءَ	Then the way (ptcl. class., def. noun)	ثُمَّ ٱلسَّبِيلَ
Pouring down in abundance (vrb. n. acc.)	صَبًّا	He made easy for him (dr. vrb. II *madi* III. msc. sing., pro.)	يَسَّرَهُۥ
Then We clove the earth (ptcl. class., *madi* I. pl., def. noun)	ثُمَّ شَقَقْنَا ٱلْأَرْضَ	Then He gave him death, caused him to die (ptcl. class., dr. vrb. IV *madi* III. msc. sing., pro.)	ثُمَّ أَمَاتَهُۥ
cleaving it asunder (vrb n. acc.)	شَقًّا	Then He buried him, brought him to the grave (ptcl., dr. vrb. IV *madi* III. msc. sing., pro.)	فَأَقْبَرَهُۥ
then We germinated in it (ptcl. class., dr. vrb. IV *madi* I. pl., ptcl., pro. هَا for the earth)	فَأَنۢبَتْنَا فِيهَا	Then when He wished (ptcl. class., ptcl., *madi* III. msc. sing.)	ثُمَّ إِذَا شَآءَ
grain (noun acc.)	حَبًّا	He raised him again to life (dr. vrb. IV *madi* III. msc. sing., pro.)	أَنشَرَهُۥ
and grapes (ptcl., noun acc.)	وَعِنَبًا	Nay, verily, by no means (ptcl.)	كَلَّا
and edible plants, vegetables (ptcl., noun acc.)	وَقَضْبًا	he has not yet[3] fulfilled (ptcl. negn.[3], *mudari* juss. md. III. msc. sing.)	لَمَّا يَقْضِ
and olives (ptcl., coll. noun acc.)	وَزَيْتُونًا	what He has ordered him enjoined upon him (ptcl., *madi* III. msc. sing., pro.)	مَآ أَمَرَهُۥ
and date palms (ptcl., coll. noun acc.)	وَنَخْلًا	So let man look (ptcl., ل ptcl. imp., *mudari* juss. md. III. msc. sing., def. noun nom.)	فَلْيَنظُرِ ٱلْإِنسَٰنُ
and walled gardens (ptc., noun br. pl.)	وَحَدَآئِقَ		
thick, lofty (noun adj. acc.)	غُلْبًا		
and fruit (ptcl., noun acc.)	وَفَٰكِهَةً	at his food (ptcl., noun *mdf*., pro. *mdfi*.)	إِلَىٰ طَعَامِهِۦٓ
and vegetation (ptcl., noun acc.)	وَأَبًّا	[3] *mudari* of negation with the particle لَمَّا has the meaning of the perfect tense with emphasis.	

Surah 80 ʿAbasa

Words	Meaning	Words	Meaning
مَتَاعًا لَّكُمْ	a benefit for you (noun acc., ptcl., att. pl. pro. كُم)	شَأْنٌ	(enough) concern (of his own) (noun nom.)
وَلِأَنْعَامِكُمْ	and for your animals (ptcls., noun br. pl. mdf., att. pl. pro. كُم mdfi.)	يُغْنِيهِ	to make him heedless, independent (of others) (dr.vrb. IV mudariʿ III. msc. sing., pro.)
فَإِذَا جَاءَتِ	So when (there) comes (ptcl., إِذَا [4] noun adv., madi III. fem. sing.)	وُجُوهٌ يَوْمَئِذٍ	faces on [5] that day (noun br. pl., noun adv. [5])
الصَّاخَّةُ	the deafening noise (act. part. fem. sing.)	مُسْفِرَةٌ	(will be) bright, shining (act. part. fem. sing.)
يَوْمَ يَفِرُّ الْمَرْءُ	the day, shall flee man (noun adv., mudariʿ III. msc. sing., def. noun)	ضَاحِكَةٌ	laughing (act. part. fem. sing.)
مِنْ أَخِيهِ	from his brother (ptcl., noun gen. mdf., pro. mdfi.)	مُسْتَبْشِرَةٌ	rejoicing (act. part. dr. vrb. X)
وَأُمِّهِ وَأَبِيهِ	and his mother and father (ptcl., noun gen. mdf., pro. mdfi., ptcl., noun gen. mdf., pro. mdfi.)	وَوُجُوهٌ يَوْمَئِذٍ	and faces on [5] that day (ptcl., noun br. pl., noun adv. [5])
وَصَاحِبَتِهِ وَبَنِيهِ	and his wife and his children (ptcl., noun fem. sing. gen. mdf., pro. mdfi., ptcl., noun msc. pl. gen. mdf., pro. mdfi.)	عَلَيْهَا غَبَرَةٌ	on them (it) dust (ptcl., pro. fem. هَا for وُجُوه, noun br. pl.)
لِكُلِّ امْرِئٍ	To every man (ptcl., noun gen. mdf., noun mdfi.)	تَرْهَقُهَا	(there) afflicted them (with troubles) (there) covered them (madi III. fem. sing., att. pro. هَا)
مِنْهُمْ يَوْمَئِذٍ	of them, on [5] that day (ptcl., pr. pl., noun adv. [5])	قَتَرَةٌ	blackness, darkness (noun nom.)
		أُولَٰئِكَ هُمُ	Those they (are) (dem. pro. pl., per. pro. msc. pl.)
		الْكَفَرَةُ	the deniers, the disbelievers (act. part. br. pl.)
		الْفَجَرَةُ	the wicked, the deviant (act. part. br. pl.)

[4] إِذَا with the madi indicates the future.
[5] يَوْمَئِذٍ is يَوْمٌ 'day' إِذْ 'then'.

Root Words of Surah 80

عَبَسَ *	he frowned, he was austere.	
تَوَلَّى	V he turned away, turned back, وَلِيَ * he was very near to someone, مَوْلًى lord, protector, companion, patron, وَلَّى II he turned back, retreated.	
يُدْرِيكَ	Makes you know, دَرَى * he knew, أَدْرَى IV he made to know.	
أَكْفَرَ	IV he made someone an unbeliever, he was ungrateful, كَفَرَ * he denied, covered, ٱلْكَفَرَةُ disbelievers, husbandmen.	
خَلَقَ *	He produced, created, measured accurately and defined the dimensions of anything.	
تَنْفَعَ	Will profit, نَفَعَ * he availed, profited, was useful to.	
ٱسْتَغْنَى	X he was able to do without, was self-sufficient, desired riches, became rich, غَنِيَ * he was rich.	
تَصَدَّى	for تَتَصَدَّى you receive with honour تَصَدَّى V he received with honour, صَدَّا * he clapped the hands.	
يَسْعَى	He who comes striving, سَعَى * he strove after, ran, went hastily.	
يَخْشَى	He fears, خَشِيَ * he feared.	
تَلَهَّى	V he was careless, unmindful of.	
قَدَّرَ	II he made possible, decreed, determined, defined, devised, planned, prepared, disposed, قَدَرَ * he was able to do.	
صُحُف	Scrolls, writs, scriptures, صَحِيفَةٌ (sing), صَحَفَ * he dug with an instrument.	
مُكَرَّمَةٌ	(fem) Honoured, مُكَرَّمٌ (msc.), كَرِيمٌ (pl.) كِرَامٌ kind, generous, noble, honourable, كَرُمَ * he was superior to another in generosity, أَكْرَمَ IV he honoured.	
مَرْفُوعَةٌ	Raised on high, exalted, elevated, رَفَعَ * he lifted up, exalted, raised up.	
مُطَهَّرَةٌ	(fem.) Purified, freed from impurity, طَهَّرَ II he purified, cleaned, طَهَرَ * he was pure, clean.	
سَفَرَةٌ	Scribes, سَافِرٌ (sing.), مُسْفِرَةٌ shining, سَفَرَ * he went on a journey.	
بَرَرَةٌ	Virtuous ones, بَارٌّ (sing.), pious, innocent, بَرَّ * he acted justly towards, he was just, he was pious, أَبْرَارٌ (pl.) the just, kind, beneficent ones, بَرٌّ dry land (sing.).	
يَسَّرَ	II he facilitated, made easy, يَسَرَ * it was easy, he played at dice.	
أَمَاتَ	IV He caused to die, مَاتَ * he died.	
أَقْبَرَ	IV He caused to be buried, قَبَرَ * he buried, قَبْرٌ grave.	
أَنْشَرَ	IV He raised the dead, نَشَرَ * he spread abroad, نُشُورٌ resurrection.	
يَقْضِي	He performs, قَضَى * he performed, fulfilled, accomplished, decreed.	
صَبَبْنَا	We poured, صَبًّا the act of pouring, صَبَّ * he poured.	
شَقَقْنَا	We clove, شَقًّا cleaving asunder, شَقَّ * شَقَّتْ (fem.) he (she) placed under a

	difficulty, clove, split.	
يَفِرُّ	He flees, will flee, فَرَّ * he fled, مَفَرٌّ a place of refuge.	
قَضْبًا	Clover, vegetables, trefoil قَضْبٌ * he cut off.	
زَيْتُونًا	Olive, زَاتَ * he dressed food with oil.	
نَخْلًا	A date palm, نَخَلَ * he sifted.	
غُلْبًا	Thick, luxuriant, غَلَبَ * he conquered, overcame.	
الصَّاخَّةُ	Deafening cry or shout, صَخَّ * he struck something solid.	
ضَاحِكَةٌ	Laughing, ضَحِكَ * he laughed.	
مُسْتَبْشِرَةٌ	One who rejoices, بَشَرَ * he peeled off the bark, بَشَرٌ human beings, بُشْرَى good news.	
غَبَرَةٌ	Dust, غَبَرَ * he delayed.	
تَرْهَقُهَا	Will cover it, رَهِقَ * he oppressed, caused to suffer, covered.	
قَتَرَةٌ	Blackness, black dust, مُقْتِرٌ one in reduced circumstances.	
الْفَجَرَةُ	The evildoers, فُجَّارٌ (pl.) فَاجِرٌ (sing.) wicked ones, evildoers, فَجَرَ * he caused water to pour forth, acted wickedly, فَجَّرَ II he made to flow, فُجِّرَتْ (fem. pass.) it was made to flow.	

Translation of Surah 80 ᶜAbasa (He Frowned)

(1) HE FROWNED and turned away (2) because the blind man approached him! (3) Yet for all thou didst know, (O Muhammad), he might perhaps have grown in purity, (4) or have been reminded (of the truth), and helped by this reminder. (5) Now as for him who believes himself to be self-sufficient - (6) to him didst thou give thy whole attention, (7) although thou art not accountable for his failure to attain to purity; (8) but as for him who came unto thee full of eagerness (9) and in awe (of Allah) - (10) him didst thou disregard! (11) NAY, VERILY, these (messages) are but a reminder: (12) and so, whoever is willing may remember Him (13) in (the light of His) revelations blessed with dignity, (14) lofty and pure, (15) (borne) by the hands of messengers (16) noble and most virtuous. (17) (But only too often) man destroys himself: how stubbornly does he deny the truth! (18) (Does man ever consider) out of what substance (Allah) creates him? (19) Out of a drop of sperm He creates him, and thereupon determines his nature, (20) and then makes it easy for him to go through life; (21) and in the end He causes him to die and brings him to the grave; (22) and then, when it is His will, He shall raise him again to life. (23) Nay, but (man) has never yet fulfilled what He has enjoined upon him! (24) Let man, then, consider (the sources of) his food: (25) (how it is) that We pour down water, pouring it down abundantly; (26) and then We cleave the earth (with new growth), cleaving it asunder, (27) and thereupon We cause grain to grow out of it, (28) and vines and edible plants, (29) and olive trees and date-palms, (30) and gardens dense with foliage, (31) and fruits and herbage, (32) for you and for your animals to enjoy. (33) And so, when the piercing call (of resurrection) is heard (34) on a Day when everyone will (want to) flee from his brother, (35) and from his mother and father, (36) and from his spouse and his children: (37) on that Day, to every one of them will his own state be of sufficient concern. (38) Some faces will on that Day be bright with happiness, (39) laughing, rejoicing at glad tidings. (40) And some faces will on that Day with dust be covered, (41) with darkness overspread: (42) these, they will be the ones who denied the truth and were immersed in iniquity!

Explanatory Notes for Surah 80

The first part of the *surah* mentions a certain incident which took place in the early days of Islam. One day, as recorded in many well authenticated Traditions, the Prophet (SAAS) was engrossed in conversation with some of the most influential chieftains of pagan Makka, hoping to convince them - and, through them, the Makkan community at large - of the truth of his message. At that point, he was approached by one of his followers, the blind ʿAbd'Allah ibn Surayh - known after his grandmother's name as Ibn Umm Maktum - with the request for a repetition or elucidation of certain earlier passages of the Qur'an. Annoyed by this interruption of what he momentarily regarded as a more important endeavour, Muhammad (SAAS) "frowned and turned away" from the blind man - and was immediately, there and then, reproved by the revelation of the first ten verses of this *surah*. In later years he often greeted Ibn Umm Maktum with these words of humility: "Welcome unto him on whose account my Sustainer has rebuked me (ʿatabani)!"

In the second part, man's ungrateful attitude to Allah (SWT) and his denial of Him is discussed. Man is reminded of his origin, of how his life is made easy, and of how Allah (SWT) determines his death and resurrection; and of how, after all, he fails to carry out his orders. He turns his back to the true faith despite his being called upon to adopt it.

The third part directs man to reflect upon things of immediate concern to him, namely his food, the provision of which is carefully planned by the Hand that created man. Man plays no role in any of its stages. The final part touches upon "the stunning blast" and its fearful effects. It makes people unaware of anything around them. The very sound of the words give an impression of horror. Their faces, however, give a lucid account of what is happening to them.

The message of the *surah* and its implications are so powerful that no human heart can avoid being deeply touched by it.

Makki Surah

بِسْمِ اللَّهِ الرَّحْمَنِ الرَّحِيمِ

29 Ayat

Surah 81 At-Takwir

Meaning	Words	Meaning	Words
And when the seas[3] (ptcls., def.noun br. pl.)	وَإِذَا الْبِحَارُ	When the sun[1] (ptcl., def. noun fem. sing.)	إِذَا الشَّمْسُ
Shall be set on fire,[2] Boil over, fill with fire (dr. vrb. II madi maj. fem. sing)	سُجِّرَتْ	Is folded up[2] (darkened) (dr. vrb. II madi maj. III. fem. sing.)	كُوِّرَتْ
And when the souls (persons)[3] (ptcls., def. noun br. pl.)	وَإِذَا النُّفُوسُ	And when the stars[3] (ptcls., def. noun br. pl.)	وَإِذَا النُّجُومُ
Shall be joined (to their bodies)[2] (dr. vrb. II madi maj. III. fem. sing.)	زُوِّجَتْ	Fall and become scattered[2] (dr. vrb. VII madi III. fem. sing.)	انكَدَرَتْ
And when the girl child buried alive (ptcls., pass. prtc. fem. sing.)	وَإِذَا الْمَوْءُودَةُ	And when the mountains[3] (ptcls., def. noun br. pl.)	وَإِذَا الْجِبَالُ
Is asked[2] (madi maj. III. fem. sing.)	سُئِلَتْ	Will be moved, uprooted,[2] made to vanish (dr. vrb. II madi maj. III. fem. sing.)	سُيِّرَتْ
For what crime (ptcl., أَيِّ inter. pro. gen. mdf., noun mdfi.)	بِأَيِّ ذَنبٍ	And when the (ten months pregnant) she camel (ptcls., def. noun fem. sing.)	وَإِذَا الْعِشَارُ
She had been slain (madi maj. III. fem. sing.)	قُتِلَتْ	Is left unattended[2] (dr. vrb. II madi maj. III. fem. sing.)	عُطِّلَتْ
And when the pages, scrolls or records[3] (ptcls., noun br. pl.)	وَإِذَا الصُّحُفُ	And when the beasts[3] (ptcls., def. noun br. pl.)	وَإِذَا الْوُحُوشُ
Are folded[2] (madi maj. III. fem. sing.)	نُشِرَتْ	Are gathered together[2] (madi maj. fem. sing.)	حُشِرَتْ
And when the Heaven/sky (ptcls. def. noun fem. sing.)	وَإِذَا السَّمَاءُ		
Is laid bare, uncovered, stripped[2] (madi maj. III. fem. sing.)	كُشِطَتْ		

[1] Sun is a feminine word in Arabic.

[2] After إِذَا madi takes the meaning of imperfect (ref.: Juz 2&3 p.129)

[3] Broken plurals of many words are treated as feminine singular.

Surah 81 At-Takwir

Meaning	Words	Meaning	Words
And when Hell (ptcls. def. noun fem. sing.)	وَإِذَا ٱلْجَحِيمُ	When it breathes to shine, when it clears away darkness with its breath (ptcl., dr. vrb. V *madi* III. msc. sing.)	إِذَا تَنَفَّسَ
Is caused to burn fiercely (dr. vrb. II *madi maj*. III. fem. sing.)	سُعِّرَتْ	Indeed it (the Qur'an) is (ptcl., pro.)	إِنَّهُ
And when the Garden/Paradise (ptcls., def. noun fem. sing.)	وَإِذَا ٱلْجَنَّةُ	Certainly the word (لَ emph., noun *mdf*.)	لَقَوْلُ
Is brought nearer (dr. vrb. IV *madi maj*. III. fem. sing.)	أُزْلِفَتْ	Of a Messenger, Noble (the angel Jibril {AS}) (noun *mdfi*., adj. *mdfi*.)	رَسُولٍ كَرِيمٍ
Came to know a (every) soul, A soul will come to know (*madi* III. fem. sing., noun fem. sing. nom.)	عَلِمَتْ نَفْسٌ	Possessor of power, strength (dem. pro. *mdfi*., noun gen.)	ذِي قُوَّةٍ
What it has put forward, presented. (ptcl., dr. vrb. IV *madi* III. fem. sing.)	مَّا أَحْضَرَتْ	(In the sight of) The Possessor of the Throne (ptcl., dem. pro. gen. *mdf*., def. noun *mdfi*.)	عِندَ ذِي ٱلْعَرْشِ
But nay *or* So no! I swear (ptcls., dr. vrb. IV *mudari*ᶜ I. sing.)	فَلَا أُقْسِمُ	(Whose rank is) firmly established (act. ptcl. msc. sing. gen.)	مَكِينٍ
By the receding stars (ptcl., def. noun br. pl. gen.)	بِٱلْخُنَّسِ	Obeyed then and there (pass. prtc. of dr. vrb. IV أَطَاعَ, dem. pro. ثَمَّ)	مُطَاعٍ ثَمَّ
The swiftly moving (noun act. prtc. br. pl. gen.)	ٱلْجَوَارِ	Faithful, trustworthy (⁵act. ptcl.)	أَمِينٍ
The hiding ones (act. prtc. br. pl. gen.)	ٱلْكُنَّسِ	And your companion is not (ptcls., noun msc. sing. *mdf*., att. pro. pl. *mdfi*.)	وَمَا صَاحِبُكُم
By the night⁴ (ptcl., def. noun gen.)	وَٱلَّيْلِ	A mad man (ptcl., noun gen.)	بِمَجْنُونٍ
When it falls, spreads (ptcl., مَزِيدٌ فِيهِ tetra. *madi* III. msc. sing.)	إِذَا عَسْعَسَ	And indeed he saw him (the angel Jibril) (ptcls., *madi* III. msc. sing., pro.)	وَلَقَدْ رَآهُ
By the morning⁴ (ptcl., def. noun gen.)	وَٱلصُّبْحِ		

⁴ وَ is for swearing an oath, the object sworn by being in the genitive case.

Surah 81 At-Takwir

Words	Meaning	Words	Meaning
بِالْأُفُقِ	On the horizon (ptcl., noun gen.)	إِنْ هُوَ إِلَّا	That it (the message, the Qur'an) is nothing but (ptcl., per. pro. msc. sing., ptcl.)
الْمُبِينِ	The clear (act. prtc. adj. msc. sing. gen.)	ذِكْرٌ	A reminder (noun nom.)
وَمَا هُوَ	And he is not (In communication) (ptcls., per. pro. msc. sing.)	لِلْعَالَمِينَ	For the worlds/creatures (ptcl., noun msc. pl. gen.)
عَلَى الْغَيْبِ	On the unseen, secrets (ptcl., def. noun gen.)	لِمَنْ شَاءَ	For whoever wished (ptcl., pro., madi III. msc. sing.)
بِضَنِينٍ	Greedy, avaracious (ptcl., act. prtc. gen.)	مِنكُمْ	Among you (ptcl., att. pro. pl. gen.)
وَمَا هُوَ بِقَوْلِ	And it (the Qur'an) is not a word of (ptcls., per. pro., ptcl., noun mdf. gen.)	أَن يَسْتَقِيمَ	That he walk a straight way (ptcl., dr. vrb. X mudari⁶ subj. md. III. msc. sing.)
شَيْطَانٍ رَجِيمٍ	A Satan, an accursed one (noun mdfi., noun adj. mdfi.)	وَمَا تَشَاءُونَ	And you do not wish cannot wish or do (anything) (ptcls., mudari⁶ II. msc. pl.)
فَأَيْنَ	So where (ptcls.)	إِلَّا أَن	Unless that (ptcls.)
تَذْهَبُونَ	Are you all going? (mudari⁶ II. msc. pl.)	يَشَاءَ اللَّهُ	Allah wishes (mudari⁶ subj. md. III. msc. sing., pro. noun sing.)
		رَبُّ الْعَالَمِينَ	Lord of the worlds/creatures (noun mdf., noun msc. pl. mdfi.)

⁵ Active participle on the measure of فَعِيلٌ that denotes a stable meaning of the root, one who possesses the quality as a permanent and inseparable nature of his personality. Some regard it as a passive participle of the form مَفْعُولٌ i.e. مَأْمُونٌ , thus meaning 'trusted'.

Root Words of Surah 81

كُوِّرَتْ Folded up, wound round, كَارَ * he twisted up a turban, كَوَّرَ II he rolled up, تَكْوِيرٌ act of folding up.

انكَدَرَتْ VII they shot downwards (the stars), fell down, became muddy, كَدَرَ * it was muddy.

الْعِشَارُ She camels ten months pregnant, عُشَرَاءُ (sing.), عَشَرَ * he took away a tenth part,

	مَعْشَر kinsfolk, عَشِيرَة race, company.	
عُطِّلَت	Left without care, عَطِلَ * he was bare of ornaments, عَطَّلَ II he left (a thing) without care.	
الْوُحُوش	The wild beasts, وَحَشَ * he threw away (arms, etc.) in flight.	
سُجِّرَت	Filled, swelled up and became turgid, سَجَرَ * it filled with water, burned.	
الْمَوْؤُودَة	(The girl) buried alive, وَأَدَ * he buried alive.	
سُئِلَت	Is asked, questioned, سَأَلَ he asked, interrogated, asked for, demanded, تُسْئَلُنَّ you will be asked, السَّائِل the one who asks, the beggar.	
ذَنْب	Wrong action, sin, fault, a crime, ذَنَبَ * he followed closely.	
كُشِطَت	Is stripped, كَشَطَ * he removed, took off a cover.	
سُعِّرَت	Caused to burn fiercely, سَعَرَ * he lit a fire, سَعَّرَ II he caused to burn fiercely, سَعِير a burning fire.	
أُزْلِفَت	Is brought near, زَلَفَ * he drew near, أَزْلَفَ IV he brought near, زُلْفَة nearness.	
أُحْضِرَت	IV Has presented, حَضَرَ * he was present to or present at, stood in presence.	
أُقْسِم	I swear, قَسَمَ * he divided into parts, قَسَم an oath, قِسْمَة apportionment, a dividing.	
الْخُنَّس	The receding stars, خَنَّاس sneaking, Shaytan, because he hides himself at the name of Allah خَنَسَ * he remained behind, hid away.	
الْجَوَار	Moving swiftly, course of a ship, جَرَى * it happened, ran, flowed.	
الْكُنَّس	Those which hide themselves (stars), كَنَسَ * to lie in a covert (a deer).	
عَسْعَسَ	It departed (quad. vrb.), approached, advanced, عَسَّ * he kept watch, he went round by night.	
تَنَفَّسَ	V he breathed away, نَفْس a person, a self, a soul, (pls.) أَنْفُس and, نُفُوس, نَفَسَ * he injured by casting an evil eye upon someone, مُتَنَافِس one who longs for, تَنَافَسَ VI he longed for.	
مُطَاع	Obeyed one, طَاعَ * he was obedient, أَطَاعَ IV he obeyed, لَا تُطِعْه do not obey him!	
أَمِين	Secure, trustworthy, faithful, أَمِنَ * he was secure, put trust in, مَأْمُون secured, آمَنَ IV he had faith in, he believed, he made sure, he secured, إِيمَان faith, آمَنُوا they believed.	
صَاحِبُكُم	Your companion, صَحِبَ أَصْحَاب (pl.), * he was a companion to someone.	
مَجْنُون	Mad, possessed by a Jinn, جَنَّ * he covered, جَنَّات (pl.) جَنَّة garden, paradise, جِنّ jinn, genii, demon, جِنَّة a jinn, madness, جُنَّة shield, cover.	
أُفْق	The horizon, أَفَقَ * he dressed leather.	
ضَنِين	Tenacious, greedy, avaricious, grudging, ضَنَّ * he was tenacious or grasping.	
رَجِيم	Thrown off with curse, driven away with stones, رَجَمَ * he stoned, رَجْم conjecture, a doubt.	
يَسْتَقِيم	He keeps straight, يَقُوم قَامَ * he stood fast or firm, he stood, he stood forth, اسْتَقَامَ X he walked uprightly (in the paths of religion), تَقْوِيم قَيِّمَة right, true, stature, mould, formation, symmetry, يُقِيمُون they establish.	

36

The Qur'an Translation and Study – Juz' 30

Translation of Surah 81 At-Takwir (Shrouding in Darkness)

(1) WHEN THE SUN is shrouded in darkness, (2) and when the stars lose their light, (3) and when the mountains are made to vanish, (4) and when she-camels big with young, about to give birth, are left unattended, (5) and when all beasts are gathered together, (6) and when the seas boil over, (7) and when men's souls are paired (like with like), (8) and when the girl-child that was buried alive is asked (9) for what crime she had been slain, (10) and when the scrolls (of men's deeds) are unfolded, (11) and when heaven is laid bare, (12) and when the blazing fire (of hell) is kindled bright, (13) and when paradise is brought into view: (14) (on that Day) every human being will come to know what he has prepared (for himself). (15) But nay! I call to witness the revolving stars, (16) the planets that run their courses and set, (17) and the night as it darkly falls, (18) and the morn as it softly breathes: (19) behold, this (divine writ) is indeed the (inspired) word of a noble apostle, (20) with strength endowed, secure with the Possessor of the Throne (21) (the word) of one to be heeded, and worthy of trust! (22) For, this fellow man of yours is not a mad-man: (23) he truly beheld him (the angel) on the clear horizon, (24) and he is not one to begrudge others the knowledge (of whatever has been revealed to him) out of that which is beyond the reach of human perception. (25) Nor is this (message) the word of any accursed *shaytan*. (26) Whither, then, will you go? (27) This (message) is no less than a reminder to all mankind - (28) to every one of you who wills to walk a straight way. (29) But you cannot will it unless Allah, the Sustainer of all the worlds, wills (to show you that way).

Explanatory Notes for Surah 81

Ayat 1 to 14 of this *surah* sketch a scene of a great upheaval, it is one of violent movement, which envelops the whole universe and which leaves nothing in its place. The *surah* aims to establish in men's hearts and minds that worldly values, riches and enjoyments have no importance as they will perish. People should establish a firm bond with the everlasting Truth, the truth of Allah the Eternal Who never changes, when everything else changes and disappears.

The darkening of the sun probably means it will cool down; the falling of the Stars probably means that they will break away from the system which holds them together and lose their light and brightness; the mountains will probably be crushed and blown away; a ten months pregnant she-camel is to an Arab his most valuable possession because she is about to give him a highly valued young camel and a lot of milk, however on that day such priceless camels will be left unattended; the overwhelming terror changes the character of the wildest beasts. What would it do to man? Seas will be overfilled with water from floods similar to those which characterised the early stages of life on earth, or the barriers now separating the seas will be removed so the water from one will flow into the other. The pairing of souls may mean the reunion of body and soul or it may mean grouping like with like. The barbaric custom of burying female infants alive seems to have been fairly widespread in pre-Islamic Arabia for fear of shame and poverty. Islam condemns this attitude, forbids it and expresses its horrifying nature. It makes it one of the subjects of the reckoning on the Day of Judgement, the murdered girl will be questioned about her murder, imagine how the murderer will be brought to account.

In present times, Muslims in general are not killing their daughters (and also sons) physically; but by depriving them of true Islamic education right from the beginning and exposing them to un-Islamic culture without Islamic guidance and allowing them to practise un-Islamic ways, they are killing them spiritually. Such children have un-Islamic thinking and attitudes towards life. This is the modern way of killing children; different from pagan Arabs and is a more heinous sin because the true message of Islam has reached us and we are no longer pagans.

Ayat 15 to 29 discuss the principle of revelation with a certain form of oath by depicting some very beautiful scenes in the universe. Qur'an is a noble, mighty and exalted message. Allah (SWT) has chosen the angel Jibril (AS) to convey His Revelation to the Prophet Muhammad (SAAS) who conveys this revelation to the people.

Surah 82 Al-Infitar

Makki Surah   بِسْمِ اللّٰهِ الرَّحْمٰنِ الرَّحِيْمِ   19 *Ayat*

Words	Meaning	Words	Meaning
اِذَا السَّمَآءُ	When the sky, heaven (ptcl., def. noun fem. sing.)	يٰٓاَيُّهَا الْاِنْسَانُ	O man[3] (ptcl. interj.,[3] def. noun msc. sing.)
انْفَطَرَتْ	Is cleft asunder[1] (dr. vrb. VII *madi* III. fem. sing.)	مَا غَرَّكَ	What seduced you (away) (ptcl., *madi* III. msc. sing., att. pro. كَ)
وَاِذَا الْكَوَاكِبُ	And when the stars (ptcls., noun br. pl.)[2]	بِرَبِّكَ الْكَرِيْمِ	From your bountiful Lord, Gracious Sustainer (ptcl., noun gen. *mdf*., att. pro. *mdfi*., def. adj.)
انْتَثَرَتْ	Are scattered[1] (dr. vrb. VII *madi* III. fem. sing.)	الَّذِيْ خَلَقَكَ	The One Who created you (rel. pro. msc. sing., *madi* III. msc. sing., att. pro. كَ)
وَاِذَا الْبِحَارُ	And when the seas (ptcl., noun br. pl.)[2]	فَسَوّٰىكَ	Then perfected, proportioned, fashioned you (ptcl., dr. vrb. II *madi* III. msc. sing., att. pro. كَ)
فُجِّرَتْ	are made to flow[1] (beyond their bounds) (dr. vrb. II *madi maj*. III. fem. sing.)		
وَاِذَا الْقُبُوْرُ	And when the graves (ptcls., noun br. pl.)[2]	فَعَدَلَكَ	He disposed you aright (ptcl., *madi* III. msc. sing., att. pro. كَ)
بُعْثِرَتْ	Are turned upside down, opened, torn forth (*madi maj*. مَزِيْد فِيْه tetra. III. fem. sing.)	فِيْٓ اَيِّ صُوْرَةٍ	In whichever form (ptcl., اَيِّ inter. pro. gen. *mdf*., noun fem. sing. *mdfi*.)
عَلِمَتْ نَفْسٌ	Shall know a soul (*madi* III. fem. sing., noun fem. sing. nom.)	مَا شَآءَ	That He willed (ptcl., *madi* III. msc. sing.)
مَّا قَدَّمَتْ	What it sent ahead (ptcl., dr. vrb. II *madi* III. fem. sing.)	رَكَّبَكَ	He put you together, constructed you (dr. vrb. II *madi* III. msc. sing., att. pro. كَ)
وَاَخَّرَتْ	And what it left undone, left behind, deferred (ptcls., dr. vrb. II *madi* III. fem. sing.)		

---

[1] After اِذَا *madi* takes the meaning of imperfect (ref. Juz 2&3 p.129).

[2] Broken plurals of many words are treated as fem. sing.

[3] Particles of interjection require a definite noun after them in the nominative case.

Surah 82 Al-Infitar

Meaning	Words	Meaning	Words
They shall roast (in) it (Hell) (*mudari*ᶜ III. msc. pl., att. pro. هَا)	يَصْلَوْنَهَا	Nay! but/rather By no means but/rather (ptcls.)	كَلَّا بَلْ
On the Day of Judgement (noun adv. acc. *mdf.*, def. noun *mdfi.*)⁴	يَوْمَ الدِّينِ	You (O men) belie (dr. vrb. II *mudari*ᶜ II. msc. pl.)	تُكَذِّبُونَ
And they (will) not (ptcls., per. pro. msc. pl.)	وَمَا هُمْ	The Judgment (the day of punishment & reward) (ptcl., def. noun gen.)	بِالدِّينِ
From it (Hell) (ptcl., att. pro. هَا)	عَنْهَا	And indeed over you (ptcls., att. pro. كُمْ)	وَإِنَّ عَلَيْكُمْ
(be able to be) absent (ptcl., act. prtc. msc. pl. gen.)	بِغَائِبِينَ	(There) certainly are guards, watchers (ptcl. لَ emph., act. prtc. msc. pl. acc.)	لَحَافِظِينَ
And what would make you know (ptcls., dr. vrb. IV *madi* III. msc. sing., att. pro. كَ)	وَمَا أَدْرَاكَ	Nobles, who record, write or noble scribes (noun br. pl. acc., act. prtc. msc. pl. acc.)	كِرَامًا كَاتِبِينَ
What the Day of Judgement is (ptcl., noun *mdf.*, def noun *mdfi.*)	مَا يَوْمُ الدِّينِ	They know (*mudari*ᶜ III. msc. pl.)	يَعْلَمُونَ
Again what would make you know (ثُمَّ ptcl. class., ptcl., dr. vrb. IV *madi* III. msc. sing., att. pro. كَ)	ثُمَّ مَا أَدْرَاكَ	What you do (ptcl., *mudari*ᶜ II. msc. pl.)	مَا تَفْعَلُونَ
What the Day of Judgement is? (ptcl., noun *mdf.*, def noun *mdfi.*)	مَا يَوْمُ الدِّينِ	Indeed the righteous ones (ptcl., def. noun br. pl. acc.)	إِنَّ الْأَبْرَارَ
(On) a day⁴ shall not possess (noun adv.⁴, ptcl. negn., *mudari*ᶜ III. fem. sing.)	يَوْمَ لَا تَمْلِكُ	Will certainly be in bliss, happiness, pleasure delight (ptcl. لَ emph., ptcl., noun gen.)	لَفِي نَعِيمٍ
		And indeed the wicked ones (ptcls., act. prtc. msc. br. pl. acc.)	وَإِنَّ الْفُجَّارَ
⁴ يَوْمَ has a *fathah* instead of the usual *dammah* because here it is adverbial ظَرْفُ زَمَانٍ or because it is the object of an unstated verb such as "Remember...!"		Will certainly (be) in Hell (ptcl. لَ emph., ptcl., noun gen.)	لَفِي جَحِيمٍ

Words	Meaning	Words	Meaning
نَفْسٌ لِنَفْسٍ	Anyone for anyone else, A self for a self (noun fem. sing. nom., ptcl., noun fem. sing. gen.)	وَالْأَمْرُ	And the command, the affair, the judgement (ptcl., def. noun sing. nom.)
شَيْئًا	Anything/A thing (noun acc.)	يَوْمَئِذٍ	On that day (shall be) (noun adv. يَوْم = day إِذْ = then {ptcl.})
		لِلَّهِ	For Allah (alone) (ptcl., proper noun gen.)

Root Words of Surah 82

انْفَطَرَتْ Was cleft asunder, فَطَرَ * He created, he split, انْفَطَرَ VII it was cloven asunder.

انْتَثَرَتْ Were scattered, نَثَرَ * he dispersed, انْتَثَرَ VIII it was scattered.

بُعْثِرَتْ Was poured forth, overturned, بَعْثَرَ * (quad. vrb.) he tore forth, it lay open, turned upside down, he exposed.

غَرَّكَ Beguiled you, deceived, غَرَّ * he deceived with vain hopes, غُرُورٌ a vain hope, غَرُورٌ a shaytan, a deceiver.

فَعَدَلَكَ Then He proportioned you, عَدَلَ * he dealt justly, he held as equal, he disposed aright, عَدْلٌ justice, recompense, ransom.

رَكَّبَكَ He constructed you, He put you together, رَكِبَ * he was carried, he rode, رَكَّبَ II he put together, تَرْكَبُنَّ surely you will ride, مُتَرَاكِبٌ (act. prtc. dr. vrb. VI) lying in heaps.

حَافِظِينَ Guardians, protectors, حَفِظَ * he kept, guarded, مَحْفُوظٌ well guarded, protected.

نَعِيمٍ Bliss, pleasure, delight, happiness, نَعِمَ * he enjoyed the comforts and conveniences of life, he was joyful, نِعْمَ he was excellent, نَاعِمَةٌ rejoicing, joyful, نَعَّمَ II he provided good things for someone.

يَصْلَوْنَهَا They will roast in it, صَلَى * he roasted, صَلِيَ he underwent roasting in the fire.

Translation of Surah 82 Al-Infitar (The Cleaving Asunder)

(1) When the sky is cleft asunder, (2) and when the stars are scattered, (3) and when the seas burst beyond their bounds, (4) and when the graves are overturned - (5) a person will (at last) comprehend what he has sent ahead and what he has held back (in this world). (6) O Man! What is it that lures thee away from thy bountiful Sustainer, (7) Who has created thee, and formed thee in accordance with what thou art meant to be, and shaped thy nature in just proportions, (8) having put thee together in whatever form He willed (thee to have)? (9) Nay, (O men,) but you (are lured away from Allah whenever you are tempted to) give the lie to Allah's Judgement! (10) And yet, verily, there are ever-watchful (forces) over you, (11) noble recording, (12) they know whatever you do! (13) Behold, (in the life to come) the truly virtuous will indeed be in bliss, (14) whereas, behold, the wicked will indeed be in a blazing fire - (15) (a fire) which they shall roast in on Judgement Day, (16) and which they shall not (be able to) evade. (17) And what could make thee conceive what that Judgement Day will be? (18) And once again: What could make thee conceive what that Judgement Day will be? (19) (It will be) a Day

when no human being shall be of the least avail to another human being: for on that Day (it will become manifest that) the sovereignty is Allah's (alone).

The Explanatory Notes for Surah 82

The opening of the *surah* mentions the violent change which overwhelms the universe as we see it, and it leaves nothing in its familiar shape and condition. The feelings generated in people when they visualise the universe undergoing such a change are, that they tend to pull man away from anything which gives him a sense of security, with the exception of Allah, the Creator of the universe, the One Who lives on after everything has died and withered away, Who is the only One worthy of being worshipped. As the graves are hurled about people are resurrected and stand up again, back in life, to face the reckoning and receive their reward or punishment.

The second part of the *surah*, by means of gentle remonstrance combined with an implicit threat, touches the hearts of men who busy themselves with trivialities. Man who is the recipient of abundant grace does not show any gratitude for Allah's gracious blessings, and continues with his erring ways and impudent behaviour towards Him.

The third part provides the reason for such an ungrateful attitude. The denial of reckoning and judgement, the *surah* tells us, is the source of every evil. How can any person disbelieve in the Judgement and still lead a life based on goodness and right guidance? The reality of the meting out of reward and punishment at the Last Judgement is re-emphasised.

The final part of the *surah* gives an idea of how fearful the Day of Judgement is, how everyone is absolutely helpless and all power belongs to Allah (SWT).

Makki Surah   بِسْمِ اللَّهِ الرَّحْمَٰنِ الرَّحِيمِ   36 *Ayat*

Surah 83 Al-Mutaffifin or At-Tatfif

Meaning	Words	Meaning	Words
They give short measure, diminish (dr. vrb. IV *mudari*ᶜ III. msc. pl.)	يُخْسِرُونَ	Woe (ptcl. interj.)[1]	وَيْلٌ
Do (they) not think[3] (*alif* ptcl. inter., ptcl. negn., *mudari*ᶜ msc. sing.)	اَلَا يَظُنُّ	To those who give short measure (ptcl., noun act. prtc. dr. vrb. II pl. gen.)	لِلْمُطَفِّفِينَ
Those, that they all (shall be) (dem. pro. msc. pl., ptcl., att. per. pro. msc. pl.)	أُولَٰئِكَ أَنَّهُم	The ones who, when (rel. pro. msc. pl., ptcl.)	الَّذِينَ إِذَا
Raised from the dead (pass. prtc. msc. pl. nom.)	مَبْعُوثُونَ	They receive their measure[2] (dr. vrb. VIII *madi* III. msc. pl.)	اكْتَالُوا
On a great or heavy day (ptcl., noun gen., adj. gen.)	لِيَوْمٍ عَظِيمٍ	From (other) people (عَلَىٰ used as مِن = from, def. coll. noun)	عَلَى النَّاسِ
A day (the Day of Judgement) (noun adv.)	يَوْمَ	They demand full measure (dr. vrb. X *mudari*ᶜ III. msc. pl.)	يَسْتَوْفُونَ
Shall stand people (*mudari*ᶜ III. msc. sing., coll. def. noun)	يَقُومُ النَّاسُ	And when they measure[2] (ptcls., *madi* III. msc. pl.)	وَإِذَا كَالُوا
Before the Lord/Sustainer of the worlds (ptcl., noun sing. gen. *mdf.*, def. noun msc. pl. *mdfi.*)	لِرَبِّ الْعَالَمِينَ	(for) them, (for other people) (per. pro. msc. pl.)	هُمْ
		or they weigh[2] (ptcl., *madi* III. msc. pl.)	أَوْ وَزَنُوهُمْ
Nay but, indeed By no means, indeed (ptcls.)	كَلَّا إِنَّ	(for) them, (for others) (per. pro. msc. pl.)	هُمْ

---

[1] وَيْلٌ is an interjection commonly used with لِ to express a big misfortune.

[2] After إِذَا *madi* takes the meaning of imperfect (ref. Juz 2&3 p.129).

[3] أ is for a question.

Surah 83 Al-Mutaffifin or At-Tatfif

Words	Meaning	Words	Meaning
كِتَٰبَ ٱلْفُجَّارِ	The book, record of the wicked (noun sing. acc. *mdf.*, act. prtc. msc. br. pl. *mdfi.*)	وَمَا يُكَذِّبُ بِهِ	And does not belie or deny it, none gives the lie to it (ptcls., dr. vrb. II *mudari'* III. msc. sing., ptcl., att. pro. ه)
لَفِى سِجِّينٍ	is (preserved) in Sijjeen[4] (لَ emph., ptcl., noun gen.)	إِلَّا كُلُّ	Except all those, everyone (who is) (ptcl., noun nom. *mdf.*)
وَمَا أَدْرَىٰكَ	And what would make you know (ptcls., dr. vrb. IV *madi* III. msc. sing., att. pro. كَ)	مُعْتَدٍ أَثِيمٍ	Wrongdoing, transgressor (act. prtc. dr. vrb. VIII *mdfi.*, noun adj. *mdfi.*)
مَا سِجِّينٌ	What Sijjeen[4] (is)? (ptcl., noun nom.)	إِذَا تُتْلَىٰ عَلَيْهِ	When there is recited on (to) him (ptcl., *mudari'* maj. III. fem. sing., ptcl., att. pro. ه)
كِتَٰبٌ مَّرْقُومٌ	A book, record (fully) inscribed (registered) (noun sing. nom., pass. prtc. sing. adj. nom.)	ءَايَٰتُنَا	Our signs, verses (noun fem. pl. nom. *mdf.*, att. pro. نَا *mdfi.*)
وَيْلٌ يَوْمَئِذٍ	Woe, on that day (ptcl. interj.[1], noun adv. يَوْمَئِذٍ يَوْمَ = day إِذْ = then{ptcl.})	قَالَ	He (the wrongdoer) said (*madi* III. msc. sing.)
لِّلْمُكَذِّبِينَ	To the beliers or deniers who give the lie to the truth (ptcl., act. prtc. dr. vrb. II msc. pl. gen.)	أَسَٰطِيرُ ٱلْأَوَّلِينَ	(they are) Tales of the ancients, those of former days (noun br. pl. *mdf.*, ord. no. pl. *mdfi.*)
ٱلَّذِينَ يُكَذِّبُونَ	The ones who belie, deny (rel. pro. msc. pl., dr. vrb. II *mudari'* III. msc. pl.)	كَلَّا بَلْ	Nay but, by no means but (ptcls.)
بِيَوْمِ ٱلدِّينِ	(With) the Day of Judgement (ptcl., noun gen. *mdf.*, def. noun *mdfi.*)	رَانَ	(their evil deeds) corroded, cast layer of rust, (*madi* III. msc. sing.)
		عَلَىٰ قُلُوبِهِم	Over their hearts (ptcl., noun br. pl. gen. *mdf.*, att. pro. هِم *mdfi.*)
		مَّا كَانُوا يَكْسِبُونَ	What they have been earning (ptcl., past. cont. III. msc. pl.)

[4] *Sijjeen* derives from *sijn* meaning prison. It has the inescapable quality of being the record of bad deeds of the wrong-doer. *Sijjeen* is the register and place where the actions of the wicked are recorded.

Meaning	Words	Meaning	Words
Nay indeed, by no means indeed (ptcls.)	كَلَّا إِنَّ	By no means, verily indeed they (ptcls., att. pro. هُمْ)	كَلَّا إِنَّهُمْ
(the) Book⁵, the record of the righteous ones (noun acc. *mdf.*, def. noun br. pl. *mdfi.*)⁵	كِتَبَ الْأَبْرَارِ	From their Lord, Sustainer (His vision) (ptcl., noun gen. *mdf.*, att. pro. هِمْ *mdfi.*)	عَن رَّبِّهِمْ
is (preserved) in ᶜIlliyeen⁶ (لَ ptcl. emph., ptcl., noun pl. gen.)	لَفِى عِلِّيِّينَ	On that day (the Day of Judgement) (noun adv. يَوْمَ = day إِذْ = then{ptcl.})	يَوْمَئِذٍ
And what would make you know (ptcls., dr. vrb. IV *madi* III. msc. sing., att. pro. كَ)	وَمَآ أَدْرَىٰكَ	(shall be) certainly shut out, debarred (لَ ptcl. emph., pass. prtc. msc. pl. nom.)	لَّمَحْجُوبُونَ
What ᶜIlliyun⁷ is (ptcl., noun pl. nom.)	مَا عِلِّيُّونَ	Then, indeed they (shall be) (ptcl. class., ptcl., att. pro. هُمْ)	ثُمَّ إِنَّهُمْ
A book, record (fully) inscribed registered (noun sing. nom., adj. pass. part. msc. sing.)	كِتَبٌ مَّرْقُومٌ	(the ones who) roast in Hell (لَ ptcl. emph., noun act. prtc. msc. pl. *mdf.*, def. noun *mdfi.*)	لَصَالُوا۟ الْجَحِيمِ
(They) witness it (the record) (*mudariᶜ* III. msc. sing., att. pro. msc. sing.)	يَشْهَدُهُ	Then it shall be said (to them) (ptcl. class., *mudariᶜ maj.* III. msc. sing.)	ثُمَّ يُقَالُ
Those who are brought nearer to or permitted to approach (Allah) (pass. prtc. dr. vrb. II pl. nom.)	الْمُقَرَّبُونَ	This is the one (reality) which (dem. pro. msc. sing., rel. pro. msc. sing.)	هَٰذَا الَّذِى
Indeed the righteous ones (ptcl., def. noun br. pl. acc.)	إِنَّ الْأَبْرَارَ	You used to belie, deny (past. cont. كُنتُم بِهِ تُكَذِّبُونَ = كُنتُم *madi* II. msc. pl., بِ ptcl., att. pro. هِ, تُكَذِّبُونَ dr. vrb. II. *mudariᶜ* msc. pl.)	كُنتُم بِهِۦ تُكَذِّبُونَ
(will certainly be) in bliss, happiness, pleasure, delight (لَ ptcl. emph., ptcl., noun gen.)	لَفِى نَعِيمٍ		
(Resting) on the couches (ptcl., def. noun br. pl. gen.)	عَلَى الْأَرَآئِكِ		

⁵ كِتَابَ which is *mudaf* has *fathah* instead of the usual *dammah* because of the action of إِنَّ.

⁶ This is genitive because it is preceded by فِى.

⁷ ᶜIlliyun is derived from ᶜilli – loftiness which is derived from عَلِىّ which means high, exalted, sublime. ᶜIlliyun is where the register of good actions is preserved.

Surah 83 Al-Mutaffifin or At-Tatfif

Meaning	Words	Meaning	Words
And it's mixture (ptcl., noun *mdf*., att. pro. ه *mdfi*.)	وَمِزَاجُهُۥ	They shall look around (*mudari'* III. msc. pl.)	يَنظُرُونَ
Is of Tasnim[8] (ptcl., noun gen.)	مِن تَسْنِيمٍ	You will discern, see, in (*mudari'* II. msc. sing., ptcl.)	تَعْرِفُ فِى
A fountain (noun acc.)	عَيْنًا	Their faces (noun br. pl. gen[6]. *mdf*., att. pro. هم *mdfi*.)	وُجُوهِهِمْ
Shall drink from it (*mudari'* III. msc. sing., ptcl., att. pro. fem.)	يَشْرَبُ بِهَا	Brightness (noun fem. sing. acc. *mdf*.)	نَضْرَةَ
Those who are brought near to or permitted to approach (Allah) (pass. prtc. dr. vrb. II msc. pl. nom.)	الْمُقَرَّبُونَ	Of bliss, happiness, delight, pleasure (def. noun sing. *mdfi*.)	النَّعِيمِ
Indeed those (ptcl., rel. pro. msc. pl.)	إِنَّ الَّذِينَ	They will be given a drink from (of) (*mudari'* maj. msc. pl., ptcl.)	يُسْقَوْنَ مِن
Who sinned, (they) were (dr. vrb. IV madi III. msc. pl., madi III. msc. pl.)	أَجْرَمُوا كَانُوا	A pure drink, wine (noun gen.)	رَحِيقٍ
At the believers (ptcl., rel. pro., dr. vrb. IV madi III. msc. pl.)	مِنَ الَّذِينَ آمَنُوا	Sealed (pass. prtc. gen.)	مَخْتُومٍ
Used[9] to laugh (past cont. *mudari'* III. msc. pl.)	يَضْحَكُونَ	Its seal (will be) of musk (noun sing. nom. *mdf*., att. pro. ه *mdfi*., noun nom.)	خِتَامُهُۥ مِسْكٌ
And whenever they passed (ptcls., madi III. msc. pl.)	وَإِذَا مَرُّوا	And in that (for this) (ptcls., dem. pro. msc. sing.)	وَفِى ذَٰلِكَ
By them (the believers) (ptcl., att. pro.)	بِهِمْ	Let long for, aspire after, strive for (ptcl., ل ptcl. exh., dr. vrb. VI *mudari'* juss. md. III. msc. sing.)	فَلْيَتَنَافَسِ
		(All) who long or aspire after strive for (act. prtc. dr. vrb. VI msc. pl. nom.)	الْمُتَنَافِسُونَ

[8] One of the fountains in Paradise.

[9] The *mudari'* verb is in the past continuous state due to the action of كَانُوا which appears before it (see above).

Meaning	Words	Meaning	Words
Over them (believers) (ptcl., pro. pl.)	عَلَيْهِمْ	They used to wink at one another (dr. vrb. VI mudariᶜ III. msc. pl.)	يَتَغَامَزُونَ
Watchers or guardians (act. prtc. pl. acc.)	حَافِظِينَ	And whenever they return (ptcls., dr. vrb. VII madi III. msc. pl.)	وَإِذَا انقَلَبُوٓا
So today (the Day of Judgement) (ptcl., def. noun adv.)	فَالْيَوْمَ	To their own people (ptcl., noun gen. mdf., att. pro. mdfi.)	إِلَىٰٓ أَهْلِهِمُ
Those who believe (rel. pro. msc. pl., dr. vrb. IV madi III. msc., pl.)	الَّذِينَ ءَامَنُوا	They returned (like the ones) (dr. vrb. VII madi III. msc. pl.)	انقَلَبُوا
Over (at) the deniers disbelievers (ptcl., def. noun br. pl. gen.)	مِنَ الْكُفَّارِ	(Who are) rejoicing, jesting, joyful (act. prtc. msc. pl. acc. adv.)	فَكِهِينَ
Shall laugh (mudariᶜ III. msc. pl.)	يَضْحَكُونَ	And when they (the kafirs) saw them (Believers) (ptcls., madi III. msc. pl., att. pro.)	وَإِذَا رَأَوْهُمْ
On the couches (ptcl., def. noun br. pl. gen.)	عَلَى الْأَرَآئِكِ	They (the kafirs, wrongdoers) said (madi III. msc. pl.)	قَالُوٓا
They shall look around (mudariᶜ III. msc. pl.)	يَنظُرُونَ	Indeed all these (the believers) (ptcl., dem. pro. msc. pl.)	إِنَّ هَٰٓؤُلَآءِ
Are (they) rewarded, recompensed (ptcl. inter., dr. vrb. II madi maj. III. msc. sing.)	هَلْ ثُوِّبَ	Are certainly those who stray (لَ emph., act. prtc. msc. pl. nom.)	لَضَآلُّونَ
The disbelievers, deniers (def. noun br. pl. nom.)	الْكُفَّارُ		
(for) what they have been doing? (ptcl., past cont. III. msc. pl.)	مَا كَانُوا يَفْعَلُونَ	And they have not been sent (ptcls., dr. vrb. IV madi maj. III. msc. pl.)	وَمَآ أُرْسِلُوا

Root Words for Surah 83

يُخْسِرُونَ They give short measure, diminish a quantity, خَسِرَ * he suffered loss, أَخْسَرَ IV he diminished (a quantity), خُسْرَ loss, a losing concern.

مُطَفِّفِينَ Those who give short measure or weight, scrimpers, طَفَّ * he was near, تَطْفِيفٌ vrb. n. II, the giving of short measure.

Surah 83 Al-Mutaffifin or At-Tatfif

كَالُوا	They measured out to anyone, كَالَ * he measured out to anyone, اِكْتَالَ VIII he received by measure from.
يَسْتَوْفُونَ	They take exactly the full, وَفَىٰ * he performed a promise, اِسْتَوْفَىٰ X he demanded full payment, he took full measure.
مَبْعُوثُونَ	Those who are sent or raised up, بَعَثَ * he raised from the dead, he sent, اِنْبَعَثَ VII he was sent, he rose up.
سِجِّين	The register in which the actions of the wicked are recorded, or the place where it is kept, سَجَنَ * he imprisoned, سِجْنٌ a prison.
مَرْقُومٌ	Written one, رَقَمَ * he wrote.
مُعْتَدٍ	A transgressor, wicked, عَدْوًا for عَدَوَ * he transgressed, he passed by, العَادِيَاتُ those who run rapidly, coursers.
أَثِيمٍ	Sinful or wicked person, أَثِمَ * he sinned, آثِمٌ one who sins.
أَسَاطِيرُ	Idle tales, fables, سَطَرَ * he wrote, مَسْطُورٌ written, مُسَيْطِرٌ or مُصَيْطِرٌ a warden, a manager of affairs.
رَانَ	for رَيْنَ * it was rusty, encrusted, it took possession (of the heart).
مَحْجُوبُونَ	Those who are shut out, the debarred ones, حَجَبَ * he covered, he shut out.
عِلِّيِّينَ	عِلِّيُّونَ name of the upper part of the Heavens where the register of men's good actions is preserved, high places, عَلَا * for عَلَوَ he was high, elevated, exalted, lofty, أَعْلَىٰ high, lofty, عَالِيَّة Highest, Most Exalted.
مُقَرَّبُونَ	Those who are made or permitted to draw near, approach, honoured, قَرُبَ * he drew near to, approached, قَرَّبَ II he set before, he caused to draw near, قُرْبَىٰ relationship, مَقْرَبَةٌ kinsfolk, مَقْرَبَةٌ relationship, اِقْتَرَبَ VIII he drew near, was nearer. الأَقْرَبُونَ
أَرَائِكِ	Couches, thrones, أَرِيكَةٌ (sing.), أَرَكَ * he fed on the tree, أَرَاكٌ a camel.
يَنْظُرُونَ	They shall contemplate, نَظَرَ * he looked at, he looked for, expected, considered, saw.
نَضْرَةَ	Brightness, نَضَرَ * he was endowed with brilliancy and beauty, he shone, نَاضِرٌ shining.
يُسْقَوْنَ	They will be given to drink, سَقَىٰ * he gave drink to, watered, أَسْقَىٰ IV he gave drink.
رَحِيقٍ	Pure wine, no verbal root.
مَخْتُومٍ	Sealed, خِتَامُهُ its sealing, خَتَمَ * he sealed, خَاتَمٌ a seal, خَاتَمُ النَّبِيِّينَ seal and close of the long line of prophets, there will be no prophet after him in any case in any shape or in any sense.
مِسْكٌ	Musk, مَسَكَ * he took hold of, مَسَّكَ II he held fast, أَمْسَكَ IV he held, إِمْسَاكٌ the act of retaining.
مِزَاجُهُ	Its mix, مَزَجَ * he mixed.
تَسْنِيمٍ	Name of a fountain in Paradise, said to be so called because conveyed to the highest part of heaven, سَنِمَ * he was tall, سَنَامٌ camel's hump.
أَجْرَمُوا	They committed sin, جَرَمَ * he commited a crime.

مَرُّوا بِ	They passed by, مَرَّ * he passed by, مَرَّةٌ one turn, one time.	
يَتَغَامَزُونَ	They wink at each other, غَمَزَ * he pointed or winked at anyone.	
انْقَلَبُوا	They returned, قَلَبَ * he returned, he turned, قَلْبٌ (pl.) قُلُوبٌ heart, تَقَلَّبَ V he was turned about, changed.	
فَاكِهِينَ	Jesting, فَكِهَ * he was very merry, فَكِهٌ one who makes game of others.	
ثُوِّبَ	Is paid, ثَابَ * he returned, ثَوَّبَ II he repaid, أَثَابَ IV he gave as a recompense, rewarded.	

Translation of Surah 83 Al-Mutaffifin (Those Who Give Short Measure)

(1) Woe be to those who give short measure: (2) those who, when they are to receive their due from (other) people, demand that it be given in full - (3) But when they have to measure or weigh whatever they owe to others, give less than what is due! (4) Do they not know that they will be raised from the dead (5) (and called to account) on an awesome Day - (6) the Day when all men shall stand before the Sustainer of all the worlds? (7) Nay, verily, the record of the wicked is indeed (set down) in a mode inescapable! (Sijjin) (8) And what do you know what that mode inescapable (Sijjin) is? (9) A record (indelibly) inscribed! (10) Woe on that Day unto those who give the lie (to the truth) - (11) those who give the lie to the (coming of) Judgement Day: (12) for, none gives the lie to it but such as are wont to transgress against all that is right (and are) immersed in sin: (13) (and so), whenever Our messages are conveyed to them, they but say, "Fables of the ancients!" (14) Nay, but their hearts are corroded by all (the evil) that they were wont to do! (15) Nay, verily, from (the grace of) their Sustainer shall they on that Day be debarred; (16) and then, behold, they shall roast in the blazing fire (17) and be told: "This is the (very thing) to which you used to give the lie! (18) NAY, VERILY, the record of the truly virtuous is (set down) in a mode most lofty (ʿIlliyun)! (19) And what do you know what that mode most lofty (ʿIlliyun) is? (20) A record (indelibly) inscribed (21) witnessed by all who are close (to Allah) (22) Behold, (in the life to come) the truly virtuous will indeed be in bliss: (23) (resting) on couches, they will look (to Allah): (24) upon their faces you will see the brightness of bliss. (25) They will be given a drink of pure wine whereon the seal (of Allah) will have been set, (26) whose seal is musk. To that (wine of paradise), then, let all such aspire as (are willing to) aspire to things of high account: (27) for it is composed of all that is most exalting (28) a source (of bliss) whereof those who are drawn close (unto Allah) shall drink. (29) Behold, those who have abandoned themselves to sin were wont to laugh at such as have attained to faith; (30) and whenever they pass by them, they wink at one another (derisively); (31) and whenever they return to people of their own kind, they return full of jests; (32) and whenever they see those (who believe,) they say, "Behold, these (people) have indeed gone astray!" (33) And, withal, they have no call to watch over (the beliefs of) them (34) but on the Day (of Judgement), they who had attained to faith will (be able to) laugh at the (erstwhile) disbelievers: (35) (for, resting in paradise) on couches, they will look on (and say to themselves): (36) "Are the disbelievers (thus) requited for (aught but) what they were wont to do?"

Explanatory Notes for Surah 83

The *Surah* may be divided into four parts. The first opens with a declaration of war against those who give short measure. Ayat 1-3 do not, of course, refer only to commercial dealings but touch upon every aspect of social relations, both practical and moral, applying to every individual's rights and obligations no less than to his physical possessions.

The second part warns the transgressors, establishes their guilt and aggression, describes their punishment on the Day of Judgement. The third part gives an account of the righteous; it describes their high rank and the bliss they will enjoy in the Hereafter. The last part of the *Surah* describes the transgressors' harsh treatment of, ridicule and bad manners towards the righteous in the worldly life. But the opposite will be the case in the eternal life.

Surah 84 Al-Inshiqaq

Makki Surah

بِسْمِ اللَّهِ الرَّحْمَٰنِ الرَّحِيمِ

25 Ayat

Surah 84 Al-Inshiqaq

Meaning	Words	Meaning	Words
And hearkens or listens in obedience (ptcl., *madi* III. fem. sing. أَذِنَ لِ = he heard in obedience)	وَأَذِنَتْ	When the sky, heaven (noun adv., def. noun fem. sing.)	إِذَا السَّمَاءُ
To it's Sustainer, Lord (ptcl., noun, pro. fem. sing.)	لِرَبِّهَا	Is split asunder[1] (dr. vrb. VII *madi* III. fem. sing.)	انْشَقَّتْ
And as in truth it must, truth shall be verified (ptcl., *madi maj.* III. fem. sing.)	وَحُقَّتْ	And hearkens, listens in obedience (ptcl., *madi* III. fem. sing. أَذِنَ لِ = he heard in obedience)	وَأَذِنَتْ
O[2] man (ptcl. interj.[2], def. noun msc. sing.)	يَا أَيُّهَا الْإِنْسَانُ	To it's Sustainer, Lord (ptcl., noun gen. *mdf.*, pro. fem. sing. *mdfi.*)	لِرَبِّهَا
You indeed labour, you toil (ptcl., att. pro. كَ, act. prtc. msc. sing. nom.)	إِنَّكَ كَادِحٌ	And as in truth it must truth shall be verified (ptcl., *madi maj.* III. fem. sing.)	وَحُقَّتْ
After your Sustainer, Lord (ptcl., noun gen. *mdf.*, att. pro. كَ *mdfi.*)	إِلَىٰ رَبِّكَ	And when the earth (ptcl., noun adv., def. noun fem. sing. nom)	وَإِذَا الْأَرْضُ
Labouring (hard) (vrb. n. acc.)	كَدْحًا	Is stretched forth flattened out, extended (*madi maj.* III. fem. sing.)	مُدَّتْ
Then you shall meet Him (ptcl., مُلَاقٍ act. prtc. dr. vrb. III, att. pro. هُ)	فَمُلَاقِيهِ	And casts forth (ptcl., dr. vrb. IV *madi* III. fem. sing.)	وَأَلْقَتْ
So as for whoever (ptcls., pro.)	فَأَمَّا مَنْ	Whatever is in it (ptcls., att. pro. fem. sing.)	مَا فِيهَا
He is given (dr. vrb. IV *madi maj.* III. msc. sing.)	أُوتِيَ	And becomes clear and empty (ptcl., dr. vrb. V *madi* III. fem. sing.)	وَتَخَلَّتْ

---

[2] Particles of Interjection require after them a definite noun in the nominative case.

[1] After إِذَا *madi* takes the meaning of imperfect, i.e. generally future tense (ref. Juz 2&3 p.129)

The Qur'an Translation and Study – Juz' 30

Meaning	Words	Meaning	Words
Behind (noun adv.)	وَرَآءَ	His book, record (of deeds) (noun msc. sing. acc. mdf., att. pro. msc. sing. mdfi.)	كِتَٰبَهُۥ
His back (noun gen. mdf., pro. msc. sing. mdfi.)	ظَهْرِهِۦ	In his right hand (ptcl., noun sing. gen. mdf., pro. msc. sing. mdfi.)	بِيَمِينِهِۦ
Then he shall[3] call (for) (ptcls.[3], mudari' (future) III. msc. sing.)	فَسَوْفَ يَدْعُوا۟	So soon shall[3] (ptcls.)[3]	فَسَوْفَ
Destruction, death (vrb. n. acc.)	ثُبُورًا	He be called to account (dr. vrb. III mudari' maj. III. msc. sing.)	يُحَاسَبُ
And he shall roast, burn (صَلِىَ he roasted) (ptcl., mudari' III. msc. sing.)	وَيَصْلَىٰ	An easy accounting, an easy reckoning (vrb. n. acc., adj. acc.)	حِسَابًا يَسِيرًا
(In) burning fire (noun msc. acc.)	سَعِيرًا	And shall return (ptcl., dr. vrb. VII mudari' III. msc. sing.)	وَيَنقَلِبُ
Indeed he was (in this world) (ptcl., att. pro., madi III. msc. sing.)	إِنَّهُۥ كَانَ	To his people or family or kin (ptcl., noun gen. mdf., att. pro. msc. sing. mdfi.)	إِلَىٰٓ أَهْلِهِۦ
Among his people, family, kin (ptcl., noun gen. mdf., pro. msc. sing. mdfi.)	فِىٓ أَهْلِهِۦ	Rejoicing (pass. prtc. msc. sing. adv.)	مَسْرُورًا
Rejoicing (pass. prtc. msc. sing. adv.)	مَسْرُورًا	And as for whoever (ptcls., pro.)	وَأَمَّا مَنْ
Indeed he thought (ptcl., att. pro., madi III. msc. sing.)	إِنَّهُۥ ظَنَّ	Is given (dr. vrb IV madi maj. III. msc. sing.)	أُوتِىَ
That he would never return (to his Sustainer) (ptcls., mudari' subj. md. III. msc. sing.)	أَن لَّن يَحُورَ	His book, record (of deeds) (noun msc. sing. acc. mdf., att. pro. msc. sing. mdfi.)	كِتَٰبَهُۥ
Nay but verily, but certainly (ptcl.)[4]	بَلَىٰٓ إِنَّ		

[4] بَلَىٰ this particle is used after a negative preposition (interrogative or otherwise) and affirms the contrary of such proposition to be the truth.

[3] سَوْفَ a particle which, when placed before mudari', confirms the meaning of the future.

Surah 84 Al-Inshiqaq

Words	Meaning	Words	Meaning
رَبَّهُ كَانَ	His Sustainer was (has always been) (noun acc. mdf., att. pro. mdfi., madi III. msc. sing.)	لَا يُؤْمِنُونَ	They do not believe? (ptcl. negn., mudari̇̂ III. msc. pl.)
بِهِ بَصِيرًا	Seeing him, watchful of him (ptcl., att. pro., act. prtc. msc. sing. acc.)	وَإِذَا قُرِئَ	And when it is recited, read (ptcls., noun adv., madi maj. III. msc. sing.)
فَلَا أُقْسِمُ	But nay, I swear (ptcls., dr. vrb. IV mudari̇̂ I. sing.)	عَلَيْهِمُ الْقُرْآنُ	On or upon them, to them the Qur'an (ptcl., att. pro. msc. pl., def. noun)
بِالشَّفَقِ	By the redness of the sky after sunset (twilight) (ptcl., def. noun. gen.)	لَا يَسْجُدُونَ	They do not prostrate (ptcl. negn., mudari̇̂ III. msc. pl.)
وَاللَّيْلِ	And the night (ptcl., def. noun gen.)	بَلِ الَّذِينَ	Nay[5] but the ones who (ptcl.[5], rel. pro. msc. pl.)
وَمَا وَسَقَ	And what it gathers together (ptcls., madi III. msc. sing.)	كَفَرُوا	Disbelieve (the truth), cover over (the truth) (madi III msc. pl.)
وَالْقَمَرِ	And the moon (ptcl., def. noun gen.)	يُكَذِّبُونَ	Give the lie, belie or deny (the Qur'an) (dr. vrb. II mudari̇̂ III. msc. pl.)
إِذَا اتَّسَقَ	When it grows to its fulness (noun adv., dr. vrb. VIII madi III. msc. sing.)	وَاللَّهُ أَعْلَمُ	And Allah knows fully (ptcl., proper noun nom., elat. noun msc. dipt.)
لَتَرْكَبُنَّ	You shall ride, mount, move onwards (لَ and نَّ emph., mudari̇̂ II. msc. pl.)	بِمَا يُوعُونَ	What they conceal (in their hearts) (ptcls., dr. vrb. IV mudari̇̂ III. msc. pl.)
طَبَقًا	(from) one state, one condition (noun acc.)	فَبَشِّرْهُمْ	Then give good news to them (ptcl., dr. vrb. II amr II. sing., pro. msc. pl.)
عَنْ طَبَقٍ	To another state or condition (ptcl., noun gen.)	بِعَذَابٍ أَلِيمٍ	Of a painful punishment (prep., noun gen., act. prtc. adj. gen.)
فَمَا لَهُمْ	Then what (is amiss) with them, what is the matter with them (ptcls., att. pro. msc. pl.)		

[5] بَلْ a particle which affirms that which follows it but contradicts or corrects that which went before.

Words	Meaning	Words	Meaning
إِلَّا الَّذِينَ آمَنُوا	Except the ones who believe (ptcl. exc., rel. pro. msc. pl., dr. vrb. IV madi III. msc. pl.)	لَهُمْ أَجْرٌ	For them a reward (ptcl., att. pro. msc. pl., noun nom.)
وَعَمِلُوا الصَّالِحَاتِ	And perform good deeds (ptcl., madi III. msc. pl., الصَّالِحَاتِ act. prtc. fem. pl. acc.)	غَيْرُ مَمْنُونٍ	Undiminished, unbroken, uninterrupted, unending (noun[6], pass. prtc. msc. sing. gen. derived from the verb مَنَّ)

[6] غَيْرُ a noun used as a preposition.

Root Words of Surah 84

مُدَّتْ — Is spread out, مَدَّ * he stretched forth, مُمَدَّدَة widely extended.

أَلْقَتْ — Cast forth, لَقِيَ * he met, مُلَاقٍ one who meets, مُلَاقِيهِ about to meet him.

تَخَلَّتْ — Became empty, خَلَا * it (he) was empty, تَخَلَّى it was clear and empty.

أَذِنَتْ — Heard, perceived, أَذِنَ * he gave ear, أَذِنَ he suffered, hearkened to, granted permission.

كَادِحٌ — One who is toiling, labours after, كَدَحَ * he laboured after a thing, to study, كَدْحًا the act of labouring after anything.

بِيَمِينِهِ — In his right hand, يَمَنَ * he placed on his right side, يَمِينٌ (pl.) أَيْمَانٌ power, oath, right hand, أَصْحَابُ الْمَيْمَنَةِ people of the right hand.

مَسْرُورًا — Delighted, rejoiced, سَرَّ * he made glad, rejoiced, سِرٌّ a secret, السَّرَائِرُ the secrets, سَرِيرٌ throne, couch, (pl.) سُرُرٌ.

كِتَابَهُ — His record, كَتَبَ * he wrote, كَاتِبٌ scribe, writer, كِتَابٌ writing, book, scripture, decree, letter, record.

وَرَاءَ — Behind, beyond, وَرَى * it ate away the interior of the body, أَوْرَى IV he struck fire, مُورِيَةٌ one who strikes fire, (pl.) الْمُورِيَاتُ the strikers of fire, وَارَى III he concealed, hid.

ظَهْرِهِ — His back, ظَهَرَ * he helped, appeared, ظَهْرٌ a back, (pl.) ظُهُورٌ.

ثُبُورًا — Destruction, ثَبَرَ * he perished, lost, kept back.

يَحُورَ — He will go back, return to, حَارَ * he returned.

الشَّفَقِ — After the glow of sunset, twilight, شَفَقَ * he feared, أَشْفَقَ IV he was afraid, مُشْفِقٌ one who is afraid.

وَسَقَ — * He gathered together, اتَّسَقَ VIII he was complete or in perfect order.

طَبَقًا — Condition, a state, طَبَقَ * he covered.

يُوعُونَ — They hide, preserve (in their hearts) وَعَى * he retained in the memory, collected.

غَيْرُ مَمْنُونٍ — Uninterrupted, undiminished, مَنَّ * he fatigued, was gracious towards.

Translation of Surah 84 Al-Inshiqaq

(1) When the sky is split asunder, (2) obeying its Sustainer, as in truth it must: (3) and when the earth is levelled, (4) and casts forth whatever is in it, and becomes utterly void, (5) obeying its Sustainer, as in truth it must -: (6) (then,) O man - thou (that) are, verily, toiling towards thy Sustainer in painful toil - then shalt thou meet Him! (7) And as for him whose record shall be placed in his right hand, (8) he will (in time) be called to account with an easy accounting, (9) and will (be able to) turn joyfully to those of his own kind. (10) But as for him whose record shall be given to him behind his back, (11) he will (in time) pray for utter destruction: (12) but he will be roasted in the blazing flame. (13) Behold, (in his earthly life) he lived joyfully among people of his own kind - (14) for, behold, he never thought that he would have to return (to Allah). (15) Yes indeed! His Sustainer did see all that was in him! (16) But no! I call to witness the sunset's (fleeting) afterglow, (17) and the night, and what it (step by step) unfolds, (18) and the moon, as it grows to its fullness: (19) (even thus, O men,) you will move onward from stage to stage. (20) What, then, is amiss with them that they will not believe (in a life to come)? - (21) and (that), when the Qur'an is read unto them, they do not fall down in prostration? (22) Nay, but the disbelievers give the lie (to this divine writ)! (23) Yet Allah has knowledge of what they conceal (in their hearts). (24) Hence, give them the tidings of grievous suffering (in the life to come) - (25) unless it be such (of them) as (repent, and) attain to faith, and do good works: for theirs shall be a reward unending!

Explanatory Notes for Surah 84

The powerful opening of the *surah,* by sketching some of the scenes of universal upheaval with its emphasis on submission to Allah, is to make man feel his humbleness in front of his Lord.

Ayah 6 gives an allusion to the fact that in man's earthly life - irrespective of whether one is consciously aware of it or not - sorrow, pain, drudgery and worry by far outweigh the rare moments of true happiness and satisfaction. Thus, the human condition is described as "painful toiling towards the Sustainer" - i.e. towards the moment when one meets Him on resurrection.

Ayat 13 to 15 sketch certain scenes of life on earth which are well known to man. The last part of the *surah* wonders at those who deny the faith. There is a *hadith* related to *ayah* 7 of this *surah*. ʿA'ishah (RA) related that the Messenger of Allah (SAAS) answered, "that is not what is meant by reckoning and accountability. Lenient reckoning signifies no more than showing his record. He who is called to account on the Day of Judgment will suffer affliction". (Bukhari, Muslim, Tirmidhi, Nasa'i).

The *surah* ends with decisive note that the righteous ones will receive good recompense which is continuous and unceasing and will be given in the hereafter, where men are immortal.

Surah 85 Al-Buruj

Makki Surah — بِسْمِ اللَّهِ الرَّحْمَنِ الرَّحِيمِ — 22 *Ayat*

Meaning	Words	Meaning	Words
(are) Those who sit Sitting or sitters (act. prtc. br. pl. nom.)	قُعُودٌ	By[1] the sky or heaven (ptcl., def. noun sing. gen.)	وَالسَّمَاءِ
And they on what (ptcl., pro., ptcls.)	وَهُمْ عَلَىٰ مَا	Having constellations, stars of zodiac (ذَاتِ fem. of ذُو dem pro. *mdf.*, def. noun br. pl. *mdfi.*)	ذَاتِ الْبُرُوجِ
They do (*mudariᶜ* III msc. pl.)	يَفْعَلُونَ	And by[1] the Day promised (ptcl., def. noun gen., adj. pass. prtc. msc. sing. gen.)	وَالْيَوْمِ الْمَوْعُودِ
With (to) the believers (ptcl., def. noun pl. gen.)	بِالْمُؤْمِنِينَ	And by a witness (ptcl., act. prtc. gen.)	وَشَاهِدٍ
(are) witnesses (shall be witnessing) (act. prtc. br. pl. nom.)	شُهُودٌ	And a witnessed one (ptcl., pass. prtc. gen.)	وَمَشْهُودٍ
And they did not take revenge (ptcl., ptcl of negn., *madi* III. msc. pl.)	وَمَا نَقَمُوا	Killed, destroyed (*madi maj.* III msc. sing. used as an imprecation i.e. 'may they be killed!')	قُتِلَ
From them (the believers) except (ptcl., pro., ptcl. exc.)	مِنْهُمْ إِلَّا	The people of the pit[2] (noun *mdf.*, noun *mdfi.*)	أَصْحَابُ الْأُخْدُودِ
That they believed in Allah (ptcl., *mudariᶜ* subj. md. III. msc. pl., ptcl., noun gen.)	أَن يُؤْمِنُوا بِاللَّهِ	(of) the fire having (def. noun fem., ذَاتِ fem of dem. pro. ذُو gen. *mdf.*)	النَّارِ ذَاتِ
The Mighty, the Praiseworthy (def. nouns gen.)	الْعَزِيزِ الْحَمِيدِ	The fuel (burning) (def. noun *mdfi.*)	الْوَقُودِ
The One to Whom belongs (rel. pro., ptcl., pro. msc. sing.)	الَّذِي لَهُ	When they over it (the pit) (ptcl., pro., ptcl., att. pro.)	إِذْ هُمْ عَلَيْهَا
The kingdom of the heavens and earth (noun *mdf.*, def. noun fem. pl. *mdfi.*, ptcl., def. noun *mdfi.*)	مُلْكُ السَّمَاوَاتِ وَالْأَرْضِ		

[1] The وَ indicates the swearing of an oath, the object sworn upon being in the genitive.

[2] See the explanatory notes to the *surah*.

Surah 85 Al-Buruj

Meaning	Words	Meaning	Words
For them (there are) gardens (ptcl., pro. msc. pl., noun fem. pl. nom.)	لَهُمْ جَنَّٰتٌ	And Allah is over (ptcl., noun, ptcl.)	وَٱللَّهُ عَلَىٰ
Flows from underneath them (the gardens) (mudari' III. fem. sing., ptcls., pro. fem. sing. ها 'gardens')	تَجْرِى مِن تَحْتِهَا	All things a Witness (noun gen. mdf., noun mdfi., act. prtc. msc. sing. nom.)	كُلِّ شَىْءٍ شَهِيدٌ
The rivers (def. noun br. pl. nom.)	ٱلْأَنْهَٰرُ	Indeed the ones (ptcl., rel. pro. msc. pl.)	إِنَّ ٱلَّذِينَ
That is the victory (dem. pro. msc. sing., def. noun nom.)	ذَٰلِكَ ٱلْفَوْزُ	Who (burnt) persecuted (madi III. msc. pl.)	فَتَنُوا
The big, the great (adj. nom.)	ٱلْكَبِيرُ	The believing men (def. noun msc. pl. acc.)	ٱلْمُؤْمِنِينَ
Indeed the force, hold, attack, assault (ptcl., vrb. n. acc. mdf.)	إِنَّ بَطْشَ	And the believing women (ptcl., def. noun fem. pl. acc.)	وَٱلْمُؤْمِنَٰتِ
Of your Lord is exceedingly strong (noun mdfi., att. pro., لَ ptcl. emph., act. prtc. msc. sing.)	رَبِّكَ لَشَدِيدٌ	Then they did not repent (ptcl. of class., ptcl. negn., mudari' juss. md. III. msc. pl.)	ثُمَّ لَمْ يَتُوبُوا
Indeed it is He Who originates (ptcl., pros., dr. vrb. IV mudari' III. msc. sing.)	إِنَّهُۥ هُوَ يُبْدِئُ	So for them punishment of Hell (ptcls., att. pro., noun msc. sing. nom. mdf., noun fem. sing. dipt. mdfi.)	فَلَهُمْ عَذَابُ جَهَنَّمَ
And He shall restore (them) cause them to return bring them forth anew (ptcl., dr. vrb. IV mudari' III. msc. sing.)	وَيُعِيدُ	And for them punishment of (ptcls., pro., noun msc. sing. nom. mdf.)	وَلَهُمْ عَذَابُ
and He is the All-Forgiving (ptcl., pro., def. noun nom.)	وَهُوَ ٱلْغَفُورُ	The burning (noun def. sing. mdfi.)	ٱلْحَرِيقِ
the All-Loving (def. noun nom.)	ٱلْوَدُودُ	Indeed the ones who believe (ptcl., rel. pro., dr. vrb. IV madi III. msc. pl.)	إِنَّ ٱلَّذِينَ ءَامَنُوا
		And perform good deeds (ptcl., madi III. msc. pl., act. prtc. fem. pl. acc.)	وَعَمِلُوا ٱلصَّٰلِحَٰتِ

Words	Meaning	Words	Meaning
ذُو الْعَرْشِ	Owner of the throne (dem. pro. *mdf*. msc. sing., ذُو def. noun *mdfi*.)	فِي تَكْذِيبٍ	(persist) in giving it the lie, in denying (ptcl., vrb. n. {dr. vrb. II} gen.)
الْمَجِيدُ	The Glorified, the Sublime (def. noun nom.)	وَاللَّهُ مِن وَرَائِهِم	But Allah from behind them (ptcl., def. noun nom., ptcl., وَرَاءٌ noun gen. *mdf*., pro. msc. pl. *mdfi*.)
فَعَّالٌ لِّمَا يُرِيدُ	Doer of what He wishes (intensive noun nom., ptcls., dr. vrb. IV *mudari'* III. msc. sing.)		
هَلْ أَتَاكَ	Has (there) come to you? (ptcl. inter., *madi* III. msc. sing., att. pro. كَ)	مُحِيطٌ	(is) All encircling, encompassing (act. prtc. {dr. vrb. IV} msc. sing. nom.)
حَدِيثُ الْجُنُودِ	The story or narration of the host, troops, army, forces (noun msc. sing. nom. *mdf*., def. noun br. pl. *mdfi*.)	بَلْ هُوَ قُرْآنٌ	Rather³, it is a Qur'an (ptcl.³, pro. msc. sing., noun nom.)
		مَجِيدٌ	Glorified, sublime (act. prtc. msc. sing. nom.)
فِرْعَوْنَ وَثَمُودَ	(of) Fir'aun and Thamud (proper nouns *mdfi*.)	فِي لَوْحٍ	(Written, inscribed) on a tablet (ptcl., noun gen.)
بَلِ الَّذِينَ كَفَرُوا	Rather³, the ones who disbelieve (ptcl.³, rel. pro. msc. pl., *madi* III. msc. pl.)	مَّحْفُوظٍ	Guarded (adj. pass. prtc. msc. sing. gen.)

³ بَلْ a particle which affirms that which follows it, but contradicts or corrects that which went before.

Root Words for Surah 85

الْبُرُوجِ The towers, constellations, بَرَجَ * he ate and drank in large quantities, تَبَرَّجَ V he displayed beauty.

الْمَوْعُودِ Promised, وَعَدَ * he promised.

شَاهِدٍ A witness, an evidence, شَهِيدٌ (pl.) شُهُودٌ , شَهِدَ * he witnessed, bore witness, he was present, witnessed.

الْأُخْدُودِ The pit or trench, خَدَّ * he made an impression.

وَقُودٌ Fuel, وَقَدَ * it burned, أَوْقَدَ IV he kindled, set fire, مَوْقُودَةٌ kindled (fire).

قُعُودٌ State of sitting, قَعَدَ * he sat.

نَقَمُوا They chastised, punished, persecuted, took revenge, نَقَمَ * he disapproved, disliked.

الْعَزِيزِ	Mighty, excellent, عَزَّ * he (or it) was precious, rare, عِزَّة pride, honour, power.
الْحَمِيدِ	Worthy of praise, حَمِدَ * he praised, حَمْدٌ praise.
الْحَرِيقِ	Burning, the fire, حَرَقَ * it burned, حَرَّقَ II he burned (a thing).
الْفَوْزُ	Salvation, safety, felicity, victory, فَازَ * he obtained his desire, received salvation, gained, got possession of, مَفَازَة place of refuge.
بَطْش	Vengeance, violence, force, بَطَشَ * he took or seized by force, he laid hold.
يُبْدِئُ	He makes to appear, بَدَأَ * he began, appeared.
يُعِيدُ	He repeats, shall repeat, عَادَ * he returned, عِيد a festivity, a feast.
الْغَفُورُ	The Fully Forgiving, غَفَرَ * he pardoned, forgave, covered.
الْوَدُودُ	The Affectionate, the Loving, وَدَّ * he liked, wished, desired, loved.
ذُوالْعَرْشِ	Possessor of the Throne, عَرَشَ * he built houses, constructed.
الْمَجِيد	Glorious, glorified, مَجَدَ * he excelled in glory.
فَعَّالٌ	Doer (with full might – Allah), فَعَلَ * he did, accomplished, performed, acted, made.
الْجُنُودِ	Troops, the army, forces, a host, companions (no verbal root), (sing.) جُنْد.
مُحِيطٌ	One who comprehends, encompasses, حَاطَ * he guarded, أَحَاطَ IV he encompassed, comprehended, surrounded.
لَوْح	A broad table or plank or tablet, لَاحَ * he appeared, it caused one to change colour.

Translation of Surah 85 Al-Buruj (The Constellations)

(1) By the sky full of constellations,

(2) By the promised Day,

(3) By a witness, and (of) that unto which witness is borne!

(4) They destroyed (but) themselves, the companions of the pit

(5) of fire fiercely burning (for all who have attained to faith)!

(6) Lo! (With glee do) they sit over that (fire),

(7) fully conscious of what they are doing to the believers,

(8) whom they took revenge upon for no other reason than that they believe in Allah, the Almighty, the One to Whom all praise is due,

(9) (and) to whom the dominion of the heavens and the earth belongs. But Allah is witness unto everything!

(10) Verily, as for those who persecute believing men and believing women, and thereafter do not repent, hell's suffering awaits them: yea, suffering through fire awaits them!

(11) (But) verily, they who attain to faith and do righteous deeds shall (in the life to come) have gardens through which running waters flow - that is the triumph most great!

(12) VERILY, thy Sustainer's grip is exceedingly strong!

(13) Behold, it is He who creates (man) in the first instance, and He (it is who) will bring him forth anew.

(14) And He alone is the All-Forgiving, All-Embracing in His love,

(15) Possessor of the Glorious Throne,

(16) a Sovereign Doer of whatever He wills.

(17) Has it ever come within thy ken, the story of the (sinful) hosts

(18) of Fir'awn, and of (the tribe of) Thamud?

(19) And yet, they who disbelieve persist in giving it the lie:

(20) but all the while Allah encompasses them (with His knowledge and might) without their being aware of it.

(21) Nay, but this (divine writ which they reject) is a glorious Qur'an,

(22) upon an imperishable tablet (inscribed).

Explanatory Notes for Surah 85

The immediate theme of the *surah* is the pit incident. Commentators identify it with one or the other event in the past ranging from Ibrahim's (AS) experiences with his idolatrous contemporaries (Qur'an 21: 68-70) to the Biblical legend of Nebuchadnezzar's attempt to burn three pious Israelites in a fiery furnace (*The Book of Daniel* iii, 19 ff.), or the persecution, in the sixth century, of the Christians of Najran by the King of Yemen, Dhu Nawas (who was a Jew by religion), or the story of a Zoroastrian king who burnt to death those of his subjects who refused to accept his dictum that a marriage of brother and sister was 'permitted by God'; and so forth. As a matter of fact, the words are perfectly general and we need not search for particular names except by way of illustration. The persecutors are people who, having no faith whatsoever, hate to see faith in others; the 'pit of fire' may also then be a metaphor for the persecution of the latter by the former: a phenomenon not restricted to any particular time or to a particular people but recurring in many forms and in varying degrees of intensity throughout recorded history.

Ayat 21 and 22 give a unique description of the Qur'an to be found only in this one instance. This divine writ is noble and sublime. It is inscribed on a well-guarded tablet the *'lawh mahfuz'*. Although some commentators understand by it an actual "heavenly tablet"; upon which the Qur'an is inscribed since all eternity, other commentators describe it as the imperishable quality of this divine writ. This interpretation is pointedly mentioned as justified by, i.e. Tabari, Baghawi, Razi and Ibn Kathir, all of whom agree that the phrase 'upon a well-guarded tablet' relates to Allah's promise that the Qur'an would never be corrupted, and would remain free of all arbitrary additions, diminutions and textual changes, as is also mentioned in *Surah* 15 Al-Hijr, *ayah* 9.

Surah 86 At-Tariq

Makki Surah   بِسْمِ اللهِ الرَّحْمٰنِ الرَّحِيْمِ   17 *Ayat*

Surah 86 At-Tariq

Words	Meaning	Words	Meaning
وَالسَّمَآءِ	By[1] the sky or heaven (ptcl.[1], def. noun fem. sing. gen.)	مِمَّ خُلِقَ	Out of what, from what he is created (ptcls. مِنْ & مَا, *madi maj.* III. msc. sing.)
وَالطَّارِقِ	And[1] the comer by night (ptcl.[1], def. noun msc. sing. gen.)	خُلِقَ مِنْ	He is created from (*madi maj.* III. msc. sing., ptcl.)
وَمَآ أَدْرَاكَ	and what would make you know (ptcls., dr. vrb. IV *madi* III. msc. sing., att. pro.)	مَّآءٍ دَافِقٍ	Water poured out (poured forth) (noun gen., act. prtc. gen.)
مَا الطَّارِقُ	What the comer by night is? (ptcl., def. noun nom.)	يَخْرُجُ مِنْ بَيْنِ	(which) Comes out from between (*mudari*ᶜ III. msc. sing., ptcls.)
النَّجْمُ	(It is) the star (def. noun nom.)	الصُّلْبِ	The loins or back bone (of men) (def. noun gen.)
الثَّاقِبُ	(Of) piercing brightness, the shining one (act. prtc. msc. sing.)	وَالتَّرَآئِبِ	and the breast bones or ribs (of women) (ptcl., def. noun br. pl. gen.)
إِنْ كُلُّ نَفْسٍ	Truly, every soul (ptcl., noun *mdf.*, noun fem. sing. *mdfi.*)	إِنَّهُ عَلَى رَجْعِهِ	Indeed He, over his (man's) return to life (again) (ptcl., pro., ptcl., noun *mdf.*, pro. *mdfi.*)
لَمَّا عَلَيْهَا	But has over it (لَمَّا ptcl. exc., ptcl., att. pro. هَا for نَفْس)	لَقَادِرٌ	Is able, has power (لَ ptcl. emph., act. prtc. msc. sing. nom.)
حَافِظٌ	A guardian, a watcher (act. prtc. dr. vrb. III msc. sing.)	يَوْمَ تُبْلَى	On a day shall be tried or scrutinised (noun acc. adv., *madi maj.* III. fem. sing.)
فَلْيَنْظُرِ الْإِنْسَانُ	Then let man consider or see (ptcl., لْ ptcl. imp., *mudari*ᶜ III. msc. sing., def. noun nom.)		

[1] The particle وَ indicates the swearing of an oath, the object sworn by being in the genitive case.

Words	Meaning	Words	Meaning
السَّرَآئِرُ	(all) the secrets (noun br. pl. nom.)	فَصْلٌ	Decisive, separating (between truth and falsehood) (vrb. n. nom.)
فَمَا لَهُ	Then he (man) shall not have (ptcls., pro. msc. sing.)	وَمَا هُوَ	And it (the Qur'an) is not (ptcls., per. pro. msc. sing.)
مِن قُوَّةٍ	Any strength (ptcl., noun fem. sing. gen.)	بِالْهَزْلِ	A joke, a jest, a false argument and amusement (ptcl., vrb. n. gen. because of prec. prep. ب)
وَلَا نَاصِرٍ	Nor helper (ptcls., act. prtc. msc. sing. gen. due to prec. prep. مِن)	إِنَّهُمْ يَكِيدُونَ	Indeed they plot (ptcl., pro., *mudari* III msc. pl.)
وَالسَّمَاءِ	By¹ the sky or heaven (ptcl.¹, def. noun fem.)	كَيْدًا	A plot, a fraud, a trick (vrb. n. acc.)
ذَاتِ الرَّجْعِ	That returns² (ذَاتِ dem. pro. fem. *mdf.*, vrb. n. *mdfi.*)	وَأَكِيدُ	And I (Allah) plot (ptcl., *mudari* I. sing.)
وَالْأَرْضِ	By¹ the earth (ptcl., def. noun fem. gen.)	كَيْدًا	A plot, a fraud, a trick (vrb. n. acc.)
ذَاتِ الصَّدْعِ	That splits³ (dem. pro. fem. *mdf.*, vrb. n. *mdfi.*)	فَمَهِّلِ الْكَافِرِينَ	So grant a delay, give respite, to the disbelievers (ptcl., dr. vrb. II *amr* II. msc. sing., def. noun msc. pl. acc. gen.)
إِنَّهُ لَقَوْلٌ	Indeed it (the Qur'an) is a word (ptcl., pro. msc., لَ ptcl. emph., vrb. n.,)	أَمْهِلْهُمْ	Act quietly towards them (dr. vrb. IV *amr* II. msc. sing., per. pro. msc. pl.)
² by sending rain repeatedly. ³ by sprouting vegetation.		رُوَيْدًا	Gently (vrb. n. acc.)

Root Words of Surah 86

الطَّارِقِ	That which appears by night, طَرَقَ he came by night.
النَّجْمِ	The star, نَجَمَ * he appeared.
الثَّاقِبُ	The shining, piercing, ثَقَبَ * he shone, penetrated, perforated.
دَافِقٍ	That which pours or is poured forth, دَفَقَ * it poured forth.

الصُّلْب	The back bone or the loins, صَلَبَ	* he crucified.
تَبْلَى	Will appear in its reality, بَلَى	* he tried, proved, experienced,
	اِبْتَلَى VIII he proved by trial.	
ذَاتِ الرَّجْعِ	That which returns, possessed of returning, رَجَعَ * he returned, رَجْعٌ a return,	
	اِرْجِعِي return! (imp. fem.), الرُّجْعَى the return.	
ذَاتِ الصَّدْعِ	That which has a fissure or a split, صَدَعَ	* it split.
فَصْلٌ	Separation, a distinction, فَصَلَ	* he made a distinction or division, depart.
الْهَزْلِ	Frivolity, the joke, هَزِلَ	* he joked.
يَكِيدُونَ	They plot, كَادَ * he plotted against, كَيْدًا a plot.	
مَهِّلْ	Grant a delay, give respite, مَهَلَ * he did a thing quietly and gently,	
	أَمْهِلْ respite gently! (imp. msc. sing.).	
رُوَيْدًا	Gently, رَادَ	* he sought.

Translation of Surah 86 At-Tariq (The Night Visitor)

(1) By the heaven and that which comes in the night! (2) And what could make thee conceive what it is that comes in the night? (3) It is the star of piercing brightness. (4) For every soul there is a guardian who watches over it.

(5) Let man, then, observe out of what he has been created: (6) he has been created out of a gushing fluid (7) issuing from between the loins (of man) and the pelvic arch (of woman). (8) Now, verily, He (Who thus creates man in the first instance) is well able to bring him back (to life) (9) on the Day when all secrets will be laid bare, (10) and (man) will have neither strength nor helper!

(11) By the heaven, ever-revolving, (12) and the earth, bursting forth with plants! (13) behold, this (divine writ) is indeed a word that cuts (between truth and falsehood), (14) and is no idle tale. (15) Behold, they (who refuse to accept it) devise a plot (many a false argument to disprove its truth); (16) but I devise a plot. (17) Then grant the disbelievers a delay: respite them for a little while!

Explanatory Notes for Surah 86

The message of this *surah* like most others in the 30th Juz is like continuous, strong, knocks; they are shouts addressed to people who are fast asleep. The warning is: "wake up! rise! reflect! look round! think! consider! God *is*. There is an organisation and a deliberate system of creation. There is trial and liability, reckoning and reward, severe chastisement and endless happiness. For every soul there is a guardian who watches over it, and accurate and immediate record is kept on the basis of which the reckoning is made.

Let man consider his origin, out of a drop of fluid how the guiding hand of Allah (SWT) transforms the gushing water into the communicative human being. Allah (SWT) Who has created him and looked after him is well able to bring him back to life after death to recompense his deeds.

Surah 87 Al-A'la

Makki Surah — بسم الله الرحمن الرحيم — **19 Ayat**

Words	Meaning	Words	Meaning
سَبِّحِ اسْمَ	Glorify, praise the name (dr. vrb. II *amr* II. msc. sing., noun acc. *mdf*.)	أَحْوَىٰ	Dead and dried up, dark coloured (adj. elat.[1] msc.)
رَبِّكَ الْأَعْلَى	Of your Lord the Highest (noun *mdfi*., pro. كَ, adj. msc. elat.[1])	سَنُقْرِئُكَ	We shall enable you to recite, to read (ptcl.[2], dr. vrb. IV *mudari'* I. pl., att. pro. كَ)
الَّذِي خَلَقَ	The One Who created (rel. pro., *madi* III. msc. sing.)	فَلَا تَنْسَىٰ	Then you shall not forget (ptcl., ptcl. negn., *mudari'* II. msc. sing.)
فَسَوَّىٰ	Then proportioned, fashioned, perfected (ptcl., dr. vrb. II *madi* III. msc. sing.)	إِلَّا مَا شَاءَ اللَّهُ	Except, what wished, Allah (ptcls., *madi* III. msc. sing., def. noun nom.)
وَالَّذِي قَدَّرَ	And the One who made possible, planned, determined, defined, decreed, devised (ptcl., rel. pro., dr. vrb. II *madi* III. msc. sing.)	إِنَّهُ يَعْلَمُ	Indeed He knows (ptcl., pro., *mudari'* III. msc. sing.)
فَهَدَىٰ	Then guided (ptcl., *madi* III. msc. sing.)	الْجَهْرَ	(That which is) open, public, manifest, loud speaking (def. noun acc.)
وَالَّذِي أَخْرَجَ	And the One Who brought forth, took out (ptcl., rel. pro., dr. vrb. IV *madi* III. msc. sing.)	وَمَا يَخْفَىٰ	And that which is hidden (ptcls., *mudari'* III. msc. sing.)
الْمَرْعَىٰ	The vegetation, pasture (def. noun acc.)	وَنُيَسِّرُكَ	We shall ease you or facilitate for you (ptcl., dr. vrb. II *mudari'* I. pl., att. pro. كَ)
فَجَعَلَهُ	Then He made it (ptcl., *madi* III. msc. sing. att. pro. هُ)	لِلْيُسْرَىٰ	To the easiest (way) (ptcl., adj. elat.[1] fem. gen.)
غُثَاءً	Light straw, stubble (noun acc.)	فَذَكِّرْ	So remind, admonish (ptcl., dr. vrb. II *amr* II. msc. sing.)

---

[2] The particle سَ prefixed to the *mudari'*, being the shortened form of سَوْفَ, denotes the future tense of the verb.

[1] The elative is the superlative degree of the adjective.

Surah 87 Al-Aʿla

Words	Meaning	Words	Meaning
اِنْ نَفَعَتِ	If it will be useful to (them), profit them (ptcl., *madi* III. fem. sing.)	فِيهَا وَلَا يَحْيٰى	In it (Hell), nor shall he (be able to) live (there) (ptcl., pro. fem. هَا for Hell, ptcl., ptcl. negn., *mudariʿ* III. msc. sing.)
الذِّكْرٰى	The remembrance, the admonition, warning (def. noun fem. nom.)	قَدْ اَفْلَحَ	Certainly attained prosperity, happiness (ptcl.[4], dr. vrb. IV *madi* III. msc. sing.)
سَيَذَّكَّرُ	Shall receive, accept admonition shall be warned (ptcl.[2], dr. vrb. V *mudariʿ* III. msc. sing. {يَذَّكَّرُ for يَتَذَكَّرُ})	مَنْ تَزَكّٰى	Who tried to be pure (pro.[3], dr. vrb. V *madi* III. msc. sing.)
مَنْ يَخْشٰى	Who fears Allah (pro.[3], *mudariʿ* III. msc. sing.)	وَذَكَرَ اسْمَ	And he remembered the name (ptcl., *madi* III. msc. sing., noun acc. *mdf*.)
وَيَتَجَنَّبُهَا	And shall turn away from it shall withdraw himself from it (admonition) (ptcl., dr. vrb. V *mudariʿ* III. msc. sing., pro. هَا for الذِّكْرٰى)	رَبِّهٖ	Of his Lord, Sustainer (noun *mdfi*., pro. msc. sing.)
الْاَشْقَى	The most wretched, miserable, unhappy (adj. elat.[1] msc.)	فَصَلّٰى	then prayed (ptcl., dr. vrb. II *madi* III. msc. sing.)
الَّذِىْ يَصْلَى	The one who shall roast or burn (صَلِىَ he roasted) (rel. pro., *mudariʿ* III. msc. sing.)	بَلْ تُؤْثِرُوْنَ	But, nay rather[5] you prefer (ptcl.[5], dr. vrb. IV *mudariʿ* II. msc. pl., اٰثَرَ = he preferred)
النَّارَ الْكُبْرٰى	The greater Fire (def. noun fem., def. adj. elat.[1] fem.)	الْحَيٰوةَ الدُّنْيَا	The worldly[1] life (def. noun acc., adj. elat.[1] fem. acc.)
ثُمَّ لَا يَمُوْتُ	Then he shall neither (be able to) die (ptcl. class., ptcl. negn., *mudariʿ* III. msc. sing.)	وَالْاٰخِرَةُ خَيْرٌ	And the Hereafter is better (ptcl., def. noun fem. sing., adj. elat.[1])
		وَّاَبْقٰى	and more lasting, permanent (ptcl, adj. elat.[1] msc.)
		اِنَّ هٰذَا لَفِى	Indeed this is in (the same message) is in (ptcl., dem. pro. msc. sing., ptcls.)

[3] مَنْ is an indeclinable conjunctive pronoun.

[4] قَدْ is a confirmatory particle that is placed before the *madi* to indicate two points: a) that the action is certainly true and, b) that the verb is in the recent past.

[5] بَلْ a particle which affirms that which follows it but contradicts or corrects that which went before.

Words	Meaning	Words	Meaning
صُحُفِ إِبْرَاهِيمَ وَمُوسَىٰ	The scrolls of Ibrahim and Musa (noun br. pl.gen., prop. noun dipt. gen., ptcl., prop. noun *gh*. gen.)	الصُّحُفِ الْأُولَىٰ	The scrolls, the former the previous scriptures (def. noun br. pl. gen., ord. no. fem.)

Root Words for Surah 87

غُثَاءً	Stubble, light straw, scum and refuse, غُثَا * it was covered with foam and dead leaves.
أَحْوَىٰ	Dark coloured foam, حَوَىٰ * he collected.
تَنسَىٰ	You forget, نَسِىَ * he forgot, neglected.
الْجَهْرَ	The open, public, manifest, visible, جَهَرَ * he was manifest, spoke aloud.
يَتَجَنَّبُهَا	Keeps himself away, avoids it, جَنَبَ * he turned aside, caused to turn from or avoid, جَنَّبَ II he removed away from, تَجَنَّبَ V he withdrew himself from, he turned away.
الْأَشْقَى	The most wretched, شَقِىَ * he was miserable, unhappy, wretched.
كُبْرَىٰ	Greater, greater, كَبُرَ * he was great, it was a weighty or grievous matter.
أَفْلَحَ	IV he attained his desires, was happy, prospered, فَلَحَ * it split.
صَلَّىٰ	II he offered prayers to Allah, with عَلَى means, he prayed for, he blessed for صَلَوَ he had the centre of the back bent, صَلَوٰةٌ a prayer, (pl.) صَلَوَاتٌ * صَلِىَ مُصَلِّينَ those who pray (five times a day).
تُؤْثِرُونَ	You prefer, أَثَرَ * he raised, excited, آثَرَ IV he preferred, chose, آثَارٌ traces, أَثَرْنَ they raised.
أَبْقَىٰ	More lasting, بَقِىَ * he remained.
الْأُولَىٰ	The first, the first beginning, prior, former, آلَ * for أَوَلَ he was before, he returned.

Translation of Surah 87 Al-Aᶜla (The Highest)

(1) Extol the limitless glory of thy Sustainer's name: (the glory of) the All-Highest,

(2) Who creates (everything), and thereupon forms it in accordance with what it is meant to be,

(3) And who determines the nature (of all that exists), and thereupon guides it (towards its fulfilment),

(4) And who brings forth herbage,

(5) And thereupon causes it to decay into rust-brown stubble!

(6) We shall make you read, and you will not forget (aught of what you read),

(7) Save what Allah may will (you to forget) - for, verily, He (alone) knows all that is open (to man's perception) as all that is hidden (from it)

(8) And (thus) shall We make easy for you the path towards (ultimate) ease.

(9) Remind then, (others of the truth, regardless of) whether this reminding (would seem to) be of use (or not):

(10) In mind will keep it he who stands in fear (of Allah),

(11) But aloof from it will remain that most hapless wretch,

(12) He who (in the life to come) shall have to endure the greatest fire,

(13) Wherein he will neither die nor remain alive.

(14) To happiness (in the life to come) has indeed attained he who attains to purity (in this world),

(15) And remembers his Sustainer's name, and prays (unto Him).

(16) But nay, (O men,) you prefer the life of this world,

(17) Although the life to come is better and more enduring.

(18) Verily, (all) this has indeed been (said) in the earlier scrolls

(19) The scrolls of Ibrahim and Musa.

Explanatory Notes for Surah 87

The Prophet (SAAS) used to read this *surah* and *surah* 88 "The Enveloper", in prayers of the Islamic festivals (ᶜEidain) and in Friday prayers. The *surah* begins with an order to glorify the Lord, it is much more than verbal repetition of glorification, it means to recognise His Supremacy and infallibility in everything, remembering His Divine attributes with a genuine feeling of the sublimity of these attributes. When this *surah* was revealed the Prophet (SAAS) told the Muslims to fulfil the Divine Order as they prostrate themselves in their daily prayers.

Everything Allah (SWT) has created is well proportioned and perfect. Every creature is given guidance so that it may know its role and play it. It is told the purpose of its creation, given what it needs for sustenance and guided to it. All things are also collectively perfected so that they may fulfil their collective role. The *surah* gives the Prophet (SAAS), and the Muslim nation in general a very welcome tiding. It starts with sparing the Prophet (SAAS) the trouble of memorising the Qur'an, Allah (SWT) will look after this task and ensure that he will never forget any part of it. The tiding is also a happy one for the Islamic nation since it is a reassurance that the faith the Prophet (SAAS) preaches is authentic, it is from Allah and He looks after it. *Ayah* number 8 describes the fundamental principle of Islam: the universe is created by Allah (SWT) with ease, if Allah (SWT) smoothes a certain person's path he finds ease in everything in his life.

Surah 88 Al-Ghashiyah

Makki Surah — 26 Ayat

Words	Meaning	Words	Meaning
هَلْ أَتَاكَ	Has (there) come to you? (ptcl. inter., *madi* III. msc. sing., att. pro. ك)	لَيْسَ لَهُمْ طَعَامٌ	There is no food for them (neg. vrb.[2], ptcl., pro., noun nom.)
حَدِيثُ الْغَاشِيَةِ	Narration of the overshadowing[1] (event) (noun nom. *mdf*., act. prtc. fem. sing. *mdfi*.)	إِلَّا مِنْ ضَرِيعٍ	Except *dari*[c][3] (ptcls., noun gen.)
وُجُوهٌ يَوْمَئِذٍ	(some) faces on that day (noun br. pl. nom., يَوْمُ = day, إِذْ = then)	لَا يُسْمِنُ	Which shall neither fatten (or nourish) (ptcl. negn., dr. vrb. IV *mudari*[c] III. msc. sing.)
خَاشِعَةٌ	(shall be) downcast, humiliated (act. prtc. fem. sing. nom.)	وَلَا يُغْنِي مِنْ	Nor shall it satisfy (ptcl., ptcl. negn., dr. vrb. IV *mudari*[c] III. msc. sing., ptcl.)
عَامِلَةٌ	Toiling or working (act. prtc. fem. sing. nom.)	جُوعٍ	Hunger (noun gen.)
نَاصِبَةٌ	Labouring, weary (act. prtc. fem. sing. nom.)	وُجُوهٌ يَوْمَئِذٍ	(some) Faces on that day (noun br. pl. nom., يَوْمُ = day, إِذْ = then)
تَصْلَى	Shall roast (*mudari*[c] III. fem. sing., صَلِيَ = he roasted)	نَاعِمَةٌ	Rejoicing, joyful (act. prtc. fem. sing. nom.)
نَارًا حَامِيَةً	(in) a fire scorching, burning hot, scalding (noun acc., act. prtc. fem. sing. acc.)	لِسَعْيِهَا	With their striving endeavour (ptcl., noun gen. *mdf*., pro. هَا *mdfi*.)
تُسْقَى	Shall be given to drink (*mudari*[c] *maj*. III. fem. sing.)	رَاضِيَةٌ	Well pleased (act. prtc. fem. sing. nom.)
مِنْ عَيْنٍ	From a fountain (ptcl., noun sing. gen.)	فِي جَنَّةٍ	In a garden (ptcl., noun fem. sing. gen.)
آنِيَةٍ	(which is) Boiling (act. prtc. fem. sing. gen.)		

[2] لَيْسَ is known as one of the 'sisters of كَانَ'; it is a negative substantive verb which has no *mudari*[c] or *amr* and it expresses the negation of existence. لَيْسَ, 'there is not', is the III person masculine singular.

[3] A plant growing in Hell, bitter, thorny and burning more than fire.

[1] The Day of Judgement or Resurrection.

Surah 88 Al-Ghashiyah

Meaning	Words	Meaning	Words
Do they not see, do they not look at [4] (ptcl. *alif* inter., ptcl., ptcl. negn., *mudari* III. msc. pl., ptcl.[4])	اَفَلَا يَنْظُرُوْنَ اِلَى	Lofty, Sublime (act. prtc. fem. sing. gen.)	عَالِيَةٍ
The camels (generic noun gen.)	الْاِبِلِ	(They) shall not hear in it (ptcl. negn., *mudari* III. fem. sing., ptcl., pro.)	لَا تَسْمَعُ فِيْهَا
How[5] they were created[6] (ptcl.[5], *madi maj.* III. fem.[6] sing.)	كَيْفَ خُلِقَتْ	Vain or obscene talk (act. prtc. fem. sing. acc.)	لَاغِيَةً
And (did they not look) at [4] the sky (ptcls., def. noun fem. sing. gen.)	وَاِلَى السَّمَآءِ	In it (there is) a spring (ptcl., pro., noun nom.)	فِيْهَا عَيْنٌ
How[5] it was raised[6] (ptcl.[5], *madi maj.* III. fem. sing.)	كَيْفَ رُفِعَتْ	Running, flowing (act. prtc. fem. sing. nom)	جَارِيَةٌ
And to[4] the mountains (ptcls., noun br. pl. gen.)	وَاِلَى الْجِبَالِ	In it (there are) couches, thrones (ptcl., pro., noun br. pl. nom.)	فِيْهَا سُرُرٌ
How[5] they were fixed[6] (they were) fixed (ptcl.[5], *madi maj.* III. fem. sing.)	كَيْفَ نُصِبَتْ	Raised high, elevated (pass. prtc. fem. sing. nom.)	مَرْفُوْعَةٌ
And to the earth (ptcls., def. noun fem. sing. gen.)	وَاِلَى الْاَرْضِ	And cups or goblets (ptcl., noun br. pl.)	وَاَكْوَابٌ
How[5] it was spread out (ptcl.[5], *madi maj.* III. fem. sing.)	كَيْفَ سُطِحَتْ	Placed (ready) (pass. prtc. fem. sing. nom.)	مَوْضُوْعَةٌ
So remind (them) (ptcl., dr. vrb. II *amr* II. msc. sing.)	فَذَكِّرْ	And cushions (ptcl., noun br. pl. dipt. nom.)	وَنَمَارِقُ
		Arranged in order (pass. prtc. fem. sing. nom.)	مَصْفُوْفَةٌ
		And rich carpets (ptcl., noun br. pl. dipt.)	وَزَرَابِيُّ
		Scattered, spread abroad (pass. prtc. fem. sing. nom.)	مَبْثُوْثَةٌ

[5] كَيْفَ is an interrogative particle which, when used with a particle of negation is used as an exclamatory particle showing a sense of wonder.

[6] The verb referring to the camels and the mountains (plurals) is feminine singular because the nouns are broken plurals denoting non-conscious beings.

[7] لَسْتَ is the second person masculine sing. of لَيْسَ.

[4] اِلَى with remaining places means 'did they not look at all these following things?'.

Words	Meaning	Words	Meaning
فَيُعَذِّبُهُ ٱللَّهُ	Then Allah shall punish him (ptcl., dr. vrb. II *mudari* III. msc. sing., att. pro., noun nom.)	إِنَّمَا أَنتَ	Only you are i.e. you are only (ptcl., per. pro. msc. sing.)
ٱلۡعَذَابَ ٱلۡأَكۡبَرَ	The punishment (greater) the greater punishment (noun acc., adj. elat. acc.)	مُذَكِّرٌ	A reminder, one who reminds (act. prtc. dr. vrb. II msc. sing. nom.)
إِنَّ إِلَيۡنَآ	Indeed to Us (shall be) (ptcls., att. pro. نَا I. pl.)	لَّسۡتَ عَلَيۡهِم	You are not[7] over them (neg. vrb.[7], ptcl., att. pro. هِم)
إِيَابَهُمۡ	Their returning (vrb. n., att. pro. هُم)	بِمُصَيۡطِرٍ	A warden, an overseer who presides over (who manages) affairs (ptcl., act. prtc. msc. sing. gen.)
ثُمَّ إِنَّ عَلَيۡنَا	Again or then indeed on Us (shall be) (ptcls., att. pro. نَا I. pl.)	إِلَّا مَن تَوَلَّىٰ	Except for one who turned away (ptcl., indecl. conj. pro., dr. vrb. V *madi* III. msc. sing.)
حِسَابَهُم	Their account-taking reckoning (vrb. n., att. pro. هُم)	وَكَفَرَ	And disbelieved (ptcl., *madi* III. msc. sing.)

Root Words for Surah 88

ٱلۡغَاشِيَةُ The covering, غَشِيَ * he came upon, covered over, غَشَّىٰ II he covered, أَغۡشَىٰ IV he covered, caused to cover, caused to be covered.

عَامِلَةٌ Toiling, travailing, عَمِلَ * he did, acted, operated, worked, عَمَلٌ (pl.) أَعۡمَالٌ act, deed, work, toil, labour, action.

نَاصِبَةٌ Fatigued, weary, tired, نَصَبَ * he erected, fixed, placed, نَصِبَ he used diligence, فَٱنصَبۡ so toil, labour! (imp. msc.).

آنِيَةٌ Boiling hot (water), أَنَىٰ * it was boiling hot, he arrived, آنِيَةٌ (pl.) إِنَاءٌ a vessel.

يُسۡمِنُ Nourishes, سَمِنَ * he was fat.

رَاضِيَةٌ Well pleased, one who is content, رَضِيَ * he was pleased, contented, مَرۡضِيَّةٌ an accepted, well pleasing, approved one.

لَاغِيَةٌ Vain or obscene discourse, idle speech, لَغَىٰ * he used vain words.

عَيۡنٌ Spring of water, fountain, (pl.) عَانَ , عُيُونٌ * it flowed, عَيۡنٌ an eye, (dual) عَيۡنَيۡنِ , (pl.) أَعۡيُنٌ , مَعِينٌ clear flowing, a fountain.

جَارِيَةٌ Running, جَرَىٰ * it happened, he (it) ran, flowed, تَجۡرِي it (she) flows.

مَوْضُوعَةٌ Ready placed ones, وَضَعَ * he laid down, placed, put, وَضَعَ عَنْ he put off, removed.

مَصْفُوفَةٌ Arranged in order, صَفَّ he set, arranged in a row or rank.

مَبْثُوثَةٌ Spread abroad, scattered, بَثَّ * he disseminated, dispersed, الْمَبْثُوث the scattered ones.

سُطِحَتْ It was spread out, سَطَحَ * he spread out.

Translation of Surah 88 Al-Ghashiyah (The Overshadowing Event)

(1) Has there come to you the news of the Overshadowing Event (i.e. the Day of Resurrection)?

(2) (Some) faces will on that Day be downcast, (3) toiling (under burdens of sin), worn out (by fear), (4) about to enter a glowing fire, (5) given to drink from a boiling spring. (6) No food for them save the bitterness of dry thorns, (7) which gives no strength and neither stills hunger.

(8) And (some) faces will on that day shine with bliss, (9) well-pleased with (the fruit of) their striving, (10) in a garden sublime, (11) wherein they will hear no empty talk. (12) Countless springs will flow therein, (13) (and) there will be raised couches, (14) and goblets placed ready, (15) and cushions are arranged, (16) and carpets spread out.

(17) Do then, they (who deny resurrection) never reflect (and observe) how the camel is created? (18) And at the sky, how it is raised aloft? (19) And at the mountains, how firmly they are reared? (20) And at the earth, how it is spread out? (21) And so, (O Prophet,) remind them; your task is only to remind: (22) You are not their overseer. (23) However, as for him who turns away, and disbelieves, (24) Allah will cause him to suffer the greatest suffering (in the life to come): (25) for, behold, unto Us will be their return, (26) and, verily, it is for Us to call them to account.

Explanatory Notes for Surah 88

The Prophet (SAAS) whenever he listened to this *Surah* would feel that the address was direct to him personally, as if he was receiving it from his Lord directly for the first time. He was extremely moved by Allah's address to him. The *Surah* warns man to be ready for the day of reckoning. We are told that there are on that day faces which look downcast and toilworn. They had laboured and toiled for something different than the cause of Allah (SWT). Their work was totally for themselves and their families, for their own ambitions and worldly life. They did not make any provisions for the life of the Hereafter, hence they face the end with a mixture of humiliation, exhaustion, misery and hopelessness. We in this world cannot fully comprehend the nature of that suffering and torture in the Hereafter. The description is made in order to give our human perceptions the feeling of the greatest possible pain, which is produced by a combination of humiliation, weakness, failure, the scorching fire, drinking and bathing in boiling water and eating thorny dry food. The true nature of the ultimate affliction is incomprehensible except to those who will actually experience it. May we be saved from it. On the other hand the righteous ones will be in total bliss, their faces bright with joy, the nature of their enjoyments are left for the experience of those successful people who struggle hard in this world to please Allah (SWT) and Allah's rewards will be enjoyed by them in the Hereafter. Then some aspects of the universe are pointed out in the *surah*.

Lastly it addresses the Prophet (SAAS) laying down the nature of his mission which is confined to reminding and conveying the Message, but the disbelievers are not to be left alone, they cannot deny Allah (SWT) and be safe. The definition of the Prophet's role and the role of every subsequent advocate of Islam is thus completed. They have only to remind that the reckoning will be made by Allah (SWT).

It must be stressed, however, that the process of reminding includes the removal of hindrances so that people may be free to listen to the call. This is the aim of *Jihad* as it is understood from the Qur'an and the history of the Prophet (SAAS). It is a process which neither admits negligence nor permits aggression.

The Qur'an Translation and Study – Juz' 30

Makki Surah بِسْمِ اللهِ الرَّحْمٰنِ الرَّحِيْمِ **30 Ayat**

Surah 89 Al-Fajr

Meaning	Words	Meaning	Words
Did you not see (inter. ptcl., ptcl. negn., *mudari'* juss. md. II. msc. sing.)	أَلَمْ تَرَ	By[1] the dawn (ptcl.[1], def. noun gen.)	وَالْفَجْرِ
How, in what way (ptcl. inter.[2])	كَيْفَ	And ten nights (generic noun br. pl. gen., card. no. gen.)	وَلَيَالٍ عَشْرٍ
Dealt, did your Lord (*madi* III. msc. sing., noun nom., att. pro. كَ)	فَعَلَ رَبُّكَ	And the even or double (def. noun gen.)	وَالشَّفْعِ
With 'Ad (ptcl., noun gen.[3])	بِعَادٍ	And the odd or single (def. noun gen.)	وَالْوَتْرِ
(Who belonged to) Iram the people of Iram[4] (noun dipt.)	إِرَمَ	And by the night (def. generic noun gen.)	وَاللَّيْلِ إِذَا
Possessor of pillars, lofty structures (dem. pro. gen. *mdf*, def. noun br. pl. *mdfi*.)	ذَاتِ الْعِمَادِ	When it passes away (ptcl., *mudari'* III. msc. sing.)	يَسْرِ
		Is there (not) in it (inter. ptcl., ptcl., dem. pro. msc. sing.)	هَلْ فِي ذٰلِكَ
which had never been created (built) (rel. pro. fem. sing., ptcl. negn., *mudari'* maj. juss. md. III. msc. sing.)	الَّتِي لَمْ يُخْلَقْ	An oath (noun nom.)	قَسَمٌ
Similar to it like of it (noun nom. *mdf*., att. pro. هَا *mdfi*.)	مِثْلُهَا	For one gifted with intelligence, for a possessor of sense (ptcl., dem. pro. ذِي gen. *mdf*., noun *mdfi*.)	لِذِي حِجْرٍ

---

[1] The particle و is used when swearing an oath, the object sworn by being in the genitive case.

[2] كَيْفَ is an interrogative particle which, when used with a particle of negation is used as an exclamatory particle showing a sense of wonder.

[3] Nouns governed by particles which are prepositions will always indicate the genitive case by the ending with *kasrah* unless they are diptotes. (Consult Juz 2 & 3 p.140).

[4] The settlement of the tribe of 'Ad.

Surah 89 Al-Fajr

Meaning	Words	Meaning	Words
your Lord (noun nom., att. pro. كَ)	رَبُّكَ	In (all) the lands, countries regions, territories (prep., def. noun br. pl. gen.)	فِى الْبِلَادِ
Mixture or scourge of punishment (vrb. n. acc. mdf., noun mdfi.)	سَوْطَ عَذَابٍ	And (with) Thamud (ptcl., noun, dipt.)	وَثَمُودَ
Indeed your Lord (ptcl., noun, att. pro. كَ)	إِنَّ رَبَّكَ	Who cut out (rel. pro., madi III. msc. pl.)	الَّذِينَ جَابُوا
Is ever on the watch observing all the time, ever lying in ambush (لَ ptcl. emph., prep., def. noun gen.)	لَبِالْمِرْصَادِ	The rocks (def. generic noun pl.)	الصَّخْرَ
		In the valley (prep., def. noun sing. gen.)	بِالْوَادِ
As for man (ptcls., def. noun msc. sing. nom.)	فَأَمَّا الْإِنْسَانُ	And Fir'aun (ptcl., noun dipt.)	وَفِرْعَوْنَ
Whenever tried him (ptcls., dr. vrb. VIII madi III. msc. sing., att. pro. هُ)	إِذَا مَا ابْتَلَاهُ	Of many tent poles of tent stakes, pegs (dem. pro., def. noun br. pl.)	ذِى الْأَوْتَادِ
his Lord (noun nom., att. pro. هُ)	رَبُّهُ	The ones who transgressed (rel. pro., madi III. msc. pl.)	الَّذِينَ طَغَوْا
and so honoured him was generous to him (ptcl., dr. vrb. IV madi III. msc. sing., att. pro. هُ)	فَأَكْرَمَهُ	In all the lands, countries, regions and territories (prep., def. noun br. pl. gen.)	فِى الْبِلَادِ
And blessed him provided him good things bestowed favours on him (ptcl., dr. vrb. II madi III. msc. sing., att. pro. هُ)	وَنَعَّمَهُ	So they multiplied (increased) in them (in the lands) (ptcl., dr. vrb. IV madi III. msc. pl., prep., att. pro. fem. sing.)	فَأَكْثَرُوا فِيهَا
		The corruption, the violence (def. noun acc.)	الْفَسَادَ
So he says, "My Lord (ptcl., mudari' III. msc. sing., noun, att. pro. ي I. sing.)	فَيَقُولُ رَبِّى	So poured over them (prep., madi III msc. sing., ptcl., att. pro. هِم)	فَصَبَّ عَلَيْهِم
Has honoured me" (dr. vrb. IV madi III. msc. sing., att. pro. نِي I. sing.)	أَكْرَمَنِ		

Words	Meaning	Words	Meaning
وَأَمَّا	And as for, (ptcls.)	طَعَامِ الْمِسْكِينِ	To feed the needy (vrb. n. gen. *mdf.*, def. noun sing. *mdfi.*)
إِذَا مَا ابْتَلَاهُ	Whenever (He) tried him (ptcls., dr. vrb. VIII *madi* III. msc. sing., att. pro. ه)	وَتَأْكُلُونَ	And you eat, devour (ptcl., *mudari*ᶜ II. msc. pl.)
فَقَدَرَ عَلَيْهِ	And straitened or restricted for him (ptcl., *madi* III. msc. sing., prep., pro. gen.)	التُّرَاثَ	The inheritence (def. noun acc.)
رِزْقَهُ	his provision (noun acc. *mdf.*, att. pro. ه *mdfi.*)	أَكْلًا	In a greedy, devouring manner (vrb. n. acc.)
فَيَقُولُ رَبِّي	So he says, "My Lord (ptcl., *mudari*ᶜ III. msc. sing., noun, att. pro. ي I. sing.)	لَمًّا	Entirely, altogether (vrb. n. acc.)
أَهَانَنِ	Disgraced me, left me humiliated (dr. vrb. IV *madi* III. msc. sing., att. pro. ني I. sing.)	وَتُحِبُّونَ الْمَالَ	And you love the wealth (ptcl., dr. vrb. IV *mudari*ᶜ II. msc. pl., def. noun acc.)
كَلَّا بَلْ	Nay but, by no means but (ptcls.)⁵	حُبًّا جَمًّا	A love, much, abounding, exceeding, boundless (both vrb. n. acc.)
لَا تُكْرِمُونَ	You are not generous kind, you do not honour (ptcl. negn., dr. vrb. IV *mudari*ᶜ II. msc. pl.)	كَلَّا إِذَا	No indeed, when (ptcls.)
الْيَتِيمَ	(to) the orphan (def. noun sing. acc.)	دُكَّتِ الْأَرْضُ	Is crushed, pounded to powder, is levelled down the earth (*madi maj.* III. fem. sing., def. noun nom.)
وَلَا تَحَاضُّونَ عَلَىٰ	And you do not urge one another (ptcl., ptcl. negn., dr. vrb. VI *mudari*ᶜ msc. pl., (عَلَى) with ptcl. تَتَحَاضُّونَ for تَحَاضُّونَ	دَكًّا دَكًّا	into a powder, a levelling, a crushing (vrb. n. acc. twice)
		وَجَاءَ رَبُّكَ	and comes your Lord (ptcl., *madi* III. msc. sing., noun nom., att. pro. ك)

⁵ كَلَّا is a particle used to indicate a reprimand. بَلْ is a particle which affirms that which follows it but contradicts or corrects that which went before.

Surah 89 Al-Fajr

Meaning	Words	Meaning	Words
Prepared beforehand / I had sent before (dr. vrb. II *madi* I. sing.)	قَدَّمْتُ	And the Angels (ptcl., def. noun sing. & pl. nom.)	وَالْمَلَكُ
For my life (ptcl., noun gen., att. pro. ي)	لِحَيَاتِي	in rows, ranks (vrb. n. acc. twice)	صَفًّا صَفًّا
So on that day (ptcl., noun, ptcl.)	فَيَوْمَئِذٍ	and shall be brought (*madi maj.* III. msc. sing., pass. of جَاءَ)	وَجِاْىءَ
No one shall punish (ptcl. negn.[7], dr. vrb. II *mudari* III. msc. sing.)	لَا يُعَذِّبُ	On that day (Day of Judgement) (يَوْمَ = day, noun, ئِذٍ = then, ptcl.)	يَوْمَئِذٍ
(Like) His punishment (noun acc., att. pro. هـ)	عَذَابَهُ	Hell (ptcl., noun dipt.)	بِجَهَنَّمَ
Anyone, (none) (card. no.)	أَحَدٌ	On that day (Day of Judgement) (يَوْمَ = day, noun, ئِذٍ = then, ptcl.)	يَوْمَئِذٍ
and no one shall bind (ptcl., ptcl. negn.[7], dr. vrb. IV *mudari* III. msc. sing.)	وَلَا يُوثِقُ	Man shall remember (dr. vrb. V *mudari* III. msc. sing., def. noun nom.)	يَتَذَكَّرُ الْإِنْسَانُ
(Like) His binding (noun acc., att. pro. هـ)	وَثَاقَهُ	and (but) how will he have / how will it help (ptcls.[6], att. pro. هـ)	وَأَنَّى لَهُ
Anyone, (None) (card. no.)	أَحَدٌ	the reminder, the admonition (def. noun dipt.)	الذِّكْرَى
O' soul (ptcl. interj., def. noun fem. sing.)	يَا أَيَّتُهَا النَّفْسُ	He shall say (*mudari* III. msc. sing.)	يَقُولُ
Become tranquil / Who enjoys peace (act. prtc. fem. sing.)	الْمُطْمَئِنَّةُ	Would that I had (يَا ptcl. interj., لَيْتَ ptcl. of desire, att. pro. نِي)	يَا لَيْتَنِي
Return to your Lord (*amr* II. fem. sing., prep., noun gen., att. pro. ك fem. sing.)	ارْجِعِي إِلَى رَبِّكِ		

[6] أَنَّى is a conjunction.

[7] The لَا governs the noun أَحَدٌ giving it the meaning of 'none'.

Meaning	Words	Meaning	Words
And enter in My Paradise. (ptcl., *amr* II. fem. sing., noun fem., att. pro. ي ⁸)	وَادْخُلِي جَنَّتِي	Contented, well pleased (act. prtc. fem. acc., pass. prtc. fem. acc.)	رَاضِيَةً مَّرْضِيَّةً
		So enter (ptcl., *amr* II. fem. sing.)	فَادْخُلِي
⁸ ي is a possessive pronoun giving the meaning 'My'.		In (among) My slaves (prep., noun br. pl., att. pro. ي)	فِي عِبَادِي

Root Words for Surah 89

- لَيَالٍ — Nights, لَيْل night, لَيْلَة a night.

- الشَّفْعِ — Double, the pair, the even (number), شَفَعَ * he was an intercessor, he interceded, he made even (in number).

- الْوَتْرِ — The single or odd (number), وَتَرَ * he defrauded someone of a thing, he hated, تَتْرَى (for وَتْرَى) one after another successively.

- ذِي حِجْرٍ — One gifted with intelligence, حَجَرَ * he hindered, حِجْرٌ unlawful, anything forbidden, a wall or dam, understanding, حِجَارَة a rock, stone.

- الْعِمَادِ — Lofty structures, columns, tent poles, (sing.) عَمَدَ , عَمَدَ * he afflicted, تَعَمَّدَ V he purposed, مُتَعَمِّدًا on purpose.

- الْبِلَادِ — The towns, territories, countries, lands, بَلَدَ * he stayed in a place.

- جَابُوا — They cut or hewed out, جَابَ * he cut out a garment at the neck.

- الصَّخْرَ — The rocks (no verbal root).

- الْوَادِ — The valley, channel of a river, وَدَى * he paid a fine as expiation for manslaughter.

- الْفَسَادَ — Corruption, violence, فَسَدَ * he was corrupt, أَفْسَدَ IV he acted corruptly, مُفْسِدٌ one who acts corruptly.

- سَوْطَ — A scourge, a mixture, سَاطَ * he mingled.

- أَهَانَ — IV He despised, هَانَ * he was quiet, vile, light, هُونٌ meekness, modesty, هَيِّنٌ light, easy, مُهِينٌ contemptible, shameful.

- تَحَاضُّونَ — You do not urge one another, حَضَّ * he incited, تَحَاضَّ VI they urged one another.

- تَأْكُلُونَ — You eat, أَكَلَ * he ate, devoured, consumed, أَكْلًا the act or state of eating in a greedy devouring manner, مَأْكُولٍ eaten.

- لَمًّا — Altogether, entirely, لَمَّ * he assembled, collected, was near, لَمَّا an adverb meaning 'when' or 'after that'.

- جَمًّا — Very much, جَمَّ * it abounded.

دُكَّتْ	Is ground or pounded into dust, دَكَّ * he pounded (it) into dust, دَكّاً dust, powder.	
يُوثِقُ	Binds, shall bind, وَثِقَ * he confided or trusted in someone, وَثَاقٌ a bond, ميثَاقٌ covenant, treaty, أَوْثَقَ IV he bound, drew tight.	
الْمُطْمَئِنَّةُ	The peaceful (fem.), طَمْنَ *quiet, إِطْمَأَنَّ IV he bequieted, rested securely in.	
ٱدْخُلي	Enter! (imp. fem.), دَخَلَ he entered, أَدْخَلَ IV he caused to enter.	
عِبَادِي	My slaves, (sing.) عَبْدٌ , عَبَدَ * he adored, worshipped, عِبَادَةٌ worship, عَبَّدَ II he enslaved.	

Translation of Surah 89 Al-Fajr (The Dawn)

(1.) By the dawn;

(2.) And by the ten nights;

(3.) And by the even and the odd;

(4.) And by the night as it journeys on;

(5.) Is there not in that an oath for those who have sense?

(6.) Have you not seen how your Lord dealt with ᶜAd;

(7.) Iram of the pillars;

(8.) The like of whom was never created in any land?

(9.) And Thamud, who used to hew out rocks in the valley?

(10.) And with Firᶜawn of the stakes?

(11.) Who were insolent in the land;

(12.) And infested the land with much corruption;

(13.) Therefore your Lord loosed upon them a scourge of chastisement;

(14.) Surely your Lord is ever watchful.

(15.) As for man, whenever his Lord tries him and honours him, and blesses him, he says "My Lord has honoured me".

(16.) But whenever He tries him by straitening his means, he says "My Lord has humiliated me."

(17.) No indeed! But you show no kindness to the orphans;

(18.) And you do not urge each other to feed the bereft;

(19.) And you devour the inheritance (of the orphans) with greed;

(20.) And you love wealth ardently;

(21.) No indeed! When the earth is systematically levelled down,

(22.) and your Lord comes, with the angels rank on rank,

(23.) and the Hell is, then, brought near, on that Day. Then on that day man will remember, but how will that remembrance profit him?

(24.) He shall say, "Oh, would that I had forwarded for my life!"

(25.) On that day none shall chastise as He chastises,

(26.) Nor shall any bind as He binds.

(27.) "Oh soul at peace,

(28.) return to your Lord, well pleased and well pleasing.

(29.) Enter you among My slaves!

(30.) Enter into My Paradise!"

Explanatory Notes for Surah 89

"By the dawn" refers to the time when the life starts to breathe and the dormant world gradually wakes up, similarly the dead will rise on the Day of Judgement thinking that it is the dawn after their night's sleep.

Several explanations have been advanced about the "ten nights". Some say it is the early part of Dhu'l-Hijjah, some say they are in Muharram, and others state that they are the last ten nights of Ramadan, the true knowledge about these ten nights lies with Allah (SWT). "By the even and the odd" may include various creations of Allah (SWT). "By the night as it journeys on" and the dawn approaches indicating a systematic arrangement and the order of the things solely controlled by the Creator.

Ayat 6-14 refer to the fates of the most powerful and despotic nations in ancient history. ᶜAd of Iram (name of place), an extinct branch of Arabs, used to dwell at *Ahqaf*, a sandy piece of land in southern Arabia. ᶜAd built high buildings, erecting edifices on lofty pillars was introduced to the world by them. No other nation in the world compared with them in strength, glory and grandeur.

Thamud lived in the valley, the *Wad-il-Qura*, where they carved out dwellings in the mountains. This place was called *Al-Hijr*, a rocky tract in northern Arabia. Possibly the pyramids of Egypt have been compared to the stakes, for they are the remnants of the grandeur and glory of the Firᶜawns. All these people were corrupt and tyrannical, and Allah (SWT) punished them severely.

With reference to *ayat* 15-16, such is man's thinking about the various forms of trial Allah (SWT) may set for him, be it comfort or hardship. He does not realise the probationary nature of what he is given. A test with abundance reveals whether a man is humble and thankful to his Lord or arrogant and haughty, while a trial of the opposite kind reveals his patient acceptance or his irritability and fretfulness.

Ayat 17-20 not only expose the true nature of their attitude but they also condemn it.

In *ayat* 21-27 stern warning is given about the Day of Judgement. Hell will be on that day very close to its prospective dwellers. Indeed, the life hereafter is the one which is worth preparing for and to forward good deeds for.

Ayat 28-30 tell us that a true Believer's soul is satisfied in all eventualities: happiness or affliction, wealth or poverty; this soul is addressed compassionately on the Day of Judgement.

Surah 90 Al-Balad

Makki Surah   بِسْمِ اللهِ الرَّحْمٰنِ الرَّحِيْمِ   *20 Ayat*

Surah 90 Al-Balad

Words	Meaning	Words	Meaning
لَا أُقْسِمُ	Nay, I swear (ptcl.[1], dr. vrb. IV *mudari*ᶜ I. sing.)	أَيَحْسَبُ أَن	Does he think that (ptcl. of inter., *mudari*ᶜ III. msc. sing., ptcl.)
بِهَٰذَا الْبَلَدِ	By this city or land country (prep., dem. pro., def. noun gen.)	لَّن يَقْدِرَ عَلَيْهِ أَحَدٌ	None has power over him None will have power over him (ptcl. negn., *mudari*ᶜ subj. md. III. msc. sing., prep., att. pro., card. no.)
وَأَنتَ حِلٌّ	And while you are an inhabitant, lawful (ptcl., per. pro. msc. sing., vrb. n. nom.)	يَقُولُ أَهْلَكْتُ	He says "I have wasted (*mudari*ᶜ III. msc. sing., dr. vrb. IV *madi* I. sing.)
بِهَٰذَا الْبَلَدِ	In this city or land or country (prep., dem. pro., def. noun gen.)	مَالًا لُّبَدًا	Wealth in heaps," much, in vast amounts" (nouns acc.)
وَوَالِدٍ	And by a father (ptcl.[2], act. prtc. gen.)	أَيَحْسَبُ أَن	Does he think that (ptcl. inter., *mudari*ᶜ III. msc. sing., ptcl.)
وَمَا وَلَدَ	And what he begets (his child) (ptcls., *madi* III. msc. sing.)	لَّمْ يَرَهُ أَحَدٌ	None has seen him none has been observing him (ptcl. negn., *mudari*ᶜ juss. md. III. msc. sing., pro., card. no.)
لَقَدْ خَلَقْنَا	We have certainly created (ptcls.[3], *madi* I. pl.)	أَلَمْ نَجْعَل	Did We not make (ptcl. inter., ptcl. negn., *mudari*ᶜ juss. md. I. pl.)
الْإِنسَانَ فِي كَبَدٍ	Man in misery, trouble, affliction, toil (def. noun acc., prep., vrb. n. gen.)	لَّهُ عَيْنَيْنِ	For him two eyes (ptcl., att. pro., noun dual acc.)
		وَلِسَانًا	And a tongue (ptcl., noun acc.)

[1] The particle لَا is held to be intensive, used to emphasise the oath, and is not used as a particle of negation.

[2] The particle وَ is used to swear oaths, the object sworn by being in the genitive case.

[3] لَقَدْ is a combination of the particle لَ which is used for emphasis and قَدْ which is a confirmatory particle placed before the *madi* confirming that the action is of the recent past.

Meaning	Words	Meaning	Words
Near of kin, close relationship (dem. pro. acc. *mdf.*, noun gen. *مَصْدَر مِيمِي mdfi.*)	ذَا مَقْرَبَةٍ	And two lips (ptcl., noun dual acc.)	وَشَفَتَيْنِ
Or a destitute one (ptcl., noun acc.)	أَوْ مِسْكِينًا	And We guided him (showed him) (ptcl., madi I. pl., pro. ه)	وَهَدَيْنَاهُ
(in) extreme poverty, down in the dust (dem. pro. acc. *mdf.*, noun *mdfi.*)	ذَا مَتْرَبَةٍ	The two highways (of good & evil) (def. noun dual acc.)	النَّجْدَيْنِ
Again he was (ptcl., madi III. msc. sing.)	ثُمَّ كَانَ	But (or yet) he did not attempt (ptcl., ptcl. negn., dr. vrb. VIII madi III. msc. sing.)	فَلَا اقْتَحَمَ
Among the believers (prep., rel. pro., dr. vrb. IV madi III. msc. pl.)	مِنَ الَّذِينَ آمَنُوا	The place hard of ascent, the difficult path (def. noun fem. sing. acc.)	الْعَقَبَةَ
And they bid each other, they enjoin upon each other (ptcl., dr. vrb. VI madi III. msc. pl.)	وَتَوَاصَوْا	And what would make you know (ptcls., dr. vrb. IV madi III. msc. sing., att. pro. ك)	وَمَا أَدْرَاكَ
To patience, (prep., def. noun gen.)	بِالصَّبْرِ	What the place hard of ascent, the difficult path, is? (ptcl., def. noun fem. sing. nom.)	مَا الْعَقَبَةُ
And they bid each other, they enjoin upon each other (ptcl., dr. vrb. VI madi III. msc. pl.)	وَتَوَاصَوْا	(it is) freeing a neck (of a slave) (vrb. n. nom. *mdf.*, noun *mdfi.*)	فَكُّ رَقَبَةٍ
To mercy, kindness (prep., def. noun gen. *مَصْدَر مِيمِي*)	بِالْمَرْحَمَةِ	Or feeding in a day (ptcl., vrb. n. nom., prep., noun gen.)	أَوْ إِطْعَامٌ فِي يَوْمٍ
Those are the people or companions (dem. pro., noun br. pl. nom. *mdf.*)	أُولَٰئِكَ أَصْحَابُ	of hunger, famine (dem pro. gen. *mdf.*, vrb. n. *mdfi.*)	ذِي مَسْغَبَةٍ
of the right hand (def. noun fem. *mdfi.*)	الْمَيْمَنَةِ	An orphan (noun acc.)	يَتِيمًا
And the ones who disbelieved (ptcl., rel. pro. pl., madi III. msc. pl.)	وَالَّذِينَ كَفَرُوا		

Words	Meaning	Words	Meaning
بِـَٔايَٰتِنَا	In Our signs, verses (prep., noun fem. br. pl. gen. *mdf.*, نَا att. pro. I. pl. *mdfi.*)	عَلَيْهِمْ نَارٌ	On them or upon them a fire (prep., pro. msc. pl., noun nom.)
هُمْ أَصْحَٰبُ	They are the companions or people (per. pro. msc. pl., noun br. pl. *mdf.*)	مُّؤْصَدَةٌ	Covering, enveloping (them) (pass. prtc. fem. nom.)
ٱلْمَشْـَٔمَةِ	Of the left hand (def. noun fem. *mdfi.*)		

Root Words for Surah 90

حَلّ	An inhabitant, anything lawful, حَلَّ * he untied (i.e. a knot), حَلَالٌ lawful.
وَالِدٍ	Father, one who begets, وَالِدَةٌ mother, وَلَدٌ child son, offspring, وَلَدَ * (*mudari*ᶜ يَلِدُ) he begot offspring, brought forth, يُولَدُ he was begotten.
كَبَدٍ	Misery, trouble, كَبَدَ * he suffered pain in the liver, faced difficulty.
أَهْلَكْتُ	I wasted, destroyed, هَلَكَ * he fell, died, perished, أَهْلَكَ IV he destroyed, wasted.
مَالًا	Property, possession, substance, wealth, riches (pl.) مَالٌ , أَمْوَالٌ * he was rich.
لُبَدًا	Much (wealth), لَبَدَ * he remained in a place.
يَرَى	He sees, رَأَى * he saw, perceived, thought, had the view, judged, رَآهُ he saw it, perceived it, thought it, أَرَأَيْتَ did you see, have you seen, لَتَرَوُنَّ you will surely see, يُرَآءُونَ they make show.
نَجْعَل	We made, جَعَلَ * he constituted, ordained, appointed, made, imposed, put, placed, جَاعِلٌ he who placed.
لِسَانًا	Tongue, speech, language, (pl.) لَسَنٌ , أَلْسِنَةٌ * he seized on someone by the tongue.
شَفَتَيْنِ	The two lips, شَفَهَ * he struck someone on the lips.
ٱلنَّجْدَيْنِ	The two open highways (of good and evil), نَجَدَ * he overcame.
ٱقْتَحَمَ	VIII attempted, rushed, plunged, قَحَمَ * he rushed headlong.
ٱلْعَقَبَةَ	Steep ascent (the difficult path), عَقَبَ * he succeeded, عُقْبَى end, عَاقِبَةٌ fortunate result.
فَكّ	Freeing, فَكَّ * he broke, مُنْفَكِّينَ ones who break off, dislocated.
رَقَبَةٍ	A slave, a neck, رَقَبَ * he observed, watched, respected, regarded.
إِطْعَامٌ	The act of feeding, طَعِمَ * he ate, tasted, أَطْعَمَ IV he fed, طَعَامٌ food.
مَسْغَبَةٍ	Famine, privation, سَغَبَ * he suffered from hunger and want.
مِسْكِينًا	Poor, submissive, humble, (pl.) سَكَنَ , مَسَاكِينُ * he inhabited, dwelt, rested, was quiet.

تَوَاصَوْا	They enjoined or recommended to one another, وَصَى * he joined together, وَصِيَّة a mandate, command, testament, legacy, وَصَّى II he commanded, تَوَاصَى VI (he) enjoined one another.
الصَّبْر	Patience, صَبَرَ * he was patient or constant, he bound.
الْمَرْحَمَة	Kindness, mercy, رَحِمَ * he was merciful, had mercy upon, رَحْمَن all-merciful and رَحِيم compassionate.
الْمَشْئَمَة	The left hand, شَأَمَ * he was sinister, unlucky.
مُؤْصَدَة	Vaulted over, covered over, أَصَدَ * he covered over (a pot).

Translation of Surah 90 Al-Balad (The Land or the City)

(1.) Nay, I swear by this city; (2.) And you are a dweller in this city; (3.) By a father and what he begot; (4.) Indeed, We have created man in struggle. (5.) Does he think that no one has power over him? (6.) He says: "I have wasted much wealth." (7.) Does he think that no one sees him? (8.) Have We not made for him two eyes (9.) and a tongue and two lips (10.) And guided him to the two paths? (11.) Yet he has not attempted the steep ascent; (12.) And how would you know what the steep ascent is? (13.) It is the freeing of a slave (14.) Or the feeding on a day of hunger (15.) Of an orphan near of kin (16.) Or a needy one down in the dust; 17. Moreover he is of those who believe, and enjoin steadfastness on each other, and enjoin mercy on each other. (18.) Those shall be the Companions of the Right Hand. (19.) And the ones who disbelieve in Our signs, they shall be the Companions of the Left Hand; (20.) With Hell-Fire close above them.

Explanatory Notes for Surah 90

The *surah* opens with forceful oaths, 'I swear by this city'. The city is said to be Makkah, the Sacred House of Allah (SWT) and all the creatures that happen to be at His House enjoy full and complete security. 'By a father and what he begot' refers to Ibrahim and Isma'il (AS) in particular who built this Sacred House. As Allah (SWT) mentions, the Prophet Muhammad (SAAS) was the resident of this city which adds to the sanctity, honour and glory of the place. The disbelievers were violating the sanctity of the House by harassing the Prophet (SAAS) and the Muslims in it. These oaths affirm an intrinsic fact in human life that it is a process of continued hardships that begin from birth and go on as life passes by. This creature, man, whose suffering struggle never comes to an end becomes so conceited with what Allah (SWT) has given him of power, ability, skill and prosperity that he behaves as if he is not accountable for what he does. He corrupts himself and others in total disregard of anything of value. When he is called upon to spend for good causes, he says, "I have wasted vast riches (and given more than enough)." He has forgotten that Allah (SWT) is watching over him. He neither follows the right guidance nor shows his gratitude, although Allah (SWT) has given him the means to do so. Allah (SWT) has given him two eyes, two lips and a tongue, and has equipped him with the ability to distinguish good from evil and right from wrong. "And shown him the two paths", so that he may choose between them; for in his make-up there exists the ability to take either way. All these bounties have not motivated man to attempt the steep ascent, which Allah (SWT) explains by saying "(The steep ascent is) the freeing of a slave, feeding in a day of hunger, an orphan near of kin, or a needy man in misery". And all those who attempt the ascent are those who believe and counsel one another to be steadfast, and enjoin mercy on one another; they shall have their dwelling place on the right hand enjoying a happy recompense for what they do in this life. Those who denied shall dwell on the left hand and they shall be encircled by fire.

Surah 91 Ash-Shams

Makki Surah — 15 *Ayat*

Surah 91 Ash-Shams

Meaning	Words	Meaning	Words
And What (i.e. Who) built As He built it (ptcls., *madi* III. msc. sing., att. pro. هَا³)	وَمَا بَنَىٰهَا	By¹ the sun (ptcl.¹, def. noun fem. gen.)	وَالشَّمْسِ
By¹ the earth (ptcl.¹, def. noun fem. gen.)	وَالْأَرْضِ	And its full brightness or and its light of the day (ptcl., noun mdf., هَا³ att. pro. mdfi.)	وَضُحَىٰهَا
And What (i.e. Who) spread it out, As He spread it out (ptcls., *madi* III. msc. sing., att. pro. هَا³)	وَمَا طَحَىٰهَا	By¹ the moon (ptcl.¹, def. noun msc. gen.)	وَالْقَمَرِ
		When² it follows her (the sun) (ptcl.², *madi* III. msc. sing., att. pro. هَا³)	إِذَا تَلَىٰهَا
By¹ a self, soul or person (ptcl.¹, noun fem. gen.)	وَنَفْسٍ	By¹ the day (ptcl.¹, def. noun msc. gen.)	وَالنَّهَارِ
And What (i.e. Who) perfected it, As He perfected, levelled, fashioned, proportioned it (ptcls., dr. vrb. II *madi* III. msc. sing., att. pro. هَا³)	وَمَا سَوَّىٰهَا	When² it reveals her (the sun) in all her splendour (ptcl.², dr. vrb. II *madi* III. msc. sing., att. pro. هَا³)	إِذَا جَلَّىٰهَا
		By¹ the night (ptcl.¹, def. noun gen.)	وَاللَّيْلِ
Then He inspired it (soul) (ptcl., dr. vrb. IV *madi* III. msc. sing., att. pro. هَا³)	فَأَلْهَمَهَا	When² it covers over her (the sun) (ptcl.², *madi* III. msc. sing., att. pro. هَا³)	إِذَا يَغْشَىٰهَا
(with) Its wickedness (vrb. n. acc. mdf., att. pro. هَا³ mdfi.)	فُجُورَهَا	By¹ the sky, heaven (ptcl.¹, def. noun fem. gen.)	وَالسَّمَاءِ
And its piety (ptcl., vrb. n. acc. mdf., att. pro. هَا³ mdfi.)	وَتَقْوَىٰهَا		

¹ The particle وَ is used for swearing an oath, the object sworn by being in the genitive case.

² The *madi* that comes after إِذَا takes the meaning of being imperfect. (Ref.: Juz 2&3 p.129).

³ The attached pronoun هَا is for those nouns treated as feminine.

Words	Meaning	Words	Meaning
قَدْ أَفْلَحَ	Has certainly prospered, attained his desires become happy (قَدْ ptcl. emph., dr. vrb. IV *madi* III. msc. sing.)	رَسُولُ اللّٰهِ	The Messenger of Allah (Salih {AS}) (noun msc. sing. nom. *mdf.*, noun *mdfi.*)
مَن زَكَّىٰهَا	Whoever purified it (soul) (indecl. conj. pro., dr. vrb. II *madi* III. msc. sing., att. pro. هَا³)	نَاقَةَ اللّٰهِ	"The she camel of Allah (His sign for you) (noun fem. sing. acc. *mdf.*, noun *mdfi.*)
وَقَدْ خَابَ	Is certainly disappointed, frustrated, has reached a hopeless state (ptcl., ptcl. emph. قَدْ, *madi* III. msc. sing.)	وَسُقْيَاهَا	And (let) her drink" (do not hinder) her drinking" (ptcl., noun *mdf.*, att. pro. *mdfi.*)
مَن دَسَّىٰهَا	Who corrupted it (soul) (indecl. conj. pro., dr. vrb. II *madi* III. msc. sing., att. pro. هَا³)	فَكَذَّبُوهُ	Then they belied him (ptcl., dr. vrb. II *madi* III. msc. pl., att. pro. هُ)
كَذَّبَتْ ثَمُودُ	Belied Thamud (dr. vrb. II *madi* III. fem. sing., noun dipt. nom.)	فَعَقَرُوهَا	And so they hamstrung her (ptcl., *madi* III. msc. pl., att. pro.)
بِطَغْوَاهَا	With their extreme wickedness (prep., noun طَغْوَىٰ *mdf.*, att. pro. هَا *mdfi.* for Thamud)	فَدَمْدَمَ عَلَيْهِم	Then He destroyed them (ptcl., quad. vrb. *madi* III. msc. sing., prep., pro. هِم)
إِذِ انبَعَثَ	When, rose up, went forth (to hamstrung the camel) (ptcl., dr. vrb. VII *madi* III. msc. sing.)	رَبُّهُم بِذَنبِهِمْ	Their Lord, for their sins (noun nom. *mdf.*, att. pro. هُم *mdfi.*, prep., noun gen. *mdf.*, att. pro. هِم *mdfi.*)
أَشْقَىٰهَا	The greatest wretch among them (noun elat. msc. sing. أَشْقَىٰ *mdf.*, att. pro. هَا *mdfi.* for Thamud)	فَسَوَّىٰهَا	Then or so He levelled it (their city to the ground) (ptcl., dr. vrb. II *madi* III msc. sing., att. pro.)
فَقَالَ لَهُمْ	Then said to them (ptcl., *madi* III. msc. sing., ptcl., att. pro. هُم)	وَلَا يَخَافُ	And He does not fear (ptcl., ptcl. negn., *mudari*ᶜ III. msc. sing.)
		عُقْبَاهَا	Its end or reward or punishment or results or what may follow (noun *mdf.*, att. pro. هَا *mdfi.*)

Root Words for Surah 91

تَلَى *	He followed, recited, declared, read, rehearsed, تِلَاوَةٌ reading, recitation.
النَّهَارِ	A day from dawn to dusk, نَهَرَ * he repulsed, reproached, نَهْرٌ river, لَا تَنْهَرْ do not brow-beat, chide, repulse.
جَلَّى	II He made clear, revealed, made manifest, brought in light, glorified, جَلَى * it was clear and manifest.
طَحَى *	He spread out, extended, expanded.
أَلْهَمَ	IV He inspired someone with, لَهِمَ * he swallowed.
تَقْوَى	Piety, righteousness, Allah consciousness, fear of Allah, وَقَى * he kept someone safe, اِتَّقَى he was fearfully cautious of, protected himself against, مُتَّقِي one who fears Allah, who is cautious and careful (in his actions).
خَابَ *	He was frustrated, disappointed, in a hopeless state.
دَسَّى	He hid (a thing), buried.
نَاقَةً	A she camel, نَاقَ * he cleaned the flesh of fat.
كَذَّبُوا	They denied, كَذَبَ * he lied, كَذَّبَ II he accused of falsehood, denied, كَاذِبَةٍ lying.
عَقَرُوا	They hamstrung, عَقَرَ * he hamstrung, wounded, cut, عَاقِرٌ barren.
دَمْدَمَ	He obliterated, destroyed (quad. vrb.), دَمَّ * he plastered, (original root).

Translation of Surah 91 Ash-Shams (The Sun)

(1.) By the sun and its radiant brightness,

(2.) By the moon as it follows it (as it reflects the sun),

(3.) By the day when it reveals its splendour,

(4.) By the night when it veils over it,

(5.) By the sky and He who constructed it,

(6.) By the earth and He who spread it,

(7.) By the human self and He Who balanced it,

(8.) Then He inspired it (with knowledge of) its wickedness and its piety,

(9.) Truly successful is he who purified it (his self)

(10.) And indeed, failed is he who corrupts it,

(11.) (To this truth) gave the lie in their overweening arrogance (the tribe of) Thamud,

(12.) When their most wretched rushed forward (to mischief),

(13.) Then the Messenger of Allah said to them: "The she-camel of Allah let her drink (and do her no harm)",

(14.) But they gave him the lie and (cruelly) slaughtered her; for their sin their Lord utterly destroyed them.

(15.) And He has no fear of any consequences thereof.

Explanatory Notes for Surah 91

Allah (SWT) swears by the objects and phenomena mentioned in *ayat* 1-7, which gives these creations an added significance and draws man's attention to them. Man ought to contemplate these phenomena and try to appreciate their value and the purpose of their creation.

In *ayat* 8-10, Allah (SWT) mentions that He has created man with the capability of recognising good and evil and he is equipped with a conscious faculty which determines his line of action and is therefore responsible for his actions and decisions; successful is the one who keeps his conscious faculty pure, and ruined is the one who corrupts it.

In order to make us understand this truth an historical event is cited in *ayat* 11-15 about the tribe of Thamud. This tribe lived in Northern Hijaz, near Makkah, i.e. the North-Western part of Arabia and is even today known by the name of *Al-Hijr*. They used to carve out grand houses in the mountains. They demanded from their Prophet Salih (AS) that he bring a clear Sign of his appointment as Messenger of Allah; the Prophet Salih (AS) presented the she-camel as a sign with a warning that they should not touch her with any bad intentions and let her drink water from a particular well, but they killed the she-camel. The whole tribe was destroyed by a terrifying earthquake. When the Prophet Muhammad (SAAS) was passing through the ruins of Thamud, he assembled together those Muslims who were enjoying a walk through the remains and said, "This is the territory of the tribe on which Allah inflicted his scourge; therefore pass through this with as much haste as you can because this is not a place of enjoyment but a place of lamentation". The tribe of Thamud is mentioned 26 times in the Qur'an. After ʿAd, the tribe of Hud (S), they were the second most widely known ancient tribe of Arabia.

Surah 92 Al-Layl

Makki Surah — بِسْمِ اللَّهِ الرَّحْمَٰنِ الرَّحِيمِ — **21 Ayat**

Words	Meaning	Words	Meaning
وَالَّيْلِ	By[1] the night (ptcl.[1], def. noun gen.)	وَاتَّقَىٰ	And he feared (Allah) and he was conscious of Allah (ptcl., dr. vrb. VIII *madi* III. msc. sing.)
إِذَا يَغْشَىٰ	When[2] it covers over (ptcl.[2], *mudari* III. msc. sing.)	وَصَدَّقَ	And affirmed (ptcl., dr. vrb. II *madi* III. msc. sing.)
وَالنَّهَارِ	By[1] the day (ptcl.[1], def. noun gen.)	بِالْحُسْنَىٰ	The best (prep., def. noun fem. elat.)
إِذَا تَجَلَّىٰ	When[2] it appears or becomes clear (ptcl.[2], dr. vrb. V *madi* III. msc. sing.)	فَسَنُيَسِّرُهُ	So We will ease him facilitate him or make easy for him (ptcl., ptcl. سَ [3], dr. vrb. II *mudari* I. pl., att. pro. هُ)
وَمَا خَلَقَ	And What (i.e. He Who) created (ptcls., *madi* III. msc. sing.)	لِلْيُسْرَىٰ	To the easiest (way) or the way of happiness (ptcl., def. noun dipt. elat. fem.)
الذَّكَرَ وَالْأُنْثَىٰ	the male and the female (def. nouns sing. acc.)	وَأَمَّا مَنْ	And as for whoever (ptcls., indecl. conj. pro.)
إِنَّ سَعْيَكُمْ	Indeed your effort or endeavour (ptcl., سَعْيَ vrb. n. acc. *mdf.*, كُمْ att. pro. pl. *mdfi.*)	بَخِلَ	Was covetous, miserly (*madi* III. msc. sing.)
لَشَتَّىٰ	Is certainly diverse, divided, separate (لَ ptcl. emph., indecl. noun sing. or pl.)	وَاسْتَغْنَىٰ	And thought himself in no need (of Allah), was contented (with the world), (ptcl., dr. vrb. X *madi* III. msc. sing.)
فَأَمَّا مَنْ	Then as for him who (ptcls., indecl. conj. pro.)	وَكَذَّبَ	And he belied, denied, charged with falsehood (ptcl., dr. vrb. II *madi* III. msc. sing.)
أَعْطَىٰ	Gave in (Allah's way) (dr. vrb. IV *madi* III. msc. sing.)		

[1] The particle وَ indicates the swearing of an oath, the object sworn by being in the genitive case.

[2] After إِذَا *madi* takes the meaning of imperfect (Ref: Juz 2&3, p.129).

[3] سَ a particle which, when placed before *mudari*, confirms the meaning of the future.

Meaning	Words	Meaning	Words
The best (prep., def. noun elat. fem.)	بِالْحُسْنَىٰ	The hereafter (لَ ptcl. emph., def. noun acc.)[4]	لَلْآخِرَةُ
So We will ease him, facilitate him, or make easy for him (ptcl., ptcl. سَ [3], dr. vrb. II *mudari* I. pl., att. pro. هُ)	فَسَنُيَسِّرُهُ	And the former (present) life (life of this world) (ptcl., def. ord. no. fem. of أَوَّلُ)	وَالْأُولَىٰ
To the most wretched, most difficult, (def. noun elat. fem. dipt.)	لِلْعُسْرَىٰ	So I have warned you (ptcl., dr. vrb. IV *madi* I. sing., att. pro. كُمْ)	فَأَنْذَرْتُكُمْ
And (there) shall not avail him (ptcl., ptcl. negn., dr. vrb. IV *mudari* III. msc. sing., ptcl., att. pro. هُ)	وَمَا يُغْنِي عَنْهُ	(of) A fire[5] blazing fiercely (noun[5] acc., dr. vrb. V *madi* III. msc.[5] sing.)	نَارًا تَلَظَّىٰ
His wealth (noun nom. *mdf.*, att. pr. *mdfi.*)	مَالُهُ	Shall not burn in it[5] (ptcl. negn., *mudari* III. msc. sing., att. pro. fem. sing. هَا for fire)	لَا يَصْلَاهَا
When he falls headlong or perishes (ptcl., dr. vrb. V *madi* III. msc. sing.)	إِذَا تَرَدَّىٰ	Except the most wretched (ptcl., def. noun elat. dipt.)	إِلَّا الْأَشْقَى
Indeed it is on Us (Allah) (ptcls., att. pro. نَا I. pl.)	إِنَّ عَلَيْنَا	The one who belied, denied (rel. pro., dr. vrb. II *madi* III. msc. sing.)	الَّذِي كَذَّبَ
(To grant you) the guidance (لَ ptcl. emph., def. noun *gh.* acc.)[4]	لَلْهُدَىٰ	And turned away (ptcl., dr. vrb. V *madi* III. msc. sing.)	وَتَوَلَّىٰ
And indeed there belong to Us, are Ours (ptcls., att. pro. نَا I. pl.)	وَإِنَّ لَنَا	And he shall be averted from it (Hell fire) (ptcl., ptcl. سَ [3], dr. vrb. II *mudari* maj. III. msc. sing., att. pro. هَا)	وَسَيُجَنَّبُهَا
		Most pious, greatly fearing (Allah) (def. noun dipt. elat.)	الْأَتْقَى
		The one who gives (rel. pro. msc. sing., dr. vrb. IV *mudari* III. msc. sing.)	الَّذِي يُؤْتِي

[4] The particle لَ joins with الْآخِرَةُ and الْهُدَىٰ with the result that the ا is assimilated i.e. لَلْهُدَىٰ and لَلْآخِرَةُ.

[5] نَارٌ 'fire' is treated both as masculine and feminine.

Meaning	Words	Meaning	Words
Except desiring (ptcl., vrb. n. {dr. vrb. VIII} acc. *mdf.*⁷)	اِلَّا ابْتِغَآءَ	His wealth (noun acc. *mdf.*, att. pro. ه *mdfi.*)	مَالَهٗ
The face of his Lord (noun gen. *mdfi. mdf.*⁷, noun *mdfi.*, att. pro. ه)	وَجْهِ رَبِّهِ	He purifies himself (by giving alms) (dr. vrb. V *mudari*ᶜ III. msc. sing.)	يَتَزَكّٰى
The most High, Exalted (def. noun elat. dipt.)	الْاَعْلٰى	And not for anyone (ptcls., card. no. gen.)	وَمَا لِاَحَدٍ
And certainly soon (ptcl., ptcl. emph. لَ, ptcl.⁸)	وَلَسَوْفَ	With him (in his mind) (ptcl., att. pro.)	عِنْدَهٗ
He shall be pleased (with what Allah rewards him with) (*mudari*ᶜ III. msc. sing.)	يَرْضٰى	(to seek) any favour, reward (in return) (prep., noun fem. gen.)	مِنْ نِعْمَةٍ
⁷ Each word is in the *idafah* relation to the following and so the phrase might be translated "…except desiring *of* the face *of* the Lord *of* him…" ⁸ This particle is prefixed to the *mudari*ᶜ to give it a future significance.		(which shall be) given or recompensed (*mudari*ᶜ *maj.* III. fem. sing.)⁶	تُجْزٰى
		⁶ The verb تُجْزٰى is used for the noun نِعْمَة	

Root Words for Surah 92

شَتّٰى	Various, divided, separate, شَتَّ * he separated, أَشْتَاتًا divided into classes or groups.
صَدَّقَ	II He affirmed, was very sincere and truthful, verified, proved the truth, صَدَقَ * he was truthful, صِدْقٌ truth, truthfulness, sincerity.
الْحُسْنٰى	The best (fem. of elat. أَحْسَنُ), happiest state, best thing, best action, حَسُنَ * he was good, beautiful.
بَخِلَ *	He was covetous, avaricious, niggardly, mean, he stinted.
الْعُسْرٰى	The most difficult, wretchedness, distress, difficulty, عَسَرَ * it was difficult.
تَرَدّٰى	He was brought to destruction, perished, رَدِيَ * he perished, أَرْدٰى IV he brought someone to destruction.
تَلَظّٰى	for تَتَلَظّٰى V it blazes fiercely, لَظِيَ * it blazed.
يُؤْتِي	He gives, أَتٰى * he came, committed, brought to, آتٰى IV he give, إِيتَاء the bestowing of gifts.
تُجْزٰى	(fem. *maj.*) Given, rewarded, recompensed, جَزٰى * he recompensed for good or evil,

gave as a reward, he satisfied.

اِبْتِغَاءً (vrb. n. dr. vrb. VIII) desiring, coveting, seeking, بَغَى * he desired, sought, passed beyond bounds, he transgressed.

Translation of Surah 92 Al-Lail (The Night)

1. By the night when it covers everything (with darkness).
2. By the day when it reveals (everything by its light).
3. By Him Who created the male and the female.
4. Your efforts are surely wasted in useless pursuits.
5. So he who gives and fears (Allah),
6. And affirms the best,
7. For him We shall smooth the way to perfect ease.
8. But as for him who is miserly and thinks himself self-sufficient,
9. And calls the best a lie.
10. We shall smooth his way to affliction.
11. His wealth will not be of any use to him when he is thrown headlong into the fire.
12. It is for Us to give guidance.
13. And to Us belong the End and the Beginning.
14. I have warn you, therefore, of the fire that burns fiercely.
15. No-one will be thrown into this fire to burn except the most grievous,
16. Who denies (the truth) and turns away.
17. The righteous shall be kept away from it (the fire),
18. Who gives his wealth to purify himself,
19. And not in recompense of any favour done to him by anyone,
20. Only seeking the countenance of his Lord, Most High,
21. And he will soon be well pleased.

Explanatory Notes for Surah 92

Allah (SWT) swears by His signs which are contrasting, i.e. the day and the night, the male and female, and then He mentions two diverse types of human efforts: the righteous ones are striving for the eternal Truth and in the way of Allah, the deniers of the Truth are striving for this world's gains only. Everyone's way will be facilitated according to his striving: the righteous ones will find their way eased and made smooth for them by Allah (SWT), they will have more faith and courage to struggle in the way of Allah and their abode shall be Paradise; whereas the deniers of Truth shall find their way smoothed for the worldly gains but shall earn Allah's wrath and shall end up in Hell-Fire. The righteous ones will be preserved from this fire. The fact is that man's life in this world and in the Hereafter are but two stages of one continuous entity. Whatever man shall sow here surely he shall reap it there.

Surah 93 Ad-Duha

Makki Surah   بِسْمِ اللهِ الرَّحْمٰنِ الرَّحِيْمِ   *11 Ayat*

Surah 93 Ad-Duha

Meaning	Words	Meaning	Words
By[1] the bright morning hours or by the brightness of the day or by the forenoon (ptcl.[1], def. noun common gender)	وَالضُّحٰى	And indeed soon (لَ ptcl. emph., ptcl.[2])	وَلَسَوْفَ
By[1] the night (ptcl.[1], def. noun gen.)	وَالَّيْلِ	Shall give or grant you (dr. vrb. IV *mudari* III. msc. sing., att. pro. كَ)	يُعْطِيْكَ
When it is tranquil and dark (ptcl., *madi* III. msc. sing.)	إِذَا سَجٰى	Your Lord (noun nom. *mdf.*, att. pro. كَ *mdfi.*)	رَبُّكَ
Has not left you has not abandoned you (ptcl. negn., dr. vrb. II *madi* III. msc. sing., att. pro. كَ)	مَا وَدَّعَكَ	Then you shall be pleased (ptcl., *mudari* II. msc. sing.)	فَتَرْضٰى
Your Lord (noun nom. *mdf.*, att. pro. كَ *mdfi.*)	رَبُّكَ	Did He not find you (ptcl. inter., ptcl. negn., *mudari* juss. md. III. msc. sing., att. pro. كَ)	أَلَمْ يَجِدْكَ
Nor does He scorn you (ptcl., ptcls. negn., *madi* III. msc. sing.)	وَمَا قَلٰى	An orphan (act. prtc. msc. sing. acc.)	يَتِيْمًا
And indeed the hereafter, the later period (لَ ptcl. emph., def. noun nom.)	وَلَلْآخِرَةُ	Then He cared, sheltered, provided refuge (for you) (ptcl., dr. vrb. IV *madi* III. msc. sing.)	فَآوٰى
Is better for you (noun elat., ptcl., att. pro. كَ)	خَيْرٌ لَّكَ	And He found you (ptcl., *madi* III. msc. sing., att. pro. كَ)	وَوَجَدَكَ
Than the former (present) life, or than the earlier period (prep., def. ord. no. fem.)	مِنَ الْأُوْلٰى	Wandering, (un-aware of the way) (act. prtc. msc. sing. acc.)	ضَالًّا
		Then He guided (you) (ptcl., *madi* III. msc. sing.)	فَهَدٰى

[1] وَ for swearing an oath, the object sworn by being in the genitive case.

[2] سَوْفَ is placed before *mudari* to confirm the meaning of the future.

Words	Meaning	Words	Meaning
وَوَجَدَكَ	And He found you (ptcl., *madi* III. msc. sing., att. pro. كَ)	فَلَا تَنْهَرْ	Do not repulse, scold, reproach (ptcl., *nahy* {ptcl. negn., *mudari*ᶜ juss. md.} II. msc. sing.)
عَائِلًا	Poor or in need (act. prtc. msc. sing. acc.)	وَأَمَّا بِنِعْمَةِ	And as for the blessing, bounty (ptcls., prep., noun fem. gen. *mdf*.³)
فَأَغْنَىٰ	Then He enriched (you) made (you) independent (ptcl., dr. vrb. IV *madi* III. msc. sing.)	رَبِّكَ فَحَدِّثْ	(Of) your Lord, then declare, narrate, over speak (noun *mdfi*.³ *mdf.*, att. pro. كَ *mdfi*., ptcl., dr. vrb. II *amr* II. msc. sing.)
فَأَمَّا الْيَتِيمَ	So as for the orphan (ptcls., def. noun acc.)		
فَلَا تَقْهَرْ	So do not be harsh (ptcl., *nahy* {ptcl. negn., *mudari*ᶜ juss. md.} II. msc. sing.)		
وَأَمَّا السَّائِلَ	And as for the beggar (ptcls., def. noun acc.)		

³ Each word is in an *idafah* relation to the following. Thus "Lord" is *mdfi*. with respect to "blessing" and *mdf*. with respect to "your" so that it might be translated "…the blessing **of** the Lord **of** you…"

Root Words of Surah 93

سَجَىٰ	*	It was quiet, tranquil or dark (the night).
وَدَّعَ		II he left, وَدَعَ * he left, مُسْتَوْدَعٌ a place of deposit (such as the womb or the grave).
قَلَىٰ	*	He hated, قَالٍ one who abhors.
يَجِدْكَ		He finds you, وَجَدَ * he found, perceived.
ضَالًّا		Wandering, ضَلَّ * he strayed, wandered, أَضَلَّ IV he led astray, تَضْلِيل error, mistake.
عَائِلًا		Poor, عَالَ * he was poor, عَيْلَة poverty.
لَا تَقْهَرْ		Do not oppress, قَهَرَ * he overcame, oppressed, قَاهِر one who subdues, الْقَهَّارُ الْقَاهِرُ the Conqueror (two names of Allah).

Translation of Surah 93 Ad-Duha (The Forenoon)

(1.) By the bright forenoon;

(2.) And the night; when it falls peacefully

(3.) Your Lord has neither forsaken you nor does He hate (you);

(4.) And surely the life to come shall be better for you than the earlier part of your life;

(5.) And certainly your Lord shall give you, and you shall be well-pleased;

(6.) Did He not find you an orphan and gave (you) shelter?

(7.) Did He not find you unaware of the Way and guided (you)?

(8.) Did he not find you impoverished and enrich (you)?

(9.) Therefore as for the orphan, do not be harsh;

(10.) And as for the beggar, do not repulse;

(11.) And as for the blessing of your Lord, then proclaim (it)!

Explanatory Notes for Surah 93

The *surah* is addressed in its entirety to the Prophet (SAAS). It is a message from his Lord which touched his heart with pleasure, joy, tranquility and contentment. Altogether it is a flow of mercy and compassion to his then restless soul, and suffering heart.

Several accounts mention that the revelation of the Qur'an to the Prophet (SAAS) came at one stage to a halt and that Jibril (AS) stopped coming to him for a while. The unbelievers therefore said, "Muhammad's Lord has bidden him farewell!" Allah therefore revealed this *surah*.

Revelation, Jibril's visits and the link with Allah (SWT) were the Prophet's (SAAS) whole support along his precarious path. They were his only solace in the face of hard rejection and his sole comfort against outright repudiation. They were the source from which he derived his strength to stand steadfast against the unbelievers who were intent on rebuff and refusal, and bent on directing a wicked, vile attack against the Prophet's (SAAS) call, faith and guidance.

So when the Revelation was withheld, the source of strength for the Prophet (SAAS) was cut off. His life spring was sapped and he longed for his heart's friend. Alone he was left in the wilderness, without sustenance, without water, without the accustomed companionship of the beloved friend. It was a situation which taxes human endurance heavily.

Then this *surah* was revealed and it came as a rich flow of compassion, mercy, hope, comfort and reassurance.

This *surah*, with its subject matter, mode of expression, scenes, connotations and rhythm is a touch of tenderness and mercy. It is a message of affection; it is a benevolent hand which soothes pains and troubles and generates an air of contentment and confident hope.

The instructions in *ayat* 9-11 reflect the needs of the day, in that greedy and materialistic society in which the weak, who could not defend their own rights, were not catered for. Islam came to reform that society with Allah's (SWT) laws which establish equity, justice and good-will.

Speaking of Allah's (SWT) bounties, especially those of guidance and faith, is a form of expressing gratitude to Him, the Giver. It is a practical manifestation of thanks on the part of the recipient.

The blessing of Allah's (SWT) guidance can be proclaimed by showing the right way to the people but first to one's own self, and enduring patiently all the bitterness and hardships of the way.

Makki Surah

بِسْمِ اللَّهِ الرَّحْمَٰنِ الرَّحِيمِ

8 Ayat

Surah 94 Ash-Sharh

Meaning	Words	Meaning	Words
Your renown, fame mention, remembrance (noun acc. *mdf.*, att. pro. كَ *mdfi.*)	ذِكْرَكَ	Did We not open, expand (ptcl. inter., ptcl. negn.[1], *mudari* juss. md. I. pl.)	أَلَمْ نَشْرَحْ
So indeed with (ptcls., noun[2])	فَإِنَّ مَعَ	For you (ptcl., att. pro. كَ)	لَكَ
The hardship, difficulty (def. vrb. n. gen.)	الْعُسْرِ	Your breast, heart (noun acc. *mdf.*, att. pro. كَ *mdfi.*)	صَدْرَكَ
(there is) ease relief (comes) ease, relief (vrb. n. acc.)	يُسْرًا	And We removed (ptcl., *madi* I. pl.)	وَوَضَعْنَا
Indeed with (ptcl., noun[2])	إِنَّ مَعَ	From you (ptcl., att. pro. كَ)	عَنكَ
The hardship, difficulty (def. vrb. n. gen.)	الْعُسْرِ	Your burden (noun acc. *mdf.*, att. pro. كَ *mdfi.*)	وِزْرَكَ
(there is) ease, relief (comes) ease, relief (vrb. n. acc.)	يُسْرًا	The one, that which (rel. pro. msc. sing.)	الَّذِي
So when you are free (ptcls., *madi* II. msc. sing.)	فَإِذَا فَرَغْتَ	Weighed down heavily (on) (dr. vrb. IV *madi* III. msc. sing.)	أَنقَضَ
Then toil or labour, work hard (in worship) (ptcl., *amr* II. msc. sing.)	فَانصَبْ	Your back (noun acc. *mdf.*, att. pro. كَ *mdfi.*)	ظَهْرَكَ
And to your Lord (ptcls., noun gen. *mdf.*, att. pro. كَ *mdfi.*)	وَإِلَىٰ رَبِّكَ	And We raised high (ptcl., *madi* I. pl.)	وَرَفَعْنَا
		For you (ptcl., att. pro. كَ)	لَكَ

---

[2] Although مَعَ is used as a preposition it is actually the accusative of a noun signifying association.

[1] لَمْ always precedes *mudari* to denote the negative meaning of a *madi* or past tense.

Words	Meaning	Words	Meaning
فَٱرْغَب	Turn all (your) attention, turn with love (ptcl., *amr* II. msc.. sing.)		

Root Words of Surah 94

نَشْرَح   We opened, enlarged, expanded, شَرَّحَ * he opened, enlarged, expanded.

صَدْر   Breast, heart, bosom, صَدَرَ * he proceeded, went forward.

وِزْر   Load, heavy weight, وَزَرَ * he bore, carried (a burden).

أَنْقَضَ   IV he wrung, weighed down, نَقَضَ * he broke or violated (a treaty), untwisted.

فَرَغْتَ   You became relieved, فَرَغَ * he brought a matter to an end, he finished.

فَٱرْغَب   So attend! desire! (imp.), رَغِبَ * he loved, he desired, رَاغِب one who supplicates earnestly.

Translation of Surah 94 Ash-Sharh (The Opening-Up of the Heart)

(1.) Have We not opened up your breast?

(2.) And lifted from you your burden

(3.) That had weighed so heavily on your back?

(4.) And have We not raised for you your dignity?

(5.) And, behold, with hardship there is ease:

(6.) Verily, with hardship there is ease!

(7.) Hence, when you are freed (from distress), remain steadfast.

(8.) And unto your Sustainer turn with love.

Explanatory Notes for Surah 94

This is one of the Makki surahs in which Allah (SWT) has consoled and encouraged the Prophet Muhammad (SAAS). The difficulties facing his mission weighed heavily on his heart, hence came this comforting address. His burden was relieved by the guidance he received on how to discharge his mission and how to appeal to men's hearts. Allah (SWT) raised his fame high; so whenever it is said, "No god but Allah," it is always said "Muhammad is the Messenger of Allah", indeed it is the highest degree of exaltation and this position is granted only to Muhammad (SAAS) and no other human being. From every mosque in the world the Prophet's (SAAS) name is cried, as that of Messenger of Allah five times a day and every Muslim prays for blessings on him when his name is mentioned. The Lord's remembrance of the Muslims is the best source of pleasure and great help to Muslims.

Surah 95 At-Tin

Makki Surah — 8 Ayat

Words	Meaning	Words	Meaning
وَالتِّينِ	By[1] the fig (ptcl.[1], def. noun gen.)	أَسْفَلَ	The lowest (adj. elat. acc. *mdf.*)
وَالزَّيْتُونِ	And[1] the olive (ptcl.[1], def. noun gen.)	سَافِلِينَ	Of the low ones (act. prtc. msc. pl. *mdfi.*)
وَطُورِ سِينِينَ	And[1] Mount Sinai (ptcl.[1], noun, gen., proper noun)	إِلَّا الَّذِينَ آمَنُوا	Except those who believe (ptcl., rel. pro., dr. vrb. IV *madi* III. msc. pl.)
وَهَٰذَا الْبَلَدِ	And[1] this city, land or country (ptcl.[1], dem pro., def. noun gen.)	وَعَمِلُوا	And perform (ptcl., *madi* III. msc. sing.)
الْأَمِينِ	The secure (def. act. prtc.[2] gen.)	الصَّالِحَاتِ	Good or righteous deeds (act. prtc. fem. pl. acc.)
لَقَدْ خَلَقْنَا	We have certainly created (لَقَدْ ptcls. emph., *madi* I. pl.)	فَلَهُمْ أَجْرٌ	So for them (there is) a reward (ptcls., att. pro. pl., vrb. n. nom.)
الْإِنْسَانَ	Man, the human (def. noun acc.)	غَيْرُ مَمْنُونٍ	Undiminished, unceasing, uninterrupted (ptcl.[3] *mdf.*, pass. prtc. msc. sing. *mdfi.*)
فِي أَحْسَنِ	In the best (prep., adj. elat. gen. *mdf.*)	فَمَا يُكَذِّبُكَ	What then shall make you belie (ptcls., dr. vrb. II *mudari'* III. msc. sing., att. pro. كَ)
تَقْوِيمٍ	Shape, symmetry, stature (vrb. n. dr. vrb. II. gen. *mdfi.*)		
ثُمَّ رَدَدْنَاهُ	Then We returned him back (to) (ptcl., *madi* I. pl., pro. هُ)		

[1] وَ is for swearing an oath, the object sworn by being in the genitive case.

[2] Active participle on the measure of فَعِيل which denotes a stable meaning of the root. In many words the same form denotes the passive participle, i.e. مَفْعُول.

[3] غَيْر noun used as a particle; it is used in 113 places in the Qur'an and here it is used for negation. It also can be taken as a particle of exception.

Words	Meaning	Words	Meaning
بَعْدُ بِالدِّينِ	Henceforth[4] the religion[5], the Judgement of the Hereafter[5] (ptcl.[4], def. noun[5] gen.)	اَلَيْسَ اللّٰهُ	Is Allah not (ptcl. inter., *madi* III. msc. sing.[6], def. noun nom.)
		بِاَحْكَمِ	More or Most Knowing, Most Wise, (prep., adj. elat. gen. *mdf.*)
		الْحَاكِمِينَ	(of all) the judges or rulers (def. act. prtc. msc. pl. *mdfi.*)

[4] بَعْدُ is a noun; used as an adverb it becomes indeclinable: it may also be used as a preposition.
[5] The noun الدِّينُ is used for the rewards and punishments of the Hereafter as well as for the way of Islam.

[6] لَيْسَ "he is not" is a negative substantive verb; it has no imperfect or imperative; it is conjugated like other *madi* verbs.

Root Words of Surah 95

التِّينِ — The fig (no root word).

طُورِ — A mountain, طَارَ * he approached, طُورِ سِينِينَ Mount Sinai, (pl. أَطْوَارٌ) طُورٌ a condition or state.

الْإِنْسَانَ — Man, (pls. النَّاسُ، أُنَاسٌ), أَنِسَ * he was familiar, آنَسَ IV he perceived, rendered familiar.

أَسْفَلَ — Lowest, سَفَلَ * he was low, السَّافِلِينَ those who are low, vile, abject.

الصَّالِحَاتِ — Righteous or good works, صَلَحَ * he was right, good, honest, upright, أَصْلَحَ he amended.

أَجْرٌ — A reward, wage, أَجَرَ * he paid wages, served for hire, أُجُورٌ wages, dowers, اِسْتَأْجَرَ X he hired.

الدِّينِ — The reckoning, the Way of Islam, دَانَ * he professed a faith, he was indebted, he judged, دِينٌ religion, obedience, judgement.

أَحْكَمِ — Most knowing and wise, حَاكِمِينَ judges, rulers, (sing. حَاكِمٌ) حُكْمٌ judgement, wisdom.

Translation of Surah 95 At-Tin (The Fig)

(1.) By the fig and the olive,

(2.) And Mount Sinai

(3.) And this land secure!

(4.) Verily, We created man in the best conformation,

(5.) And thereafter We reduced him to the lowest of low,

(6.) Excepting only such as believe and do good works; and theirs shall be a reward unending!

(7.) What, then, (O man,) could henceforth cause thee to give the lie to the reckoning?

(8.) Is not Allah the Most Just of Judges?

Explanatory Notes for Surah 95

The title is derived from the mention of the fig in the first *ayah*.

This *surah* formulates a fundamental moral verity, stressing the fact that it is common to all true religious teachings.

(1) The "fig" and the "olive" are said to symbolise, in this context, the lands in which these trees predominate: i.e. the countries bordering on the eastern part of the Mediterranean, especially Palestine and Syria. As it was in these lands that most of the Abrahamic prophets mentioned in the Qur'an lived and preached, these two species of tree may possibly be taken as metonyms for the religious teachings voiced by the long line of those Allah-inspired men, culminating in the person of the last Judaic prophet, ʿIsa (AS). "Mount Sinai", on the other hand, stresses specifically the apostleship of Musa (AS), inasmuch as the religious law valid before, and up to, the advent of Muhammad (SAAS) – and in its essentials binding on ʿIsa (AS) – was revealed on a mountain of the Sinai Desert. Finally, "this land secure" signifies undoubtedly (as is evident from 2:126) Makkah, where Muhammad (SAAS), the last Prophet, was born and received his divine call. Thus *ayat* 1-3 draw our attention to the fundamental ethical unity underlying the teachings – the genuine teachings – of all the three historic phases of monotheistic religion, metonymically personified by Musa (AS), ʿIsa (AS) and Muhammad (SAAS).

(2) Endowed with all the positive qualities, physical as well as mental, corresponding to the functions which this particular creature, i.e. the human being, is meant to perform. The concept of "the best conformation" is related to the Qur'anic statement that everything which Allah (SWT) creates, including the human being or self (*nafs*), is "formed in accordance with what it is meant to be". This statement does not in any way imply that all human beings have the same "best conformation" in respect of their bodily or mental endowments: it implies simply that irrespective of his natural advantages or disadvantages, each human being is endowed with the ability to make the best possible use of his inborn qualities and of the environment to which he is exposed.

(3) The "reduction to the lowest of low" is a consequence of man's betrayal – in another word, corruption – of his original, positive disposition: that is to say, a consequence of man's own doings and omissions.

(4) The validity of the moral law may be the meaning of the term *din* in this context – outlined in the preceding three *ayat*. The above rhetorical question has this implication: Since the moral law referred to here has been stressed in the teachings of all monotheistic religions, its truth ought to be self-evident to any unprejudiced person; its negation, moreover, amounts to a negation of all freedom of moral choice on man's part and, hence, of justice on the part of Allah, Who, as the next *ayah* points out, is – by definition – "the Most Just of Judges".

Surah 96 Al-ʿAlaq

Makki Surah بِسْمِ اللهِ الرَّحْمٰنِ الرَّحِيْمِ **19 *Ayat***

Surah 96 Al-ʿAlaq

Words	Meaning	Words	Meaning
اِقْرَأْ	Read, recite (*amr* II. msc. sing.)	مَا لَمْ يَعْلَمْ	What he did not know (ptcl., ptcl. negn.[2], *mudariʿ* juss. md. III. msc. sing.)
بِاسْمِ رَبِّكَ	In the name of your Lord (prep., noun gen. *mdf*., att. pro. ك *mdfi*.)	كَلَّا إِنَّ الْإِنْسَانَ	Nay but, indeed the man (ptcls., def. noun acc.)
الَّذِيْ خَلَقَ	The One Who created (rel. pro. sing., *madi* III. msc. sing.)	لَيَطْغٰى	Certainly exceeds the bounds or limits (لَ ptcl. emph., *mudariʿ* III. msc. sing.)
خَلَقَ الْإِنْسَانَ	He created man (*madi* III. msc. sing., def. noun acc.)	أَنْ رَّآهُ	That he saw (believed or regarded) himself (ptcl., *madi* III. msc. sing., pro. ه)
مِنْ عَلَقٍ	From a clot of blood (prep., noun gen.)	اسْتَغْنٰى	(that) he is self sufficient (dr. vrb. X *madi* III. msc. sing.)
اِقْرَأْ	Read, recite (*amr* II. msc. sing.)	إِنَّ إِلٰى رَبِّكَ	Verily unto your Lord (ptcls., noun gen. *mdf*., att. pro. ك *mdfi*.)
وَرَبُّكَ	And[1] your Lord is (ptcl.[1], noun nom. *mdf*., att. pro. ك *mdfi*.)	الرُّجْعٰى	(is) the return (def. vrb. n.)
الْأَكْرَمُ	The most bountiful (def. noun elat. nom.)	أَرَأَيْتَ الَّذِيْ	Did you see the one (ptcl. inter., *madi* II. msc. sing., rel. pro. msc. sing.)
الَّذِيْ عَلَّمَ	The One Who taught (rel. pro. sing., dr. vrb. II *madi* III. msc. sing.)	يَنْهٰى	Who forbids, stops from (*mudariʿ* III. msc. sing.)
بِالْقَلَمِ	With the pen (prep., def. noun gen.)	عَبْدًا	A slave (noun acc.)
عَلَّمَ الْإِنْسَانَ	He taught man (dr. vrb. II *madi* III. msc. sing., def. noun acc.)		

---

[1] The particle وَ is used as a conjunctive particle with the meaning 'for'. It can also mean 'also', 'and', 'whilst' and 'but'.

[2] The particle of negation لَمْ precedes the *mudariʿ* to denote the emphatic negative meaning of the *madi*.

Words	Meaning	Words	Meaning
إِذَا صَلَّىٰ	When he prays (ptcl., dr. vrb. II madi III. msc. sing.)	لَمْ يَنتَهِ	He does not desist or refrain (ptcl. negn.², dr. vrb. VIII mudari' juss. md. III. msc. sing.)
أَرَءَيْتَ	Did you see (ptcl. inter., madi II. msc. sing.)	لَنَسْفَعًا	Verily we will drag or sieze (him) (لَ ptcl. emph., نَسْفَعُ mudari' I. pl.⁴)
إِن كَانَ	If he was (ptcl., madi III. msc. sing.)	بِٱلنَّاصِيَةِ	By the forelock (prep., def. noun fem. sing. gen.)
عَلَى ٱلْهُدَىٰ	On the guidance (ptcl., def. vrb. n.)	نَاصِيَةٍ	A forelock (noun fem. sing. gen.)
أَوْ أَمَرَ	Or he commanded, enjoined (ptcl., madi III. msc. sing.)	كَاذِبَةٍ	Lying, denying (act. prtc. fem. sing. gen.)
بِٱلتَّقْوَىٰ	With Allah consciousness, piety, fear of Allah (prep., def. noun)	خَاطِئَةٍ	Wrongdoing (act. prtc. fem. sing. gen.)
أَرَءَيْتَ	Did you see (ptcl. inter., madi II. msc. sing.)	فَلْيَدْعُ	Then he should call or let him call (ptcl., ptcl. exh. لِ, mudari' juss. md. III. msc. sing.)
إِن كَذَّبَ	If he gave the lie to, denied the (truth) (ptcl., dr. vrb. II madi III. msc. sing.)	نَادِيَهُ	His council or assembly (noun acc. mdf., att. pro. هُ mdfi.)
وَتَوَلَّىٰ	And turned away (ptcl., dr. vrb. V madi III. msc. sing.)	سَنَدْعُ	We shall call or summon (ptcl. fut., mudari' I. pl.)
أَلَمْ يَعْلَم	Did he not know (ptcl. inter., ptcl. negn.², mudari' juss. md. III. msc. sing.)	ٱلزَّبَانِيَةَ	The infernal guards (angels of Hell) (def. noun br. pl.)
بِأَنَّ ٱللَّهَ يَرَىٰ	That Allah sees (all) (ptcls.³, def. noun acc., mudari' III. msc. sing.)	كَلَّا لَا تُطِعْهُ	Nay but, do not obey him (ptcl., nahy {ptcl. negn., dr. vrb. IV mudari' juss. md.} II. msc. sing., att. pro. هُ)
كَلَّا لَئِن	Nay but, verily if (ptcls., لَ prefixed to إِن for emph.)	وَٱسْجُدْ	And prostrate yourself (before Allah) (ptcl., amr II. msc. sing.)

³ The preposition بِ is additional to the conjunction أَنَّ.
⁴ The suffix نَّ of emphasis is here assimilated and replaced by tanween, i.e. نَسْفَعًا for نَسْفَعَنَّ.

Words	Meaning	Words	Meaning
وَاقْتَرِب ۩	And draw close, be nearer to (Him) (ptcl., dr. vrb. VIII *amr* II. msc. sing.)		

Root Words for Surah 96

اِقْرَأْ   Read! recite! (imp.), قَرَأَ * he read, recited, قُرْآن reading, reciting, recitation.

عَلَقٍ   Clotted blood, عَلَقَ * he adhered to, hung from, مُعَلَّقَة (fem.) one in suspense.

عَلَّمَ   II He taught, عَلَمَ * he marked, signed, عَلِمَ * he knew, عِلْم knowledge, learning.

نَسْفَعًا   (for intensive نَسْفَعَنَّ) We will drag, سَفَعَ * he dragged along.

نَاصِيَة   A forelock, نَصَا * he seized by the forelock.

خَاطِئَة   A wrongdoer, خَطِئَ * he did wrong, خَطَاء an error, fault.

لِيَدْعُ   Let him call, دَعَا * he called out, called upon, he invited, دُعَاء a prayer, دَاعٍ one who calls or invites others.

الزَّبَانِيَة   Angels who keep guard over Hell, infernal guards, زَبَنَ * he sold dates on the tree by guess.

وَاسْجُدْ   And prostrate! (imp.), سَجَدَ * he prostrated, مَسْجِد a place of prostration, a mosque.

Translation of Surah 96 Al-ʿAlaq (Germ-Cell)

(1.) Read in the name of your Sustainer Who has created,

(2.) Created man out of a germ-cell!

(3.) Read – for your Sustainer is the Most Bountiful One,

(4.) Who has taught (man) by the pen,

(5.) Taught man what he did not know!

(6.) Truly man becomes insolent,

(7.) Whenever he believes himself to be self-sufficient:

(8.) Truly to your Sustainer is your return,

(9.) Have you ever considered him who prevents

(10.) A slave (of Allah) from praying?

(11.) Have you considered whether he is on the guidance,

(12.) Or enjoins *taqwa*

(13.) Have you considered whether he denies (the truth) and turns his back (upon it).

(14.) Does he, then, not know that Allah sees (all)?

(15.) Nay, if he desist not, We shall most surely drag him down upon his forehead,

(16.) The lying rebellious forehead!

(17.) And then let him call (to his aid) his own counsels,

(18.) We shall call the guards of Hell.

(19.) No, do not obey him, but prostrate yourself (before Allah) and draw closer (to Him)!

Explanatory Notes for Surah 96

There is no doubt that the first five *ayat* of this *surah* represent the very beginning of the revelation of the Qur'an. Although the exact date cannot be established with certainty, all authorities agree that these five *ayat* were revealed in the last third of the month of Ramadan, thirteen years before the *hijrah* (corresponding to July or August, 610, of the Christian era). The Prophet (SAAS) was then forty years old. At that period of his life "solitude became dear to him, and he used to withdraw into seclusion in a cave of Mount Hira (near Makka) and there apply himself to ardent devotions" consisting of long vigils and prayers (Bukhari). One night, the Angel of Revelation suddenly appeared to him and said, "Read!" The Messenger of Allah (SAAS) at first thought that he was expected to read actual script, which, being unlettered, he was unable to do. So he answered, "I cannot read" - whereupon, in his own words, the angel "seized me again and pressed me to himself until all strength went out of me; then he released me and said, 'Read!' I answered, 'I cannot read.' Then he seized me again and pressed me to himself until all strength went out of me; then he released me and said 'Read!' - to which I (again) answered, 'I cannot read.' Then he seized me and pressed me to himself a third time; then released me and said, 'Read in the name of your Sustainer, Who has created - created man out of a germ-cell! Read - for thy Sustainer is the Most Bountiful One ...'": and so the Messenger (SAAS) understood, in sudden illumination, that he was called upon to "read", that is, to receive and understand, Allah's message to man.

It is no exaggeration to describe this event as the greatest in the long history of humanity. This event specified the source man should look to in order to derive his ideals, values and criteria. The source is heaven and the Divine revelations, not this world and man's own desires. When this great event took place the people who recognised its true nature and adapted their lives accordingly enjoyed Allah's protection and manifest care. They looked to Him directly for guidance in all their affairs, great and small. They lived and moved under His supervision. It needs to be remembered that this event was a rebirth for humanity and such a rebirth can take place only once in history.

The above excerpts are quoted from the third Tradition of the section *Bad' al-Wahy*, which forms the introductory chapter of Bukhari's *Sahih*; almost identical versions of this Tradition are found in two other places in Bukhari as well as in Muslim, Nasa'i and Tirmidhi.

Ayat 6-19 of this *surah* are of somewhat later date, yet there is perfect harmony between all parts of the *surah*.

The *surah* concludes with an instruction to the obedient slaves of Allah (SWT) to persevere and follow the path of faith. As for the tyrant, leave him to the guards of Hell who are sure to mete out to him what he deserves. Some authentic reports say that the one mentioned in *ayah* 9 onwards who prevented the Prophet (SAAS) from practising and preaching Islam was Abu-Jahl.

Surah 97 Al-Qadr

Makki Surah   بِسْمِ اللهِ الرَّحْمٰنِ الرَّحِيْمِ   5 *Ayat*

Surah 97 Al-Qadr

Meaning	Words	Meaning	Words
Descends or comes down gently and gradually (dr. vrb. V تَنَزَّلُ for تَتَنَزَّلُ *madi* III. fem. sing. for the br. pl. الْمَلَائِكَة)	تَنَزَّلُ	Verily We, We sent it down (ptcl., dr. vrb. IV *madi* I. pl., att. pro. هُ)	إِنَّا أَنْزَلْنٰهُ
The angels (def. noun br. pl. nom.)	الْمَلَائِكَةُ	In the night (prep., noun gen. *mdf.*)	فِىْ لَيْلَةِ
And the spirit (the angel Jibril [A.S.]) (ptcl., def. noun)	وَالرُّوْحُ	Of the power, honour, decree, destiny (def. noun *mdfi.*)	الْقَدْرِ
In it (in that night) (prep., att. pro. هَا)	فِيْهَا	And what made you know And what will make you know (ptcls., dr. vrb. IV *madi* III. msc. sing., att. pro. كَ)	وَمَا أَدْرٰىكَ
With permission of (prep., noun gen. *mdf.*[2])	بِإِذْنِ	What the night (ptcl., noun nom. *mdf.*)	مَا لَيْلَةُ
Their Lord (noun *mdfi. mdf.*, att. pro. هِمْ *mdfi.*)[2]	رَبِّهِمْ	Of the power, honour, decree, destiny is (def. noun *mdfi.*)	الْقَدْرِ
For every affair (ptcl., كُلِّ noun gen. *mdf.*, noun *mdfi.*)	مِنْ كُلِّ أَمْرٍ	The night of the power, honour, decree, destiny (noun nom. *mdf.*, def. noun *mdfi.*)	لَيْلَةُ الْقَدْرِ
Peace, safety it (the night) is (سَلَامٌ vrb. n. nom., هِيَ pro. fem. sing.)	سَلٰمٌ هِيَ	Is better than (noun elat. nom., prep.)	خَيْرٌ مِنْ
Until the time of rising (prep., noun of time & place gen. *mdf.*)	حَتّٰى مَطْلَعِ	A thousand months (card. no. gen. *mdf.*, noun sing. *mdfi.*)	أَلْفِ شَهْرٍ
The dawn, day-break (def. noun *mdfi.*)	الْفَجْرِ		

---

[2] There are three terms in an *idafah* relationship so that رَبّ is *mdfi.* with respect to إِذْن and *mdf.* with respect to the attached pronoun هِمْ.

[1] The particle إِنَّ is prefixed to the pronoun نَا thus meaning 'Verily, We...'. The pronoun هُ is for the Qur'an.

Root Words for Surah 97

أَنْزَلْنَا We sent down, نَزَلَ * he descended, نَزَّلَ II he sent down (periodically and repeatedly), أَنْزَلَ IV he sent down, تَنَزَّلَ V he descended gently and gradually.

أَلْف A thousand, أَلِفَ * he joined together, he was accustomed (to a place), إِيلَاف a compact, uniting together, protecting, taming, keeping.

شَهْر (شُهُورٌ أَشْهُرٌ pls.) A month, شَهَرَ * he published abroad.

الْمَلَائِكَة The angels, مَلَكَ * he had power over, possessed, owned, مَالِك one who is lord over, مَلِك king, مُلْك kingdom.

أَمْر A command, decree, matter, thing, business, أَمَرَ * he commanded, ordered, enjoin.

سَلَام Peace, safety, security, greeting of peace, سَلِمَ * he was safe and sound.

مَطْلَع The time of rising (of the dawn), طَلَعَ * he ascended, rose, طُلُوع the rising, يَطَّلِعُ اِطَّلَعَ VIII he mounted above, came upon, met with, أَطْلَعَ IV he caused one to understand.

Translation of Surah 97 Al-Qadr (Power or Decree)

(1.) We revealed it (the Qur'an) on the Night of Power.

(2.) What will make you grasp what the Night of Power is?

(3.) The Night of Power is better than a thousand months.

(4.) The angels and the Spirit descend in it (that Night) by their Lord's permission, with all His decrees.

(5.) Peace it is, till the break of dawn.

Explanatory Notes for Surah 97

This *surah* speaks about the promised great night which the whole universe marks with joy and prayers. It is the night of perfect communion between this world and the Highest Society. It is the night which marked the beginning of the revelation of the Qur'an to the Messenger of Allah (SAAS), an event unparalleled in the history of mankind for its splendour and the significance it has for the life of mankind as a whole. Its greatness is far beyond human realisation. *"We revealed it on the Night of Power. What will make you grasp what the Night of Power is? The Night of Power is better than a thousand months."*

The Qur'anic statements which relate this great event radiate with Allah's clear and shining light: *"We revealed it on the Night of Power."* There is also the light of the angels and the Spirit moving between the earth and the highest Society. *"The angels and the Spirit descend in it (that night) by their Lord's permission with all His decrees."* In addition, there is also the light of dawn which the *surah* represents as perfectly harmonious with the light of the Qur'an and the angels as well as with the spirit of peace: *"Peace it is, till the break of dawn."*

The night in question here is the same night referred to in *Surah* 44, ("Smoke"): *"We revealed it (the Qur'an) on a blessed night, for We would warn (mankind), on a night when ever precept was made plain as a commandment from Us. We have ever sent forth messengers as a blessing from your Lord, Who hears all and knows all."* It is established that it is a night in the month of Ramadan, as stated in *Surah* 2, ("The Cow"): *"The month of Ramadan in which the Qur'an was revealed, a book of guidance (distinguishing right from wrong)."* This means that the Night of Power marked the beginning of the revelation of the Qur'an to the Prophet (SAAS) and his being charged with conveying it to mankind. Ibn Ishaq related that the first revelation, consisting of the opening of *Surah* 96, ("The Blood Clot"), took place in the month of Ramadan, when the Messenger of Allah was at his devotion in the cave of Hira (*Jabl-Noor*).

A number of traditions specifying this night have come down to us: some stress that it is the twenty-seventh of Ramadan, others the twenty-first; others say it is one of the last ten days and some others do not go beyond saying that it is in Ramadan.

Its title "The Night of Power" may be taken to mean decree, assignment, designation and organisation, or it may mean value, position and rank. Both meanings are relevant to that great universal event of the revelation of the Qur'an and the assigning of the message to the Prophet (SAAS). For it is one of the greatest and most precious of all events which the universe has witnessed. It is also the event which explains more clearly than any other the place of assignment, designation and organisation in the life of mankind. This night is better than a thousand months. The figure here and elsewhere in the Qur'an does not signify its precise number. It simply denotes a very high number. Many thousand months and many thousand years have passed without leaving behind a fraction of the changes and results brought about in that blessed and happy night.

This night is of an essence too sublime to be understood by human intellect: *"What will make you grasp what the Night of Power is?"* There is no reason to attach any value to the legends circulating among the masses concerning this night. It is great because Allah has chosen it for the revelation of the Qur'an, so that its light may spread throughout the universe, and Divine peace may spread in human life and consciences. That night is great because of what the Qur'an includes: an ideology, a basis for values and standards and a comprehensive code of moral and social behaviour, all of which promote peace within the human soul and in the world at large. It is great because of the descent of the angels, and Jibril (AS) in particular, by their Lord's permission carrying the Qur'an which was first sent down on that night. They fill all the space between heaven and earth in such a splendid, universal celebration, as is vividly portrayed in this *surah*.

On that night every matter of significance was made plain and distinct, new values and standards were established, the fortunes of nations were determined, and values and standards were sifted.

Humanity, out of ignorance and to its misfortune, may overlook the value and importance of the Night of Power. When humanity ignores all that, it loses the happiest and most beautiful sign of grace which Allah (SWT) bestowed on it. It loses the real happiness and peace gifted to it by Islam, namely, the peace of conscience, family and society. What it has otherwise gained of material civilisation cannot be adequate compensation for its loss. Humanity is miserable in spite of higher productivity and better means of existence. The splendid light which once illuminated its soul has been put out, the brilliant touch of happiness which carried it high up to the Highest Society has been smothered, the peace which overflowed over the hearts and minds has disappeared. Nothing can compensate for the happiness of the soul, the heavenly light and the elevation to the loftiest ranks.

We, believers in Allah, are commanded not to forget or neglect this event. The Prophet (SAAS) has taught us an easy and enjoyable way to commemorate that night, so that our souls may always be in close communion with it and with the universal event which took place in it. He has urged us to spend this night of each year in devotion. He said, *"Seek the Night of Power in the last ten nights of Ramadan." "He who spends the Night of Power in worship, out of faith and anticipation (of a reward) will have all his past sins forgiven."* Islam is not mere formalities. Hence, the Prophet (SAAS) specified that the consecration of that night must be motivated by faith and anticpation. This would make its consecration by an individual an indication of his full awareness of the far-reaching effects of what took place in that night.

The Islamic method of character building links worship with faith and the truth it establishes in the heart and conscience of the individual. In this method, worship is considered a means for maintaining full awareness of this truth, its clarification and firm establishment in one's mind, heart and soul. This method has been proved to be the best for the revival of this truth so that it may have a constant influence on men's consciences and behaviour. The theoretical understanding of this truth cannot, on its own and without worship, establish it or give it the necessary impetus for its operation in the life of the individual or the life of the society. This link between the anniversary of the Night of Power and its consecration in faith and devotion is a part of the successful and upright method of Islam.

Surah 98 Al-Bayyinah

Early Makki or Early Madani Surah — *8 Ayat*

بِسْمِ اللَّهِ الرَّحْمَٰنِ الرَّحِيمِ

Meaning	Words	Meaning	Words
Scrolls, scriptures, books (noun br. pl. acc.)	صُحُفًا	Was not[1] (They) were not (ptcl. negn.[1], *mudari‛* juss. md. III. msc. sing.)	لَمْ يَكُنْ
Purified, clean, pure (pass. prtc. dr. vrb. II fem. sing. acc.)	مُطَهَّرَةً	Those who disbelieved (rel. pro. msc. pl., *madi* III. msc. pl.)	الَّذِينَ كَفَرُوا
In it writings, written revelations, ordinances, decrees (prep., att. pro., noun br. pl. nom.)	فِيهَا كُتُبٌ	Of[2] the people of the book (prep.[2], noun gen. mdf., def. noun mdfi.)	مِنْ أَهْلِ الْكِتَابِ
Right, true, lasting (noun fem. sing. nom.)	قَيِّمَةٌ	and those who associate partners (with Allah) (ptcl., def. act. prtc. dr. vrb. IV msc. pl. gen.)	وَالْمُشْرِكِينَ
And did not divide among themselves (ptcl., ptcl. negn., dr. vrb. V *madi* III. msc. sing.)	وَمَا تَفَرَّقَ	Those who vacillate or breakers off (in their faith) (act. prtc. dr. vrb. VII msc. pl. acc.)	مُنْفَكِّينَ
The ones who were given the Book (afore time) (rel. pro. pl., dr. vrb. IV *madi maj.* III. msc. pl., def. noun acc.)	الَّذِينَ أُوتُوا الْكِتَابَ	Until comes to them (prep., *mudari‛* III. fem. sing., att. pro. هُمْ)	حَتَّىٰ تَأْتِيَهُمُ
Except after (ptcl. exc., prep., noun gen.)	إِلَّا مِنْ بَعْدِ	The evidence (of the truth) (def. noun fem. nom.)	الْبَيِّنَةُ
(what) there came to them (ptcl., *madi* III. fem. sing., att. pro. هُمْ)	مَا جَاءَتْهُمُ	A messenger from Allah (noun nom., prep., noun gen.)	رَسُولٌ مِنَ اللَّهِ
The evidence (of the truth) (def. noun fem. nom.)	الْبَيِّنَةُ	He recites, reads (*mudari‛* III. msc. sing.)	يَتْلُو
And they were not enjoined but (ptcl., ptcl. negn., *madi maj.* III. msc. pl., ptcl. exc.)	وَمَا أُمِرُوا إِلَّا		

[1] The particle of negation لَمْ always precedes the *mudari‛* to denote an emphatic negative meaning of the *madi*.

[2] The particle مِنْ here is for بَيَان (explanation) and means 'of'; it explains the composition of the group 'the ones who disbelieve' that they are the 'people of the book' and 'those who associate partners (with Allah)'.

Surah 98 Al-Bayyinah

Meaning	Words	Meaning	Words
(are) in fire of Hell / (will be) in fire of Hell (prep., noun gen. *mdf.*, noun dipt. *mdfi.*)	فِى نَارِ جَهَنَّمَ	They should worship Allah (لِ ptcl. exh., *mudari'* juss. md. III. msc. pl., noun acc.)	لِيَعْبُدُوا اللَّهَ
Ever-remaining or ever-abiding in it (act. prtc. msc. pl. acc., prep., att. pro. هَا for جَهَنَّمَ)	خَالِدِينَ فِيهَا	(as) sincere ones (act. prtc. dr. vrb. IV msc. pl. acc.)	مُخْلِصِينَ
Those they are (dem. & per. pros. msc. pl.)	أُولَٰئِكَ هُمْ	(keeping pure) for Him the religion (لِ prep., att. pro. هِ, def. noun acc.)	لَهُ الدِّينَ
The worst of creatures (adj. elat.[3] nom. *mdf.*, def. noun *mdfi.*)	شَرُّ الْبَرِيَّةِ	(as) Upright men (noun br. pl. dipt. acc.)	حُنَفَاءَ
Indeed the ones who believe (ptcl., rel. pro. pl., *madi* III. msc. pl.)	إِنَّ الَّذِينَ آمَنُوا	And that they should establish the *salah* (ptcl., *mudari'* juss. md. III. msc. pl., def. noun acc.)	وَيُقِيمُوا الصَّلَاةَ
And perform good deeds (ptcl., *madi* III. msc. pl., act. prtc. fem. pl. acc.)	وَعَمِلُوا الصَّالِحَاتِ	And that they should produce the *zakah* (ptcl., *mudari'* juss. md. III. msc. pl., def. noun acc.)	وَيُؤْتُوا الزَّكَاةَ
Those they are (dem. & per. pros. msc. pl.)	أُولَٰئِكَ هُمْ	And that is the right, true religion (ptcl., dem. pro., noun nom *mdf.*, def. adj. *mdfi.*)	وَذَٰلِكَ دِينُ الْقَيِّمَةِ
The best of creatures (adj. elat.[3] nom. *mdf.*, def. noun *mdfi.*)	خَيْرُ الْبَرِيَّةِ	Indeed the ones who disbelieve (ptcl., rel. pro. pl., *madi* III. msc. pl.)	إِنَّ الَّذِينَ كَفَرُوا
Their reward, recompense is (noun, *mdf.* & pro. *mdfi.*)	جَزَاؤُهُمْ	Of[2] the people of the book (prep.[2], noun gen. *mdf.*, def. noun *mdfi.*)	مِنْ أَهْلِ الْكِتَابِ
With their Lord (ptcl., noun gen. *mdf.*, att. pro. هِمْ *mdfi.*)	عِنْدَ رَبِّهِمْ	And the ones who associate partners (with Allah) (ptcl., def. act. prtc. dr. vrb. IV msc. pl. gen.)	وَالْمُشْرِكِينَ

[3] The adjectives شَرُّ and خَيْرُ are exceptional as elative adjectives as they do not follow the usual form for such adjectives أَفْعَلُ.

Words	Meaning	Words	Meaning
جَنَّاتُ عَدْنٍ	Gardens everlasting, (Gardens of residence) (noun fem. pl. nom. *mdf.*, vrb. noun *mdfi*.)	رَضِيَ اللَّهُ عَنْهُمْ	Allah is pleased with them (*madi* III. msc. sing., noun nom., prep., att. pro. هُمْ)
تَجْرِي مِنْ تَحْتِهَا	(there) Flows beneath it (*mudari*ᶜ III. fem. sing., ptcls., att. pro. هَا for جَنَّاتٌ)	وَرَضُوا عَنْهُ	And they are pleased with Him (ptcl., *madi* III. msc. pl., ptcl., att. pro. هـ)
الْأَنْهَارُ	The rivers (def. noun br. pl.)	ذَلِكَ لِمَنْ	That is for him who (dem. pro., prep. لِ, conj. pro. مَنْ)
خَالِدِينَ فِيهَا	Ever-remaining or ever-abiding in it (act. prtc. msc. pl. acc., prep., att. pro. هَا for جَنَّاتٌ)	خَشِيَ رَبَّهُ	Was (is) fearful of his Lord (*madi* III. msc. sing., رَبّ noun acc. *mdf.*, att. pro. هـ *mdfi*.)
أَبَدًا	For ever, eternally (vrb. n. مَصْدَر acc.)		

Root Words for Surah 98

مُشْرِكِينَ Those who ascribe associates to Allah, idolators, شَرِكَ * he was a companion or one who shared, شِرْكٌ polytheism, idolatry.

الْبَيِّنَةُ The evidence, proof, testimony, بَانَ * it was distinct and separate, بَيْنَ between, بَيَّنَ II he showed, made manifest, declared, explained.

تَفَرَّقَ V (they were) divided (among themselves), فَرَقَ * he divided, split, فَرِيقٌ a party, band of men, فُرْقَانٌ criterion to judge between right and wrong.

مُخْلِصِينَ Those who are sincere (in their faith), خَلَصَ * he was pure and sincere.

حُنَفَاءُ (sing. حَنِيفٌ) Ones naturally inclined to the truth, حَنَفَ * he inclined.

خَالِدِينَ Living forever, خَلَدَ * he was eternal, lived forever, أَخْلَدَ IV he rendered immortal, he inclined towards.

شَرٌّ Evil, bad, mischief, also worse, worst, شَرُّ الْبَرِيَّةِ the worst of creatures, شَرَّ * he did evil, شَرَرٌ sparks of fire.

خَيْرٌ Good, agreeable, wealth, also better, best, خَارَ * he was in good circumstances, he was favourable to, الْخَيْرَاتُ good things.

عَدْنٍ Everlasting, عَدَنَ * he remained, abode constantly.

أَبَدًا Eternally, forever, أَبَدَ * he remain in a place.

Translation of Surah 98 Al-Bayyinah (The Evidence of the Truth)

(1.) The disbelievers (both) the People of the Book and the ones who ascribe partners (to Allah) would not break off until there comes to them the (full) evidence of the truth:

(2.) A messenger from Allah reciting (unto them) purified scrolls,

(3.) Wherein there are ordinances of ever-true soundness and clarity.

(4.) Now those who have been vouchsafed revelation aforetime did not break up their unity (of faith) until after such an evidence of the truth had come to them.

(5.) And withal, they were not enjoined aught but that they should worship Allah, sincere in their faith in Him alone, turning away from all that is false, and that they should establish the prayer, and that they should produce the *zakah* for this is a moral law endowed with ever-true soundness and clarity.

(6.) Verily, the disbelievers (both) the People of the Book and the ones who ascribe partners (to Allah) will be in the fire of hell, therein to abide; those, they are the worst of all creatures.

(7.) (And), verily, those who believe and do right actions; those, they are the best of all creatures.

(8.) Their reward is with their Lord, gardens of perpetual bliss, rivers running from underneath them, therein to abide beyond the count of time; well-pleased is Allah with them, and well-pleased are they with Him; that is for whoever fears his Sustainer.

Explanatory Notes for Surah 98

The sending of the Prophet Muhammad (SAAS) was essential to the transformation of those of the people of the earlier revelations and the polytheists who had ended up in disbelief and could not have departed from their erring ways without the help of his prophetic mission. The Clear Proof and the True Knowledge was given to the people of earlier revelations but after receiving all that from their Lord they still ran into discord, and conflicts arose among them. The religion – its fundamentals are simple and clear, without conflicts and divisions. Those who disbelieved after receiving the clear proof are the worst creatures of all, while those who believe and do good deeds are the best creatures; hence the rewards of the two types are totally different. The 6th Century of the Christian era represented the darkest phase in the history of the human race. Corruption had spread around the whole world to the extent that there was no hope of reform except by means of the Final and Most Perfect Message, which the world so badly needed. Hence this Message and the Messenger (SAAS) came at a perfectly suitable time. Muhammad (SAAS) was the last Messenger and Islam which he [preached was the Final Message. Those who follow the message and the Messenger (SAAS), are the right-acting ones; Allah (SWT) is well pleased with them and they with Him. It is said that *Al-Bayyinah* (the Evidence of the Truth or The Clear Truth) is the Prophet Muhammad (SAAS) and it is also said that it is al-Qur'an al-Karim.

Surah 99 Az-Zilzal

Madani Surah — بِسْمِ اللهِ الرَّحْمٰنِ الرَّحِيْمِ — *8 Ayat*

Words	Meaning	Words	Meaning
إِذَا زُلْزِلَتِ	When is shaken (ptcl., madi maj. III, fem. sing.)	بِأَنَّ رَبَّكَ	Because your Lord (ptcls., noun acc. *mdf.*, att. pro. *mdfi.*)
الْأَرْضُ	The earth (def. noun nom.)	أَوْحٰى لَهَا	(will have) inspired her (to do so) (dr. vrb. IV madi III. msc. sing., ptcl. لَ, هَا for earth)
زِلْزَالَهَا	(by) its shaking (vrb. n. acc. *mdf.*, att. pro. *mdfi.*)	يَوْمَئِذٍ	On that day (of Judgment) (noun sing. acc., ptcl.)
وَأَخْرَجَتِ	And brings forth (ptcl., dr. vrb. IV madi III. fem. sing.)	يَصْدُرُ	Will proceed, come forth (*mudari^c* III. msc. sing.)
الْأَرْضُ	The earth (def. noun nom.)	النَّاسُ	People, mankind (coll. def. noun nom.)
أَثْقَالَهَا	Its burdens (noun br. pl. acc. *mdf.*, att. pro. هَا for earth *mdfi.*)	أَشْتَاتًا	Separately (noun br. pl. acc.)
وَقَالَ الْإِنْسَانُ	And says man (ptcl., madi III. msc. sing., def. noun sing. nom.)	لِيُرَوْا	That they may be shown (ptcl., *mudari^c* maj. subj. md. III. msc. pl.)
مَا لَهَا	What (has happened) to it (her) (ptcls., att. pro. fem. sing. هَا for earth)	أَعْمَالَهُمْ	Their deeds (noun br. pl. acc. *mdf.*, att. pro. *mdfi.*)
يَوْمَئِذٍ	Then on that day (the Day of Judgment) (noun acc., ptcl.)	فَمَنْ يَعْمَلْ	So he who does he who shall have done (ptcl., pro., *mudari^c* juss. md. III. msc. sing.)
تُحَدِّثُ	She will tell or inform (dr. vrb. II *mudari^c* III. fem. sing.)	مِثْقَالَ ذَرَّةٍ	The weight of a particle[1] (noun acc. *mdf.*, noun *mdfi.*)
أَخْبَارَهَا	Its tidings, news, information (noun br. pl. acc. *mdf.*, att. pro. هَا for earth *mdfi.*)		

[1] ذَرَّة does not mean an atom, for which there is no word in Arabic, but rather it means the tiniest type of ant.

Words	Meaning	Words	Meaning
خَيْرًا	(in the way) of good[2] (adv. noun acc.)	وَمَن يَعْمَلْ	And he who does shall have done (ptcl., pro., *mudari* juss. md. III. msc. sing.)
يَرَهُ	He shall see it (*mudari* juss. md. III. msc. sing., att. pro.)	مِثْقَالَ ذَرَّةٍ	The weight of a particle[1] (noun acc. *mdf.*, noun *mdfi.*)
		شَرًّا	(in the way) of evil[2] (adv. noun acc.)
[2] خَيْر good, and شَرّ evil, can be used both as nouns and adjectives.		يَرَهُ	He shall see it (*mudari* juss. md. III. msc. sing., att. pro.)

Root Words for Surah 99

زُلْزِلَتْ   Is shaken, زَلْزَلَ * it shook (quad. vrb.), زِلْزَالٌ the act of shaking.

أَخْرَجَتْ   IV (She) brought out, cast forth, خَرَجَ * he went out, went forth, came forth.

أَثْقَالٌ   (sing. ثِقْلٌ) Burdens, ثَقُلَ * it was grievous, heavy, مِثْقَالٌ a weight.

أَخْبَارٌ   (sing. خَبَرٌ) News, tidings, reports, خَبَرَ * he knew, خَبِيرٌ one who knows, is aware.

أَوْحَى   IV He revealed, وَحَى * he indicated, revealed, وَحْيٌ revelation.

ذَرَّةٍ   A grain, particle, tiny ant, ذَرَّ * he scattered, ذُرِّيَّةٌ progeny, offspring.

Translation of Surah 99 Az-Zilzal (The Earthquake)

(1.) When the Earth quakes with her (last) mighty quaking,

(2.) And (when) the earth yields up her burdens,

(3.) And man says, "what has happened to her?"

(4.) On that day will she recount all her tidings,

(5.) Because thy Sustainer will have inspired her.

(6.) On that day will all men come forward, cut off from one another, to be shown their (past) deeds.

(7.) And so, he who shall have done an particle weight of good, shall behold it;

(8.) And he who shall have done an particle weight of evil, shall behold it.

Explanatory Notes for Surah 99

The *surah* gives a fierce shake to drowsy hearts; It is a powerful blast that makes the earth and all that is on it quake and tremble. Men hardly recover their senses when they find themselves confronted with the reckoning, weighing and evaluating of actions and deeds, and with recompense.

It is the Day of Judgement when the firm earth trembles and quakes violently, yields up her long-carried loads of bodies and metals and other matters which have weighed heavily on her, i.e. all that was hitherto hidden in it, including the bodies - or the remnants - of the dead. On the Day of Judgement the earth will bear witness, as it were to all that has ever been done by man: an explanation given by the Prophet (SAAS), according to a Tradition on the authority of Abu Hurairah (quoted by Ibn Hanbal and Tirmidhi). It is a scene which cuts the heart from everything on earth which it clings to, thinking it to be firm and everlasting. This impact is all the more forceful because man is portrayed as confronting the scene described with the *ayat* revealing his reaction and reflexes while beholding it: *"And man cried: What is the matter with her?"*

When man witnesses the quake of the Day of Resurrection he sees no similarity between it and the earthquakes and volcanoes of this world *"On that day"*, when this quake occurs, leaving man entirely shaken, *"She (the Earth) will tell her news, because your Lord has inspired her"*. She will relate her news because what will be taking place is a simple and clear account of what lies behind it of Allah's orders and inspiration to the earth.

In the blinking of an eye we behold the scene of people coming out of their graves; We behold them issuing forth from all over the globe: *"as if they were swarming locusts"*. This is also a scene unknown to man; it is something unprecedented, unique in nature, with all human generations issuing forth here and there, all over the globe.

They all are *"rushing to the Summoner"*, with their heads down and their eyes staring forward, *"for each one of them will on that day have enough preoccupations of his own"*. It is a scene indescribable in human language. They go to where they will be shown their deeds. They have to face their deeds and their rewards or punishments. Encountering one's deeds may be, sometimes, far more severe than any punishment. Man sometimes does things which he avoids even thinking about when he is alone.

In a spell of repentance and remorse, man would even turn his face from some of his deeds because they are ghastly. Then, in what condition will he be on that day when he faces his deeds in front of all mankind and in the presence of Allah, the Great, the Almighty, the All-Powerful? It is a terrible and frightful punishment, although it is only that they are shown their deeds and have to confront their labours. But following this confrontation (between men and their deeds) comes the accurate reckoning which does not leave an ant's weight of good or evil unassessed or without reward. *"Whoever has done an ant's weight of good will see it then, and whoever has done an ant's weight of evil will see it."* For the believing heart is sensitive to even an ant's weight of either good or evil, but the heart of a non-believer is unmoved even by mountains of sins and crimes. These hearts are concealed in this earth, but on the Day of Judgement they are crushed under their own burdens.

Surah 100 Al-ʿAdiyat

Makki Surah

بِسْمِ اللَّهِ الرَّحْمَٰنِ الرَّحِيمِ

11 Ayat

Meaning	Words	Meaning	Words
Together, in multitude (vrb. n. acc.)	جَمْعًا	By the swift mares, coursers (ptcl.[1], def. act. prtc. fem. pl. gen.)	وَالْعَادِيَاتِ
Indeed man (ptcl., def. noun acc.)	إِنَّ الْإِنْسَانَ	Panting, breathing hard in running (vrb. n. acc.)	ضَبْحًا
Towards his Lord (ptcl., noun gen. *mdf.*, att. pro. *mdfi.*)	لِرَبِّهِ	And the strikers of fire (ptcl.[2], def. act. prtc. fem. pl. gen.)	فَالْمُورِيَاتِ
Is most ungrateful (لَ ptcl. emph., vrb. n. nom.)	لَكَنُودٌ	Striking fire (vrb. n. acc.)	قَدْحًا
And indeed he (man) (ptcls., pro.)	وَإِنَّهُ	And the raiders (rushing to assault) (ptcl.[2], def. act. prtc. dr. vrb. IV fem. pl. gen.)	فَالْمُغِيرَاتِ
To that (ptcl., dem. pro. msc. sing.)	عَلَىٰ ذَٰلِكَ	(at the) Dawn, morning (vrb. noun acc.)	صُبْحًا
Is certainly a witness (لَ ptcl. emph., vrb. n. nom.)	لَشَهِيدٌ	Thereby they raised (ptcl.[2], *madi* III. fem. pl., prep., att. pro.)	فَأَثَرْنَ بِهِ
And indeed he (man) (ptcls., pro.)	وَإِنَّهُ	(clouds of) Dust (vrb. n. acc.)	نَقْعًا
For the love (prep., noun gen. *mdf.*)	لِحُبِّ	And they penetrated into the midst (ptcl.[2], *madi* III. fem. pl., prep., att. pro.)	فَوَسَطْنَ بِهِ
Of good (wealth) (noun def. gen. *mdfi.*)	الْخَيْرِ		
(He) is vehement, most ardently devoted (لَ ptcl. emph., vrb. n. nom.)	لَشَدِيدٌ		
Does he not know (ptcl. inter., ptcl., ptcl. negn., *mudariʿ* III. msc. sing.)	أَفَلَا يَعْلَمُ		

[1] The particle وَ is used when swearing an oath, the object sworn by being in the genitive case.

[2] The prefixed particle فَ is particle of sequence as well as inference whose meaning can be: and, therefore, thereby, so that, in order that, in that case, afterwards, at least, truly. Most of these significations are found in the Qur'an.

Meaning	Words	Meaning	Words
Indeed their Lord (ptcl. noun acc. *mdf.*, att. pro. *mdfi.*)	إِنَّ رَبَّهُمْ	When is exposed, poured forth, over-turned (ptcl., quad. *madi maj.* III. msc. sing.)	إِذَا بُعْثِرَ
Of them (prep., att. pro.)	بِهِمْ	What is in the graves (ptcls., noun br. pl. gen.)	مَا فِي الْقُبُورِ
On that day (of judgment) (noun acc., att. ptcl.)	يَوْمَئِذٍ	And is brought to light, made manifest (dr. vrb. II *madi maj.* III. msc. sing.)	وَحُصِّلَ
Is Ever-Aware (of them) (لَ ptcl. emph., intensive vrb. n. nom.)	لَخَبِيرٌ	What is in the breasts What is in (men's) breasts (ptcls., def. noun br. pl. gen.)	مَا فِي الصُّدُورِ

Root Words for Surah 100

الْعَادِيَاتِ	Those who run rapidly, coursers, swift mares, عَدَا * he ran aside, transgressed, عَدَاوَةٌ enmity
ضَبْحًا	Panting, ضَبَحَ * he breathed hard in running.
قَدْحًا	The act of striking fire, قَدَحَ * he struck fire.
الْمُغِيرَاتِ	Horses making an hostile excursion, raiders, غَارَ * he came into a hollow place, غَارٌ a cavern, غَيْرُ other than, an other.
صُبْحًا	The morning, صَبَحَ * he gave someone a morning draught, صَبَّحَ II he came upon in the morning, أَصْبَحَ IV he became, happened.
نَقْعًا	Dust raising and floating in the air, نَقَعَ * he soaked, raised a sound.
وَسَطْنَ	They penetrated into the midst of, وَسَطَ * he was in the midst, وَسَطٌ middle, best.
جَمْعًا	Assembly, multitude, gathering, جَمَعَ * he collected, gathered, assembled, united.
كَنُودٌ	Ungrateful, كَنَدَ * he cut, he was ungrateful.
حُصِّلَ	Is brought to light, حَصَلَ * he was over and above, it was manifest, حَصَّلَ II he made manifest.

Translation of Surah 100 Al-ᶜAdiyat (The Chargers)

(1.) By the chargers that run panting,

(2.) By the strikers of sparks of fire,

(3.) By the raiders rushing to assault at morn,

(4.) So they thereby raise clouds of dust,

(5.) And they thereby storm into a host!

(6.) Truly, towards his Sustainer man is most ungrateful,

(7.) And to this, behold, he (himself) bears witness indeed,

(8.) And truly, to the love of wealth is he most ardently devoted.

(9.) But does he not know that (on the Last Day) when all that is in the graves is raised and brought out,

(10.) And all that is (hidden) in (men's) breasts is bared,

(11.) Truly on that day their Sustainer (will show that He has always been) fully aware of them.

Explanatory Notes for Surah 100

The term Al-ᶜAdiyat either denotes the camels employed in the Hajj or war-horses and chargers, employed by the Arabs from time immemorial down to the Middle Ages (the feminine gender for this term being due to the fact that, as a rule, they preferred mares to stallions).

The *surah* provides the cure for ingratitude, greed and miserliness. It portrays the scene of resurrection in a way which makes man shudder, and puts his love for wealth and indulgence in worldly riches out of his mind, unshackling his soul and setting it free from earthly attachments. The *surah* reflects a unique method of expression.

Surah 101 Al-Qari'ah

Makki Surah — بِسْمِ اللهِ الرَّحْمٰنِ الرَّحِيْمِ — *11 Ayat*

Meaning	Words	Meaning	Words
Carded (fluffy tufts) (def. pass. prtc. msc. sing. gen.)	الْمَنفُوشِ	The Striking[1], the Adversity (act. prtc. fem. sing. nom.)	الْقَارِعَةُ
Then as for whoever (ptcls., pro.[2])	فَأَمَّا مَن	What is the Striking[1]? (ptcl., act. prtc. fem. sing. nom.)	مَا الْقَارِعَةُ
Became heavy (madi III. fem. sing.)	ثَقُلَتْ	And what made you know / And what will make you know (ptcls., dr. vrb. IV madi III. msc. sing., att. pro. كَ)	وَمَا أَدْرَاكَ
His balances or scales (noun br. pl. nom. mdf., att. pro. mdfi.)	مَوَازِينُهُ	What the striking is (ptcl., act. prtc. fem. sing. nom.)	مَا الْقَارِعَةُ
Then he (shall be) in (ptcl., pro., prep.)	فَهُوَ فِي	A day (on which) shall become (noun acc., mudari' III. msc. sing.)	يَوْمَ يَكُونُ
A life (vrb. n. gen.)	عِيشَةٍ	The people, mankind (def. noun)	النَّاسُ
Well pleased, pleasant, agreeable (act. prtc. fem. sing. gen.)	رَاضِيَةٍ	As moths (prep., coll. noun gen.)	كَالْفَرَاشِ
But as for whoever (ptcls., pro.[2])	وَأَمَّا مَن	Scattered (def. pass. prtc. msc. sing. gen.)	الْمَبْثُوثِ
Became light (madi III. fem. sing.)	خَفَّتْ	And shall become (ptcl., mudari' III. fem., sing.)	وَتَكُونُ
His balances or scales (noun br. pl. nom. mdf., att. pro. mdfi.)	مَوَازِينُهُ	The mountains (noun br. pl. nom.)	الْجِبَالُ
Then his dwelling (shall be) (ptcl., noun nom. mdf., att. pro. mdfi.)	فَأُمُّهُ	As wool (prep., def. noun gen.)	كَالْعِهْنِ

---

[2] مَنْ is an indeclinable conjunctive pronoun.

[1] A name of the Day of Judgement.

Words	Meaning	Words	Meaning
هَاوِيَةٌ	The lowest pit of Hell, Abyss (noun fem. nom.)		(ptcls., dr. vrb. IV madi III. msc. sing., att. pro. كَ)
وَمَا أَدْرَاكَ	And what made you know (And what will make you know)	مَاهِيَهْ	What³ it is (ptcl., pro. fem.)
	³ An additional ه is suffixed to the pronoun هِيَ to indicate the final letter's vocalisation.	نَارٌ حَامِيَةٌ	(it is) Fire, vehemently hot, burning hot (noun nom., act. prtc. fem. sing. nom.)

Root Words for Surah 101

الْقَارِعَةُ — The adversity, striking, a name of the Day of Judgement, قَرَعَ * he struck.

الْفَرَاشُ — The moths, فَرَشَ * he spread a carpet on the ground.

الْعِهْنِ — The carded or particoloured wool, عَهَنَ * it withered.

الْمَنْفُوشُ — Teased or carded, نَفَشَ * he picked or teased wool, he strayed for food by night.

مَوَازِينْ — Balances (sing. مِيزَانٌ), وَزَنَ * he weighed.

خَفَّتْ — It was light, خَفَّ * it was light, خَفَّفَ II he made light, تَخْفِيفٌ an alleviation.

أُمُّ — Mother, أُمّ * he sought, intended, purposed, أُمَّةٌ (pl. أُمَمٌ) people, nation, race, party.

هَاوِيَةٌ — The lowest pit of Hell, هَوَى * he fell, هَوِيَ he loved, desired, أَهْوَى IV he overthrew, أَهْوَاءٌ desires, lusts.

Translation of Surah 101 Al-Qari'ah (The Sudden Calamity)

(1.) The sudden calamity! (2.) What is the sudden calamity? (3.) And what will make you grasp what that sudden calamity will be?

(4.) (It will occur) on the Day when men will be like moths swarming in confusion, (5.) And the mountains will be like fluffy tufts of wool,

(6.) And then, he whose balance is heavy (with good deeds) (7.) Shall find himself in a happy state of life;

(8.) Whereas he whose balance is light (without good deeds) (9.) Shall be engulfed by an abyss (lit: his mother will be an abyss)

(10.) And what will make you grasp what that (abyss) will be? (11.) A fire hotly burning.

Explanatory Notes for Surah 101

The scene of the sudden calamity leaves the hearts in panic and makes the limbs tremble with fear. The listener feels that everything he clings to in this world is flying all around him like dust. According to Allah's (SWT) evaluation and measures those whose scales would be light shall have raging fire for their home, their mother whom one turns for protection and help, but what would he find with such a mother? The abyss and the raging fire. On the Day of Judgement good and bad deeds will not be counted but weighed; fewer good deeds with faith and sincerity will be heavier than many good deeds without faith.

Surah 102 At-Takathur

Makki Surah — 8 Ayat

Words	Meaning	Words	Meaning
اَلْهٰىكُمُ	Distracted, diverted, pre-occupied you (dr. vrb. IV madi III msc. sing., att. pro. msc. pl.)	عِلْمَ الْيَقِيْنِ	(with) the surety of knowledge (noun acc. mdf., def. noun mdfi.)
التَّكَاثُرُ	Desire of abundance, rivalry in worldly increase (def. vrb. n. dr. vrb. VI nom.)	لَتَرَوُنَّ	(that) Certainly you will see (لَ ptcl. emph.[2], mudari' II. msc. pl. نَّ for emph.[2])
حَتّٰى زُرْتُمُ	Until you visited (ptcl., madi II. msc. pl.)	الْجَحِيْمَ	Hell, Hell fire (def. noun fem. acc.)
الْمَقَابِرَ	The graves (def. noun br. pl. acc.)	ثُمَّ	Once again (ptcl. class.)
كَلَّا سَوْفَ	Nay but soon will[1] (ptcls.[1])	لَتَرَوُنَّهَا	Certainly you will see it (Hell) (لَ ptcl. emph.[2], mudari' II. msc. pl. نَّ for emph.[2], att. pro. هَا for Hell)
تَعْلَمُوْنَ	You come to know (mudari' II. msc. pl.)	عَيْنَ الْيَقِيْنِ	(with) The eye of certainty (noun fem. sing. acc. mdf., def. noun mdfi.)
ثُمَّ	Once again (ptcl. class.)	ثُمَّ	Once again (ptcl. class.)
كَلَّا سَوْفَ	Nay but soon will[1] (ptcls.[1])	لَتُسْـَٔلُنَّ	Certainly you shall be questioned (لَ ptcl. emph.[2], mudari' maj. II. msc. pl. نَّ for emph.[2])
تَعْلَمُوْنَ	You come to know (mudari' II. msc. pl.)		
كَلَّا لَوْ	Nay but if (now) (ptcls.)	يَوْمَئِذٍ	On that day (Day of Judgment) (noun sing. acc., ptcl.)
تَعْلَمُوْنَ	You come to know (mudari' II. msc. pl.)		

---

[1] سَوْفَ is placed before the mudari' to indicate the future meaning of the verb.

[2] The prefixed لَ and the suffixed نَّ both intensify the action and underline its surety.

Words	Meaning	Words	Meaning
عَنِ النَّعِيمِ	About the pleasure[3] (of life) About bliss (prep., def. noun gen.)		[3] The pleasure one indulged while in this world and what one did with the gift of life.

Root Words for Surah 102

الـتَّكَاثُر Rivalry, vying (in respect of riches), كَثُرَ * it was much, many, numerous, أَكْثَرَ IV he multiplied, كَثِير much, many, الـكَوْثَر name of a river in Paradise, abundance of good things.

زُرْتُم You visited, زَارَ * he visited, زُور a falsehood.

الـيَقِين Certainty, يَقِنَ * he was certain.

Translation of Surah 102 At-Takathur (Rivalry for Worldly Gain)

(1.) Rivalry for worldly gain distracts you,

(2.) Until you visit the graves.

(3.) Indeed you shall certainly come to know.

(4.) Again, you shall certainly come to know.

(5.) Indeed, were you to have certain knowledge,

(6.) You shall certainly see the fire of Hell.

(7.) Yes, you shall see it with the eye of certainty.

(8.) Then, on that day, you shall be questioned about bliss."

Explanatory Notes on Surah 102

The above *surah* is a warning to mankind about becoming too preoccupied with materialistic gains and worldly pleasures. A very important question that one must think about every day is: "Am I prepared, right now, to die?" Death is a topic which people are reluctant to think about because of our great fear of it, the fear of being separated from our loved ones and most of all the fear of facing the Almighty Lord with the shameful burden of the sins we commited during life. It is as if we are walking towards the edge of a steep precipice with our eyes closed.

We will all die. The Qur'an says: *"Every person will taste death."* (Qur'an 3: 185) Death is a natural event and it is inescapable. Our temporary life on this Earth will be brought to an end by death and we have to keep in mind that death can occur at any time (in the next second or in the next minute or in the next hour). Will we have enough time to repent for our sins in this ever shortening life?

We should question even the smallest of the tasks we perform in this life so that we can be penitent while we have the time to be. The very thought of seeing the fire of Hell should make us conscious and attentive and tremble at our indulgence in comforts and pleasures. Our hearts and minds should be burdened with thoughts of the Hereafter, rather than with the trivialities and petty concerns of this temporary life.

Mankind have become so blinded by the thoughts of attaining great wealth or power or simply by pursuing worldly pleasures that there is no realisation that this life is nothing more than a mere moment in existence Without faith, one has chosen a very temporary and insignificant materiality that will lead to a torturous and dismal eternity.

Makki Surah

بِسْمِ اللَّهِ الرَّحْمَنِ الرَّحِيمِ

3 *Ayat*

Surah 103 Al-ᶜAsr

Meaning	Words	Meaning	Words
Good or righteous deeds (def. act. prtc. fem. pl. acc.)	الصَّٰلِحَٰتِ	By¹ the passing time (ptcl.¹, def. noun gen.)	وَالْعَصْرِ
And they enjoin upon each other (ptcl., dr. vrb. VI *madi* III. msc. pl.)	وَتَوَاصَوْا	Indeed the man (ptcl., def. noun acc.)	إِنَّ الْإِنسَٰنَ
(with) The truth, that which is right and proper (def. noun gen. because prec. prep. بِ)	بِالْحَقِّ	Is certainly in loss (ptcl. emph., prep., vrb. n. gen.)	لَفِى خُسْرٍ
And they enjoin upon each other (ptcl., dr. vrb. VI *madi* III. msc. pl.)	وَتَوَاصَوْا	Except the ones (ptcl. exc., rel. pro. msc. pl.)	إِلَّا الَّذِينَ
		Who believe (dr. vrb. IV *madi* III. msc. pl.)	ءَامَنُوا
(with) patience, endurance (in adversity) (def. noun gen. because prec. prep. بِ)	بِالصَّبْرِ	And perform (ptcl., *madi* III. msc. pl.)	وَعَمِلُوا

¹ وَ is used for an oath, the object sworn by being in the genitive case.

Root Words for Surah 103

الْعَصْرِ   The passing time, عَصَرَ * he pressed (grapes), عَصْرٌ time, age.

Translation of Surah 103 Al-ᶜAsr (The Flight of Time)

(1.) By time!

(2.) Truly, man is in loss,

(3.) Except those who believe, and do good works, and enjoin upon one another the truth, and enjoin upon one another patience.

Explanatory Notes for Surah 103

The three *ayat* of this *surah* outline a complete system for human life based on the Islamic viewpoint. The nation of Islam is described in its essential qualities and its message in one *ayah* only: the third. This is the eloquence of which Allah (SWT) alone is capable.

The *surah* affirms that there is only one trustworthy path, that path is first the adoption of faith, followed up with good deeds and exhortation to follow the truth and steadfastness. Good deeds without faith are completely disregarded by the Qur'an. Faith is the great root of life from which goodness springs in its various forms and to which all its fruits are bound.

Counselling one another to and with the truth and steadfastness is a necessity for the sustenance of faith and good deeds, and catering for right and equity are the hardest tasks ever to carry out. This makes endurance utterly indispensable. Endurance is also necessary when adapting oneself for the Islamic way of life. Steadfastness is necessary when evil and falsehood triumph.

The *surah* is unequivocal in indicating the path leading humanity away from loss.

Whenever two companions of the Prophet Muhammad (SAAS) were about to part, they would read this *surah*, after which they would shake hands. This was indicative of a pledge to accept this doctrine fully, to preserve this faith, piety and a willingness to counsel each other to follow the truth and remain steadfast. It was a mutual pact to remain good elements in an Islamic society established according to that doctrine and to preserve the foundation of this society.

Surah 104 Al-Humazah

Makki Surah — بِسْمِ اللهِ الرَّحْمٰنِ الرَّحِيْمِ — *9 Ayat*

Meaning	Words	Meaning	Words
Will make him live for-ever (dr. vrb. IV *madi* III. msc. sing., att. pro.)	اَخْلَدَهٗ	Woe[1] to every (interj., prep., noun subst. gen.)	وَيْلٌ لِّكُلِّ
Nay but he shall surely be cast or thrown (ptcl., ل ptcl. emph., *mudari* maj. msc. sing. نّ for emphasis)	كَلَّا لَيُنۢبَذَنَّ	Back-biter, slanderer, defamer (intensive form of noun gen.)	هُمَزَةٍ
Into the crushing fire (a name of Hell) (prep., def. noun fem. gen.)	فِى الْحُطَمَةِ	Traducer, making sign with the eye to traduce (intensive form of noun gen.)	لُّمَزَةِ
And what made you know And what will make you know (ptcls., dr, vrb. IV *madi* III. msc. sing., att. pro. كَ)	وَمَآ اَدْرٰىكَ	The one who (rel. pro. msc. sing.)	اِلَّذِىْ
What the crushing fire is (ptcl., def. noun nom.)	مَا الْحُطَمَةُ	Who amassed, collected, gathered (*madi* III. msc. sing.)	جَمَعَ
The Fire of Allah (noun nom. *mdf.*, noun *mdfi.*)	نَارُ اللهِ	Wealth, riches, substance (noun acc.)	مَالًا
Kindled (def. pass. prtc. fem. sing. nom.)	الْمُوْقَدَةُ	And counted it (a safeguard against the future) (ptcl., dr. vrb. II *madi* III. msc. sing., att. pro.)	وَّعَدَّدَهٗ
The one which (rel. pro. fem. sing.)	الَّتِىْ	He thinks, considers (*mudari* III. msc. sing.)	يَحْسَبُ
Rises, mounts (dr. vrb. VIII *madi* III. fem. sing.)	تَطَّلِعُ	That his wealth, riches, substance (ptcl., noun acc. *mdf.*, att. pro. *mdfi.*)	اَنَّ مَالَهٗٓ
Up to (or over) the hearts, (prep., def. noun br. pl. gen.)	عَلَى الْاَفْـِٕدَةِ		
Indeed it (the Fire) (ptcl., pro.)	اِنَّهَا		

---

[1] وَيْلٌ is an interjection commonly used with the preposition لِ to express a great misfortune.

Words	Meaning	Words	Meaning
عَلَيْهِمْ	Is (shall be) upon them (prep., att. pro.)	فِى عَمَدٍ	In columns, pillars (prep., noun pl. gen.)
مُّؤْصَدَةٌ	Closed over (pass. prtc. dr. vrb. IV fem. sing. nom.)	مُّمَدَّدَةٍ	Stretched forth, extended (pass. prtc. dr. vrb. II fem. sing. gen.)

Root Words of Surah 104

وَيْلٌ — A great misfortune, woe, (no verbal root), this word is commonly employed as an interjection with لِ

هُمَزَةٍ — A back-biter, هَمَزَ * he squeezed in the hand, he bit, هَمَّازٌ a slanderer, هَمَزَاتٌ evil suggestions of Shaytan.

لُمَزَةٍ — One who make signs with the eye to slander, traduce, defame, لَمَزَ * he winked, defamed.

عَدَدَ — II he prepared or laid up anything against the future, عَدَّ * he numbered, reckoned, عِدَّةٌ a number, prescribed term (as in divorce).

يَنۢبَذَنَّ — Shall certainly be thrown or cast, نَبَذَ * he throw, rejected.

الْحُطَمَةِ — A name of Hell, حَطَمَ * he broke into small pieces, حُطَامٌ that which crumbles away through dryness.

الْأَفْئِدَةِ — The hearts, (sing. فُؤَادٌ), فَأَدَ * he hurt anyone in the heart.

Translation of Surah 104 Al-Humazah (The Slanderer)

(1.) Woe to every slanderer and backbiter.

(2.) Who gathers wealth and counts it,

(3.) Thinking that his wealth will make him live forever,

(4.) By no means this is true. He will be thrown into the crushing torment (al-Hutama).

(5.) And what will make you grasp what the crushing torment (al-Hutama) is?

(6.) It is the Fire kindled by Allah,

(7.) Which will rise over the (guilty) hearts.

(8.) It will close in upon them,

(9.) In endless columns.

Explanatory Notes for Surah 104

This Makkan *Surah* condemns all sorts of scandal, backbiting and selfish hoarding of wealth, as destroying the hearts and affections of men, who slander others because of their pride of wealth. Man is so engrossed in amassing wealth that he has forgotten that empty-handed departing time from the world will come sooner or later. *Hutama* is described as *"the Fire kindled by Allah"* expressing in its dreadfulness the wrath and contempt of Allah for those who become proud and arrogant with worldly wealth. This fire will reach the heart of every culprit, discover the nature of his crime and then punish him according to his guilt. All that exists of this Fire will be closed, and tall columns will be erected on them without leaving any slit or opening anywhere. The people have been asked the question: "What should such a character deserve if not loss and perdition?"

In this *Surah* the warning comes in the form of a scene of the hereafter portraying the mental and physical sufferings and giving an image of Hell which is both palpable and telling. The tone and vocabulary used in this *surah* is very strong.

The crushing torment is Allah's own kindled fire which encloses the wrongdoer from all directions and locks him in. Inside he is tied to a column, as animals are tied, without respect. He has no escape from this torment.

Surah 105 Al-Fil

Makki Surah بِسْمِ اللَّهِ الرَّحْمَنِ الرَّحِيمِ **5 Ayat**

Surah 105 Al-Fil

Meaning	Words	Meaning	Words
And He sent (ptcl., dr. vrb. IV *madi* III. msc. sing.)	وَأَرْسَلَ	Did you not see or observe (ptcl. inter., ptcl. negn., *mudari*ᶜ juss. md.[1] II. msc. sing.)	أَلَمْ
Upon (against) them (prep., att. pro.)	عَلَيْهِمْ	How, in which manner (ptcl. inter.)	تَرَ كَيْفَ
Birds (noun pl. acc.)	طَيْرًا	Acted, dealt (*madi* III. msc. sing.)	فَعَلَ
(in) Flocks (noun br. pl. dipt.)	أَبَابِيلَ	Your Lord (noun nom. *mdf*., att. pro. *mdfi*.)	رَبُّكَ
They throw upon them They shooting them (*mudari*ᶜ III. fem. sing., att. pro.)	تَرْمِيهِمْ	With the fellows of (prep., noun. br. pl. gen. *mdf*.)	بِأَصْحَابِ
With stones (prep., noun br. pl. gen.)	بِحِجَارَةٍ	The Elephant (def. noun *mdfi*.)	الْفِيلِ
of baked clay (prep., noun gen.)	مِنْ سِجِّيلٍ	Did He not make (ptcl. inter., ptcl. negn.[2], *mudari*ᶜ juss. md. III. msc. sing.)	أَلَمْ يَجْعَلْ
So He made them (ptcl., *madi* III. msc. sing., att. pro.)	فَجَعَلَهُمْ	Their plot or trick (to go) (vrb. n. acc. *mdf*., att. pro. *mdfi*.)	كَيْدَهُمْ
Like straw, leaves and stalks of corn (prep., noun gen.)	كَعَصْفٍ	In error (prep., vrb. n. dr. vrb. II gen.)	فِي تَضْلِيلٍ
Eaten up (by cattle) (pass. prtc. msc. sing.)	مَأْكُولٍ		

[1] The *mudari*ᶜ due to the action of the particle of negation لَمْ upon it, has its end ي elided from تَرَى to تَرَ.
[2] لَمْ precedes *mudari*ᶜ to denote the negative meaning of a *madi*.

Root Words for Surah 105

كَيْفَ How, in what way, كَافَ * he cut.

الْفِيلِ The Elephant, فَالَ * he was weak-minded.

أَرْسَلَ IV he sent, رَسَلَ * he sent a messenger, رَسُولٌ a messenger (pl. رُسُلٌ).

طَيْرًا Birds, طَارَ * he flew, طَائِرٌ a flying thing, a bird, an omen, and especially an evil one.

أَبَابِيلَ Flocks (of birds), أَبَلَ * he had many camels, إِبِلٌ and إِبْلٌ camels.

تَرْمِي Throws, رَمَى * he threw, cast, threw out.

سِجِّيلٍ Baked clay of which the stones were formed, سَجَلَ * he poured forth.

عَصْفٍ Leaves and stalks of corn of which the grain has been eaten by cattle, عَصَفَ * it blew violently, عَاصِفَةٌ a violent wind.

Translation of Surah 105 Al-Fil (The Elephant)

(1.) Do you not see how your Lord dealt with the people of the Elephant?

(2.) Did He not make their plan go astray?

(3.) And He sent birds in flocks against them

(4.) Which threw stones of baked clay at them.

(5.) And so He made them look like leaves and stalks of corn devoured (by cattle).

Explanatory Notes for Surah 105

In "the Year of the Elephant" the Prophet Muhammad (SAAS) was born. The majority of traditionalists and historians state that he (SAAS) was born 50 days after the event of the elephant.

The various reports on this incident relate that the Abyssinian governor of Yemen, Abrahah, built a superbly luxurious church in his area. He did this after he had witnessed the love and enthusiasm of Yemeni Arabs - which were the same as those felt all over the Arab land - for the Ka'bah, the Holy Mosque at Makkah, with the aim of making them forsake their attachment to the Mosque of Makkah and turn instead to his new luxurious church.

But the Arabs did not turn away from their Holy House. As a result, Abrahah made up his mind to pull down the Ka'bah in order to achieve his objective of turning the Arabs away from it. He therefore marched at the head of a great army equipped with elephants. In the front was a very big elephant which enjoyed special fame among Abrahah's men. When the Abyssinian governor approached Ta'if, a town fifty miles from Makkah, a number of its leaders went to him to say that the House he wanted to pull down was in Makkah and not at Ta'if.

Then on arrival at Al-Mughammas (a valley mid-way between Ta'if and Makkah), Abrahah despatched one of his commanders to Makkah where he looted some belongings of the Quraysh and other Arabs, including two hundred camels which belonged to 'Abdu'l-Muttalib ibn Hashim, the chief of Makkah and the Prophet's (SAAS) grandfather. Then Abrahah sent a messenger to Makkah to meet its chief and ordered him to bring with him the Makkan chief if the latter did not propose to fight. When the messenger communicated his master's message to 'Abdu'l-Muttalib, the latter said: "By Allah, we do not want to fight him and we have no power to resist him. This is Allah's sacred House, built by His chosen friend, Ibrahim. If He protects it against him, it is because the House is His, and if He leaves it to him to destroy, we cannot defend it".

'Abdu'l-Muttalib, who was a most handsome, charming and attractive person, then went with the messenger to Abrahah. When Abrahah saw him he felt great respect for him. Abrahah ordered his interpreter to ask his guest what he wanted. 'Abdu'l-Muttalib said he wanted to request the king to give him back his two hundred camels which were looted by his commander. Abrahah ordered his interpreter to tell 'Abdu'l-Muttalib on his behalf: "I admired you when I first saw you but when I spoke to you I was disappointed. Do you come to talk to me about two hundred looted camels and forget about the House which is an embodiment of you and your forefathers' religion and which I have come to destroy? You did not even say a word to persuade me to spare it". 'Abdu'l-Muttalib said, "I am only the master of my camels, but the House has its own Lord who is sure to protect it". Abrahah snapped, "It cannot be defended against me." The Makkan chief said: "You take your chance!" Abrahah returned his camels to him.

ʿAbduʾl-Muttalib went back to Quraysh and told them of his encounter with the Abyssinian commander and ordered them to leave Makkah and seek shelter in the mountains surrounding it. Then he went with a few figures of Quraysh to the Kaʿbah where he held the ring on its door in his hand. They all prayed hard to Allah for His help and for His protection of the House. Abrahah, on the other hand, ordered his army to march with the elephants to complete their mission. Just outside Makkah the renowned great elephant sat down and refused to go any further. The soldiers exerted all efforts to persuade the elephant to enter the city but their efforts were in vain. This incident is a fact acknowledged by the Prophet (SAAS). When his she-camel, *Al-Qaswaʾ*, sat down some distance away from Makkah, on the day when the *Hubaibiyah* peace agreement was concluded, the Prophet (SAAS) said to those of his companions who claimed she had become mulish, that she had not and that mulishness was not part of her nature. "But", the Prophet (SAAS) added, "she has been prevented by the same will which debarred the Elephant from entering Makkah." (Bukhari) On the day of the conquest of Makkah, the Prophet said: "Allah protected Makkah against the Elephant but He allowed His Messenger and the Believers to conquer it. Its sanctity today is the same as yesterday. Let those who hear this convey it to those absent." (Bukhari and Muslim)

Then Allah's will to destroy the Abyssinian army and its commander was fulfilled. He sent groups of birds to stone the attackers with pebbles of sand and clay, leaving them like dry and torn leaves, as the Holy Qurʾan tells. Abrahah suffered physical injuries. The remainder of the army carried him on their way back to Yemen but his limbs began to separate from the rest of his body and he started losing one finger after another, until they arrived at Sanʿa. Abrahah died after his chest was broken apart, according to various reports.

Versions relating this event vary with regard to the description of those groups of birds, their size and the nature of stones and the manner of their effect. Some of these versions add that smallpox and measles broke out in Makkah in that year. Those who are inclined to limit the scale of miracles and imperceptible phenomena and who seek to explain all events as resulting from the operation of familiar natural phenomena, prefer to explain this event as an actual outbreak of smallpox and measles among the army. They further explain that "the birds" could have been flies or mosquitoes carrying germs. The word "bird" in Arabic refers to all that flies.

The significance of this event is far reaching and lessons deduced from mentioning it in the Qurʾan are numerous. It first suggests that Allah did not want the polytheists to take the responsibility of protecting His House, in spite of the fact that they held it in deep respect and sought security in being its neighbours. When He willed to preserve the House and made it clear that He Himself was its protector Who looked after it, He left the polytheists to be defeated by the Abyssinians. The Divine Will then directly intervened to repel the aggression and preserve the sacred House of Allah. Thus the polytheists did not have the chance to hold the protection of the House as a 'favour they did to Allah' or as 'an act of honour'. If they did, they would have been prompted by the fanatic impulses of ignorance This point gives considerable weight to the argument that the Divine Will of destroying the aggressors was accomplished through preternatural rules.

This direct intervention by Allah to protect the Holy House should have prompted the Quraysh and the rest of the Arabian tribes to embrace Islam, the Divine religion, when it was conveyed to them by the Prophet (SAAS). Surely, their respect and guardianship of the House, and the paganism they spread around it, should not have been their reason for rejecting Islam! Allah's reminder to them of this event is a part of His campaign against them and His drawing attention to their amazingly stubborn attitude.

The event also suggests that Allah (SWT) did not allow the people of earlier revelations, represented in this case by Abrahah and his army, to destroy the sacred House or to impose their authority over the Holy land, even when it was surrounded by the impurity of polytheism and the polytheists were its custodians. Thus the House remained free from any human authority, safe against all plottings and designs. Allah preserved the freedom of the land in order that the new faith would grow up there completely free, not subjected to the authority of any despot. Allah revealed this religion as the force which keeps under its fold all other religions and all mankind and takes over the leadership of humanity. This was Allah's will concerning His House and religion. It was accomplished long before any human being knew that the Prophet (SAAS), who was to convey the new message, was born in the same year. The general tone of this *surah* indicates that Allah had a scheme for the House. He wanted to preserve it as a refuge for mankind where everyone finds peace and to make it a gathering point for the followers of Islam.

Surah 106 Quraysh

Makki Surah — بِسْمِ اللَّهِ الرَّحْمَٰنِ الرَّحِيمِ — **4 Ayat**

Words	Meaning	Words	Meaning
لِإِيلَافِ	For safeguarding, taming, uniting together (prep., vrb. n. dr. vrb. IV gen.)	فَلْيَعْبُدُوا	So they should worship (ptcl., ptcl. exh., *mudari°* juss. md. III. msc. pl.)
قُرَيْشٍ[1]	Quraysh[1] (noun gen.)	رَبَّ	The Lord, Sustainer (noun acc. *mdf.*)
إِيلَافِهِمْ	For their safeguarding, taming, uniting together (vrb. n. dr. vrb. IV gen. *mdf.*, att. pro. *mdfi.*)	هَٰذَا الْبَيْتِ	(of) This House (Ka°bah) (dem. pro. msc. sing., def. noun *mdfi.*)
رِحْلَةَ	(in) Journey, travelling (vrb. n. acc. *mdf.*)	الَّذِي	The One Who (rel. pro. msc. sing.)
الشِّتَاءِ	(of) The winter (def. noun gen. *mdfi.*)	أَطْعَمَهُمْ	Provided them with food, Fed them (dr. vrb. IV *madi* III. msc. sing., att. pro.)
وَالصَّيْفِ	And the summer (ptcl., def. noun gen.)	مِنْ جُوعٍ	In (their) hunger (prep., noun gen.)
		وَآمَنَهُمْ	And made them safe (ptcl., dr. vrb. IV *madi* III. msc. sing., att. pro.)
		مِنْ خَوْفٍ	From fear (prep., vrb. n. gen.)

[1] The name of a noble Arab tribe which descended from Isma°il عَلَيْهِ السَّلَامُ and from which the Last Messenger صَلَّى اللَّهُ عَلَيْهِ وَسَلَّمَ was to appear.

Root Words for Surah 106

قُرَيْش	قُرَيْش	Name of a noble tribe descended from Isma°il (AS) of which the Prophet's (SAAS) grandfather was head.
رِحْلَة	رِحْلَة	(pl. رِحَال) A journey, travelling, رَحَلَ * he placed saddle bags on a camel, رَحْل a saddle bag.
الشِّتَاء	الشِّتَاء	The winter, شَتَا * he wintered.
الصَّيْف	الصَّيْف	The summer, صَافَ * he passed the summer.
رَبّ	رَبّ	Lord, رَبَّ * he was a lord and master, رَبَائِب (sing. رَبِيبَة) a daughter in law, step

الْبَيْت	The house, (pl. بُيُوت) بَاتَ * he passed the night, بَيَّتَ II he meditated by night, he attacked by night.
جُوع	Hunger, جَاعَ * he hungered.
خَوْف	Fear, dread, خَافَ * he feared, dreaded, apprehended.

above: daughter.

Translation of Surah 106 Quraysh

(1.) For the safeguarding of Quraysh,

(2.) Their safeguarding of the journey of the winter and the summer,

(3.) Therefore, let them worship the Lord of this House,

(4.) Who fed them against hunger and gave them security from fear.

Commentary for Surah 106

Quraysh were originally nomads, and they had been settled in Makkah for about two hundred years.

Makka is placed almost at an equal distance, a month's journey, between Yemen to the south, and Syria to the north. The former was the winter, the latter the summer, stations of her caravans: and their seasonal arrival relieved the ships of India from the tedious and troublesome navigation of the Red Sea. "The lucrative exchange diffused plenty and riches in the streets of Makkah and the noblest of her sons united the love of arms with the profession of merchandise." The extent and degree of business actively carried by means of these caravans were truly astonishing. "Few caravans set forth in which the whole population, men and women, had not a financial interest." "... On departure the caravans carried leather, spices, precious essences, and metals, particularly silver from Arabian mines." On their return everyone received a part of the profits proportionate to his stake and the number of share subscribed.

"Makkah owed its economic prosperity to its geographical position and to its relations with the important trade route to India ... From Babylonia, from the ports of the Persian Gulf as well as from the Yemen, flowed the rich products of the Middle East and of India: from Syria those of the Mediterranean world. We see Makkah opening negotiations with the neighbouring states, obtaining safe conducts, free passage for her caravans and concluding the equivalent of commercial treaties with Byzantium, Abyssinian, Persia and the Emirs of Yemen."

The Quraysh remained secure from the fear of attack on their caravan because they were custodians of the Ka'bah. They engaged the central position of Makkah and its guaranteed security, so let them be grateful to the Lord of this House, i.e. Ka'bah, and worship Him alone.

Makki Surah

بِسْمِ اللَّهِ الرَّحْمَٰنِ الرَّحِيمِ

7 Ayat

Surah 107 Al-Maʿun

Meaning	Words	Meaning	Words
(of) the poor (def. noun *mdfi.*)	الْمِسْكِينِ	Have you seen (ptcl. inter., *madi* II. msc. sing.)	أَرَأَيْتَ
So woe² be (ptcls.²)	فَوَيْلٌ	The One (rel. pro. msc. sing.)	الَّذِي
To those who pray (prep., act. prtc. dr. vrb. II msc. pl. gen.)	لِلْمُصَلِّينَ	Who gives the lie or denies (dr. vrb. II *mudari* III. msc. sing.)	يُكَذِّبُ
The ones who, they (rel. pro. msc. pl., pro. msc. pl.)	الَّذِينَ هُمْ	The judgement of the Hereafter, the religion (prep., def. noun gen.)	بِالدِّينِ
From their *salah* (prayer) (prep., noun fem. gen. *mdf.*, att. pro. *mdfi*)	عَنْ صَلَاتِهِمْ	So that is (ptcl., dem. pro. msc., sing.)	فَذَٰلِكَ
(are) negligent, unmindful (act. prtc. msc. pl.)	سَاهُونَ	The one who (rel. pro. msc. sing.)	الَّذِي
The ones who, they (rel. pro. msc. pl., pro. msc. pl.)	الَّذِينَ هُمْ	Drives away with violence or pushes back violently (*mudariʿ* III. msc. sing.)	يَدُعُّ
Make show (of their *salah*) (dr. vrb. III *mudariʿ* III. msc. pl.)	يُرَاءُونَ	The orphan (def. noun acc.)	الْيَتِيمَ
And they refuse or withhold (ptcl., *mudariʿ* III. msc. pl.)	وَيَمْنَعُونَ	And he does not urge (himself) (ptcl., ptcl. negn., *mudariʿ* III. msc. sing., prep.)	وَلَا يَحُضُّ عَلَىٰ
Small kindnesses, common necessities (def. coll. noun acc..)	الْمَاعُونَ	Feeding, (to give) Food, (vrb. n. gen. *mdf.*)	طَعَامِ

---

¹ The word الدِّين is used for the accounting, rewards and punishments of the hereafter as well as for the way of Islam.

² The noun وَيْلٌ commonly appears with لِ in the Qur'an and in such instances is used as an interjection denoting a great misfortune.

Root Words for Surah 107

يَدَعُ	Repels, دَعَّ	* he pushed, drove away with violence, دَعَّ a thrusting.
الْيَتِيمَ	The orphan يَتَمَ (*mudari*ᶜ يَيْتَمُ)	* he was an orphan.
سَاهُونَ	Those who are unmindful, سَهَا	* he forgot, neglected, overlooked, سَهْوًا heedlessness, unmindfulness.
يَمْنَعُونَ	They refuse, مَنَعَ	* he refused, prohibited, hindered, forbade, prevented.
الْمَاعُونَ	Household stuff, common necessities, small kindnesses, مَعَنَ	* he travelled fast and far, مَعِينٌ running water.

Translation of Surah 107 Al-Maᶜun (Assistance)

(1.) Have you seen the one who gives the lie to the reckoning,

(2.) For that is the who thrusts the orphan scornfully away (from what is rightfully his),

(3.) And he does not urge the feeding of the needy.

(4.) So woe to those praying ones

(5.) The ones who are careless about their prayers

(6.) The ones who do good to be seen.

(7.) And they prevent small kindnesses.

Explanatory Notes for Surah 107

Abu Jahl was the testator of an orphan. The child one day came to him in the condition that he had no shred of a garment on his body and he implored him to be given something out of his father's heritage. But the cruel man paid no attention to him and the poor child had to go back disappointed. The Quraysh said to him out of fun: "Go to Muhammad and put your complaint before him. He will recommend your case to Abu Jahl and get you your property." The child not knowing any background of the nature of relationship between Abu Jahl and the Prophet (SAAS) and not understanding the motives of the mischief-mongers, went straight to the Prophet (SAAS) and apprised him of his misfortune. The Prophet (SAAS) immediately rose and accompanied the child to the house of Abu Jahl, his bitterest enemy. Abu Jahl received him well and when the latter told him to restore to the child his right, he yielded and brought out whatever he owed to him. The chiefs of Quraysh were watching all this earnestly in the hope that an interesting altercation would take place between them. But when they saw what actually happened they were astounded and went to Abu Jahl and taunted him saying that he too perhaps had abandoned his religion. He said: "By Allah, I have not abandoned my religion, but I felt that on the right and left of Muhammad (SAAS) there was a spear which would enter my body if I acted against what he desired."

This incident not only shows what was the attitude and conduct of the principal chiefs of the most civilised and noble tribe of Arabia towards orphans and other helpless people in those days but it also shows what sublime character the Prophet (SAAS) possessed and what impact it had on even his bitterest enemies.

There are Muslims who are not regular at the prayers and when they perform them, they do not observe the prescribed times, but offer them carelessly at the eleventh hour. Or, when they rise up for the prayer, they rise up soullessly and perform it with an unwilling heart, as if it were a calamity imposed on them. They play with their garments, yawn and betray absence of every trace of Allah's remembrance in their hearts. Throughout they show no feeling at all that they are performing the prayer, nor of what they are reciting; their minds wander and they perform parts of the prayer without due attention; they somehow perform a semblance of the prayer and try to be rid of it as soon as possible. And there are many people who would perform the prayer only when they must, otherwise it has no place in their lives. The prayer time comes but they show no concern that it is the prayer time; they hear the call to the prayer but do not understand what the caller is calling to, to whom he is calling and for what purpose. These in fact are the signs of absence of faith in the Hereafter. The claimants to Islam behave thus only because they do not believe that they would be rewarded for performing the prayer, nor do they have the faith that they would be punished for not performing it.

The prayer (*Salah*) of hypocrites is described in *Surah* 4 An-Nisa *ayah* 142 in the following words: *"And when they rise to pray, they rise reluctantly, only to be seen and praised by men, seldom remembering Allah."* (Qur'an 4: 142)

The Qur'an at another place has described this state of the hypocrites, thus: *"They come to offer their Prayer but reluctantly, and they expend in the way of Allah with unwilling hearts."* (Qur'an 9: 54) The Messenger of Allah (SAAS) has said: "This is the Prayer of the hypocrite; this the prayer of the hypocrite; this is the prayer of the hypocrite! He watches the sun at the ᶜAsr time until when it reaches between the two horns of Shaytan, (i.e. when the time of sunset approaches), he gets up and performs the prayer carelessly, in which he remembers Allah but little." (Bukhari, Muslim, Musnad Ahmad)

The term *Al-Maᶜun* comprises the many small items needed for one's daily use, as well as the occasional act of kindness consisting in helping out one's fellow men with such items. In its wider sense, it denotes aid or assistance in any difficulty.

Surah 108 Al-Kawthar

Makki Surah — بِسْمِ اللهِ الرَّحْمٰنِ الرَّحِيْمِ — 3 Ayat

Surah 108 Al-Kawthar

Meaning	Words	Meaning	Words
And sacrifice[2] (an animal) (ptcl., amr II. msc. sing.)	وَانْحَرْ	Indeed We (ptcl. إِنَّ, prefixed to per. pro. نَ)	إِنَّا
Indeed your traducer, or insulter (ptcl., act. prtc. msc. sing. acc. mdf., att. pro. كَ mdfi.)	إِنَّ شَانِئَكَ	We granted you (dr. vrb. IV madi I pl., att. pro. كَ)	أَعْطَيْنٰكَ
He is the one cut off (from all future hope) (per. pro., def. noun)	هُوَ الْأَبْتَرُ	The abundance of good[1] (intensive form of noun acc.)	الْكَوْثَرَ
		Hence pray (ptcl., dr. vrb. II amr II. msc. sing.)	فَصَلِّ
		To your Lord (prep., noun gen. mdf., att. pro. mdfi)	لِرَبِّكَ

[2] The verb نَحَرَ can be taken here to mean sacrifice, but its immediate meaning is to sacrifice an animal and in this sense it is said that it is the command to sacrifice an animal after the ᶜEid prayer of Hajj.

[1] The word الْكَوْثَرَ is also taken to be the proper name of the lake granted to the Prophet صَلَّى اللهُ عَلَيْهِ وَسَلَّمَ in the Hereafter by Allah تَعَالٰى.

Root Words of Surah 108

أَنْحَرْ — Sacrifice, slaughter! (imp.) نَحَرَ * he sacrificed by stabbing upwards into the jugular vein (the way of slaughter for camels as opposed to other cattle), يَوْمُ النَّحْرِ ᶜEidul Adha day.

شَانِئًا — One who hates, traducer, insulter, شَنَّأَ * he hated.

أَبْتَرُ — Cut off from all future hopes, childless, بَتَرَ * he cut off the tail.

Translation of Surah 108 Al-Kawthar (The Abundance)

(1.) Indeed We have given you abundance (of all that is good).

(2.) So pray to your Lord and sacrifice (to Him).

(3.) Surely, he that hates you has indeed been cut off (from all that is good).

Explanatory Notes for Surah 108

The three *ayat* of the *surah* are addressed, in the first instance to the Prophet (SAAS) and through him to every believing man and woman. It is an instance of Allah's direct support to the believers in their struggle, supplying them with the fortitude, restraint and promise, while threatening a terrible fate to their antagonists. This *surah* is the sole instance in the Qur'an where the word *al-Kawthar* is used.

The abundance which Allah has given to His Prophet (SAAS) reflects in his prophethood itself, in this Qur'an which was revealed to the Messenger of Allah (SAAS). This *Kawthar* or abundance is manifest in the Prophet's *Sunnah* (way of life) throughout the centuries, in the far-flung corners of the earth, and in the goodness and prosperity which have accrued to the human race as a result of his message, and which reach those who know and believe in him.

This indeed is abundance in its absolute unlimited sense. The *surah* therefore does not give it a specific definition.

Several accounts relate that "Al-Kawthar" is a river in Paradise granted to the Prophet (SAAS) but Ibn Abbas, a learned companion of the Prophet, contended that the river is but one part of the abundance which Allah has furnished for His Prophet (SAAS).

"So pray to your Lord and sacrifice to Him". Having assured the Prophet of this munificent gift, which disproves what the calumniators and conspirators say, Allah directs the Prophet (SAAS) to be completely and sincerely thankful to Him for His bounty, as should the Believers. Islam frequently lays emphasis on the pronouncing of Allah's name when slaughtering animals. It prohibits anything that is consecrated to any other being, which indicates the importance Islam attaches to the purification of human life from all forms of polytheism and all that leads to it. Islam does not aim merely at purifying the imagination and conscience, for it is the religion based on the unity of Allah in every sense.

"Surely he who hates you is the one cut off." In the first *ayah*, Allah specified that Muhammad (SAAS) was not the one who had no prosperity but, on the contrary, was the one endowed with abundance. In this *ayah*, Allah throws back the taunt of those who hated and reviled the Prophet (SAAS). Indeed, the promise of Allah (SWT) has come true. For, the influence and the legacy of the Messenger of Allah's enemies was short-lived, while his impact on human history and human life has grown and deepened.

Surah 109 Al-Kafirun

Makki Surah — بِسْمِ اللَّهِ الرَّحْمَنِ الرَّحِيمِ — 6 Ayat

Meaning	Words	Meaning	Words
What you worshipped (ptcl., *madi* II. msc. pl.)	مَا عَبَدتُّمْ	Say: (*amr* II. msc. sing.)	قُلْ
And neither are you (ptcl., ptcl. negn., per. pro. II. msc. pl.)	وَلَا أَنتُمْ	O (you) (ptcls. interj.[1])	يَٰٓأَيُّهَا
Worshippers (of) (act. prtc. msc. pl. nom.)	عَٰبِدُونَ	Who have no belief (in Allah and His Messenger) (def. act. prtc. pl. nom.)	ٱلْكَٰفِرُونَ
What I worship (ptcl., *mudari* I. sing.)	مَآ أَعْبُدُ	I do not worship (ptcl. negn., *mudari* I. sing.)	لَآ أَعْبُدُ
To you (prep.[2], att. pro. II. msc. pl.)	لَكُمْ	What you worship (ptcl., *mudari* II. msc. pl.)	مَا تَعْبُدُونَ
Your religion, faith, religious law (noun nom. *mdf.*, att. pro. II. msc. pl. *mdfi.*)	دِينُكُمْ	And neither are you (ptcl., ptcl. negn., per. pro. II. msc. pl.)	وَلَآ أَنتُمْ
And to me (ptcl., prep., att. pro. I. sing.)	وَلِيَ	Worshippers (of) (act. prtc. msc. pl. nom.)	عَٰبِدُونَ
My religion, faith, religious law (noun, att. pro. I. sing.[3])	دِينِ	What I worship (ptcl., *mudari* I. sing.)	مَآ أَعْبُدُ
		And nor I (shall be) (ptcl., ptcl. negn., per. pro. I. sing.)	وَلَآ أَنَا۠
		A worshipper (of) (act. prtc. msc. sing. nom.)	عَابِدٌ

---

[2] The *kasra* of the preposition لِ changes into a *fathah* when prefixed to personal pronouns هُ giving لَهُ 'to him', كُمْ giving لَكُمْ 'to you (pl.)', and نَا giving لَنَا 'to us'.

[3] ي of the first person singular attached pronoun نِي is omitted if the preceding نْ occurs at the end of a sentence.

[1] يَٰٓأَيُّهَا is made up of two interjections both of which require the following noun to be definite and in the nominative case.

Root Words of Surah 109

قُلْ   Say! (imp.), قَالَ * he said, spoke, قَوْلٌ a saying, speech, قَائِلٌ a speaker.

الْكَافِرُونَ (sing. كَافِرٌ) the unbelievers, those ungrateful for benefits received, كَفَرَ * he covered, denied.

أَعْبُدُ   I worship, عَبَدَ * he adored, worshipped, served (a slave), تَعْبُدُونَ you worship, عَبْدٌ a slave, عَابِدٌ a worshipper.

Translation of Surah 109 Al-Karifun (Those Who Cover Over [The Truth])

(1.) Say: "O you who cover over (the truth),

(2.) I do not worship that which you worship,

(3.) And neither do you worship that which I worship.

(4.) And I will not worship that which you have (ever) worshipped,

(5.) And neither will you (ever) worship that which I worship.

(6.) To you, your *din*, and to me, my *din*."

Explanatory Notes for Surah 109

The word "*Al-Kafirun*" in this *surah* is used for those who do not believe in the messengership and teachings of the last Prophet Muhammad (SAAS). The word used is "*O kafirs*" and not "*O mushriks*"; therefore, those addressed are not only the *mushriks* but all those people who do not acknowledge Muhammad (SAAS) as Allah's Last Messenger and the teachings and guidance brought by him as the teaching and guidance given by Allah Himself, whether they be Jews, Christians, Zoroastrians, or the disbelievers, polytheists and pagans of the entire world. There is no reason why this address be restricted to the pagans of Quraysh or of Arabia only.

To address the deniers with the word "*O Kafirs*" is just like addressing certain people as "*O enemies*", or "*O opponents*".

In *ayat* 3 and 5 above "*that which I worship*" alludes, on the one hand, to all positive concepts and ethical values - e.g. belief in Allah (SWT) and the believer's self-surrender to Him - as opposed to false objects of worship and false values, such as man's belief in his own supposed "*self-sufficiency*" (Qur'an 96: 6-7), or his overriding, almost compulsive "*greed for more and more*", (Qur'an 102).

The primary significance of *din* is "obedience" in particular obedience to a law or to what is conceived as a system of established - and therefore binding - usages, i.e. something endowed with moral authority: hence "religion", "faith" or "religious law" in the widest sense of these terms. *Ad-Din* is the normative, natural and perfect way of life which Allah (SWT) has ordained for humanity, including faith, ethics, ways, customs, law, obedience, devotions, institutions and judgements. All Prophets were sent to preach the same Right-Way which was completed and perfected on the last Prophet Muhammad (SAAS).

Surah 110 An-Nasr

Madani Surah   بِسْمِ اللهِ الرَّحْمٰنِ الرَّحِيْمِ   3 Ayat

Surah 110 An-Nasr

Meaning	Words	Meaning	Words
With praise (prep., vrb. n. *mdf.*)	بِحَمْدِ	When comes (ptcl.[1], *madi* III. msc. sing.)	اِذَا جَآءَ
Of your Lord (noun *mdfi. mdf.*[2], att. pro. كَ *mdfi*)	رَبِّكَ	The help of Allah (vrb. n. nom. *mdf.*, proper noun *mdfi.*)	نَصْرُ اللهِ
And seek His forgiveness (ptcl., dr. vrb. X *amr* II. msc. sing., att. pro.)	وَاسْتَغْفِرْهُ	And the victory (ptcl., def. noun nom.)	وَالْفَتْحُ
Indeed He (always) is (ptcl., att. pro., *madi* III. msc. sing.[3])	اِنَّهُ كَانَ	And you see (ptcl., *madi* II. msc. sing.)	وَرَاَيْتَ
An acceptor of repentence (intensive noun acc.)	تَوَّابًا	The people, mankind (def. noun pl. acc.)	النَّاسَ
		They enter in (*mudari*ᶜ III. msc. pl., prep.)	يَدْخُلُوْنَ فِيْ
		the religion of Allah (noun gen. *mdf.*, proper noun *mdfi.*)	دِيْنِ اللهِ
		(in) Hosts, crowds, groups (noun br. pl. acc.)	اَفْوَاجًا
		Then glorify (ptcl., dr. vrb. II *amr* II. msc. sing.)	فَسَبِّحْ

[2] The word رَبّ is *mdfi.* with respect to حَمْد and *mdf.* with respect to the pronoun كَ literally meaning 'praise of the Lord of you.'

[3] The verb كَانَ which means 'was', 'happened', etc..., when used in the Qur'an in association with the attributes of Allah (SWT) means 'was, is and always will be'. The predicate of this verb, in this case تَوَّابًا, is always in the accusative case ending.

[1] The particle اِذَ when preceding the *madi* gives it the meaning of the *mudari*ᶜ.

Root Words of Surah 110

جَآءَ	*	He came, came to, arrived at, brought.
نَصَرَ		Aid, assistance, victory, نَصَرَ * her aided, assisted, succoured, protected, delivered, اَنْصَار ones who aid.
الْفَتْحُ		The victory, فَتَحَ * he opened, explained, revealed, granted victory, فَتْح victory, decision or judgement, الْفَتَّاح the Judge (Allah's attribute), الْفَاتِحَة the opening chapter of the Qur'an.

يَدْخُلُونَ	They shall enter, دَخَلَ * he entered, went in to, he joined himself in company with.	
بِحَمْدِ	With praise (of), حَمِدَ * he praised, حَمِيدٌ worthy of praise, أَحْمَدُ most praiseworthy, مُحَمَّدٌ much praised.	
اِسْتَغْفِرْ	X Seek pardon! (imp.), غَفَرَ * he covered, forgave, pardoned, غَفُورٌ fully forgiving, غَفَّارٌ oft-forgiving.	
تَوَّابًا	relenting, very repentant, تَابَ * he repented towards Allah, He (Allah) relented towards men, تَوْبَةٌ repentance.	

Translation of Surah 110 An-Nasr (Succour)

(1.) When comes the help of Allah and the victory (in the conquest of Makkah),

(2.) And you see people entering the *din* of Allah in throngs,

(3.) Then, glorify with praise of your Lord and seek His forgiveness, for He is ever-turning (towards His slaves).

Explanatory Notes for Surah 110

The *din* of Allah is the religion of self-surrender to Allah: *"the only (true) religion in the sight of Allah is Islam (man's self-surrender to Him)."* (surah 3:19)

Ayah 3 implies that even if people should embrace the true religion in great numbers, a believer ought not to grow self-complacent but should, rather, become more humble and more conscious of his own failings. Moreover, the Prophet (SAAS) is reported to have said, "Behold, people have entered Allah's religion in hosts - and in time they will leave it in hosts." (Ibn Hanbal, on the authority of Jabir ibn ʿAbdullah (RA); a similar Tradition, on the authority of Abu Hurairah (RA), is found in the *Mustadrak*).

Surah An-Nasr was revealed at Mina during the Prophet's (SAAS) Farewell Pilgrimage in the month of Dhu'l-Hijjah, 10AH. - that is, a little over two months before his death. This is unquestionably the last complete *surah* conveyed by him to the world. It was preceded one day earlier (on Friday, the 9th of Dhu'l-Hijjah) by the revelation of the words, *"Today have I perfected your din for you, and bestowed upon you the full measure of My blessings, and willed that self-surrender unto Me (al-Islam) shall be your din"* (Qur'an 5: 3) and since those words were almost immediately followed by the present *surah*, some of the Prophet's (SAAS) companions concluded that his mission was fulfilled, and that he was about to die (Bukhari). The only revelation which the Prophet received after *An-Nasr* was *ayah* 281 of *Al-Baqarah*.

Narrated ʿA'ishah (RA): "When the Surah An-Nasr, *'when comes the help of Allah and the conquest'*, had been revealed to the Prophet (SAAS) he did not offer any prayer except that he said therein, *'Subhanaka Rabbana wa bihamdika; Allahumma'ghfirli* (Glory be to You, our Lord, and with praise of You, O Allah, forgive me)'" Narrated ʿA'ishah (RA): "Allah's Messenger (SAAS) used to say very often in bowing and prostration (during his prayers), *'Subhanaka'llahumma Rabbana wa bihamdika; Allahumma'ghfirli.'* (Glory be to You, O Allah our Lord, and with praise of You, O Allah, forgive me), according to the order of the Qur'an." (Al-Bukhari)

Narrated Ibn ʿAbbas (RA): ʿUmar (RA) asked the people regarding Allah's statement:- *"When comes the help of Allah and the conquest..."* (Qur'an 110: 1)

They replied, "It indicates the future conquest of towns and places (by Muslims)." ʿUmar (RA) said, "What do you say about it, Ibn ʿAbbas?" I replied, "(This *Surah*) indicates the termination of the life of Muhammad (SAAS). Through it he was informed of the nearness of his death." (Al-Bukhari)

Surah 111 Al-Lahab or Al-Masad

Makki Surah   بِسْمِ اللهِ الرَّحْمٰنِ الرَّحِيْمِ   **5 Ayat**

Surah 111 Al-Lahab or Al-Masad

Meaning	Words	Meaning	Words
He shall roast (ptcl. fut., *mudari'* III. msc. sing.)	سَيَصْلٰى	Perished (are) (*madi* III. fem. sing.)	تَبَّتْ
(in) a fire (noun acc.)	نَارًا	The two hands (noun dual nom. *mdf*.)	يَدَآ
Having flame (dem. pro. fem. sing. acc. *mdf.*, noun *mdfi*.)	ذَاتَ لَهَبٍ	Abu Lahab[1] (noun *mdfi. mdf.*[2], noun *mdfi*.)	اَبِىْ لَهَبٍ
And his wife (ptcl., noun fem. sing. nom. *mdf.*, att. pro. *mdfi*.)	وَّامْرَاَتُهٗ	And he suffered loss, perished (ptcl., *madi* III. msc. sing.)	وَّتَبَّ
The carrier (of) (noun fem. sing. nom. *mdf*.)	حَمَّالَةَ	Did not avail him (ptcl. negn., dr. vrb IV *madi* III. msc. sing., prep., att pro. ه)	مَاۤ اَغْنٰى عَنْهُ
The firewood (def. noun *mdfi*.)	الْحَطَبِ	His wealth, property (noun nom. *mdf.*, att. pro. *mdfi*.)	مَالُهٗ
Around her neck (in Hell) (prep., noun gen. *mdf.*, att. pro. *mdfi*.)	فِىْ جِيْدِهَا	and what he earned (ptcls., *madi* III. msc. sing.)	وَمَا كَسَبَ
A rope or cord (noun nom.)	حَبْلٌ	[1] Abu Lahab (literally 'The Father of Flame') came to be the nickname of ʿAbdul-ʿUzza, one of the uncles of the Prophet صَلَّى اللّٰهُ عَلَيْهِ وَسَلَّمَ and one of the bitterest and most powerful opponents of Islam. [2] The word اَبِىْ is *mdfi.* with respect to يَدَا and *mdf.* with respect to the noun لَهَبٍ literally meaning 'the two hands of the father of flame.'	
Of twisted palm-fibres or strands (prep., noun gen.)	مِّنْ مَّسَدٍ		

Root Words of Surah 111

تَبَّتْ	Perished, تَبَّ * he cut off, perished, تَتْبِيْبٌ a loss, detriment.
يَدَا	Two hands, يَدٰى * he touched or injured in the hand.
كَسَبَ	* He gained, acquired, sought after.
لَهَبٍ	Flaming fire, لَهَبٌ * it blazed.

اِمْرَأَةٌ	A woman, wife, مَرَأٌ * it was wholesome (food), مَرْءٌ a man, مَرِيئًا salutary.
حَمَّالَةُ	(fem.) The bearer (who professionally carries loads of wool), حَمَلٌ * he carried, bore, bore away, loaded.
الْحَطَبِ	The firewood, fuel, حَطَبٌ * he bound wood.
جِيدٌ	A neck, جَادَ * for جَيِدٌ he had a long and beautiful neck.
حَبْلٌ	A rope, vein, compact, or covenant, حَبَلٌ * he took a wild beast with a snare or halter.
مَسَدٌ	Twisted fibres of palm tree, coil, مَسَدٌ * he twisted (a rope) strongly.

Translation of Surah 111 Al-Lahab

(1.) Perished are the hands of Abu Lahab and he has perished.

(2.) Neither will his wealth avail him nor all that he has gained.

(3.) (In the life to come) he shall roast at a fire of blazing flames.

(4.) Along with his wife, the carrier of the firewood,

(5.) Around her neck a cord of twisted palm fibres.

Explanatory Notes for Surah 111

This *surah* is about Abu Lahab, the paternal uncle of the Prophet (SAAS), who opposed him vehemently with abuse and force of arms. The real name of this uncle of the Prophet (SAAS) was ʿAbd al-ʿUzza. He was popularly nicknamed Abu Lahab (lit., "Father of Flame") on account of his most notable glowing countenance.

This very early Makkan *surah* relates to the bitter hostility always shown to the Prophet's message by his uncle Abu Lahab; a hostility rooted in his inborn arrogance, pride in his great wealth and a dislike of the idea, propounded by the Messenger of Allah (SAAS) that all human beings will be judged by Allah on their merits alone.

As reported by several unimpeachable authorities - Bukhari and Muslim among them - the Prophet (SAAS) ascended one day the hillock of *As-Safa* in Makkah and called together all who could hear him from among his tribe, Quraysh. When they had assembled, he asked them: "O sons of ʿAbda'l-Muttalib! O sons of Fihr! if I were to inform you that enemy warriors are about to fall upon you from behind that hill, would you believe me?" They answered: "Yes, we would." Thereupon he said: "Behold, then, I am here to warn you of the coming of the Last Hour!" At that, Abu Lahab exclaimed: "Was it for this purpose that you have summoned us? Perish you!" And shortly afterwards this *surah* was revealed. When the Prophet (SAAS) said that he was sent to warn the Quraysh of a terrible punishment which was sure to come if they did not believe in Allah, Abu Lahab cried out abusively, "You will be destroyed for calling us to hear such talk." Then he picked up a stone and threw it at the Prophet (SAAS).

Makki Surah   بِسْمِ اللَّهِ الرَّحْمَٰنِ الرَّحِيمِ   4 Ayat

Surah 112 Al-Ikhlas

Meaning	Words	Meaning	Words
And He was not begotten (ptcl., ptcl. negn.[2], *mudari^c maj.* III. msc. sing.)	وَلَمْ يُولَدْ	Say, He is (*amr* II. msc. sing., per. pro. msc. sing.)	قُلْ هُوَ
And there has never been with Him (ptcl., ptcl. negn.[2], *mudari^c juss. md.* III msc. sing., prep.[3], att. pro.)	وَلَمْ يَكُنْ لَهُ	Allah (the only) One (proper noun nom., card. no. msc. nom.)	اللَّهُ أَحَدٌ
Anyone like or co-equal or that could be compared (vrb. n. acc., card. no. msc. sing. nom.)	كُفُوًا أَحَدٌ	Allah is the Self-Sufficient, Absolute and Ever-lasting[1] (proper noun, adj., nom.)	اللَّهُ الصَّمَدُ
		He did not beget (ptcl. negn.[2], *mudari^c juss. md.* III. msc. sing.)	لَمْ يَلِدْ

[2] The particle of negation لَمْ precedes the *mudari^c* in order to denote the emphatic negative meaning of the *madi*.

[3] When prefixed to attached pronouns the preposition لِ changes its vowelisation from a *kasra* to a *fatha*.

[1] The name الصَّمَدُ occurs only once in the Qur'an and is applied to Allah (SWT) alone. He is Besought by all, Independent of everyone and everything, the Absolute, the Eternal.

Root Words of Surah 112

أَحَدٌ   One (fem. إِحْدَى) anyone, وَاحِدٌ one, single, * he was one, alone, unique, تَوْحِيدٌ unification, the act of making One, knowledge of the unity of Allah, وَحِيدٌ alone, unique.

الصَّمَدُ   (Allah's attribute) Besought of all, independent of everyone and everything, صَمَدَ * he wished to approach someone.

كُفُوًا   Co-equal, equal, like, كَفَأَ * he turned back (transitive).

Translation of Surah 112 Al-Ikhlas

(1.) Say, "He Allah is One.

(2.) Allah is the Eternally Besought of All.

(3.) He did not give birth, and was not begotten.

(4.) And there is no one like Him (in any respect)."

Explanatory Notes for Surah 112

Narrated Abu Hurairah (RA): Allah's Apostle said, "Allah said: 'The son of Adam tells a lie against Me and he hasn't the right to do so; and he abuses Me and he hasn't the right to do so. His telling a lie against Me is his saying that I will not recreate him as I created him for the first time; and his abusing Me is his saying that Allah has begotten children, while I am (*As-Samad*) the Self-Sufficient Master, Whom all creatures need, Who begets not, nor was He begotten, and there is none like unto Me.'" (Al-Bukhari).

The divine name "Allah" was not an unfamiliar word for the Arabs who had been using this very word for the Creator of the Universe since the earliest times. For other gods they use the word *ilah* (a god). This extraordinary use by itself shows that being single, unique and matchless is a fundamental attribute of Allah, He has no equal.

All lexicographers agree that the word *samad* means the chief who has no superior and to whom the people turn for the fulfilment of their desires and needs and in connection with other affairs. The term *as-samad*, which occurs in the Qur'an only once, is applied to Allah alone. It comprises the concepts of Primary Cause and eternal, independent Being, combined with the fact that everything existing or conceivable goes back to Him as its source and is, therefore, dependent on Him for its beginning as well as for its continued existence.

The word *kufu'*, as used in the original, means an example, a similar thing, one equal in rank and position. In the matter of marriage, *kufu'* means that the boy and girl should match each other socially. Thus this *ayah* means that there is no one in the entire universe, nor ever was, nor ever can be, who is similar to Allah, or equal in rank with Him, or resembling Him in His attributes, works and powers in any degree whatsoever.

Anas (RA) said: "One of the Ansar used to lead the Ansar in prayer in the Quba mosque and it was his habit to recite *'Qul huwa'llahu ahad'* (Say: 'He Allah is One.'), (after *Al-Fatihah*), whenever he wanted to recite something in the prayer. When he finished that *surah*, he would recite another one with it. He followed the same procedure in each *rak'ah*. His companions discussed this with him and said, "You recite this *surah* and do not consider it sufficient and then you recite another. So would you recite it alone or leave it."

He said, "I will never leave it and if you want me to be your Imam on this condition then it is alright; otherwise I will leave you." They knew that he was the best amongst them and they did not like someone else to lead them. When the Prophet (SAAS) went to them as usual they informed him about it. The Prophet (SAAS) addressed him and said, "O so and so, what forbids you from doing what your companions ask you to do? Why do you read this *surah* particularly in every *rak'ah*? He replied "I love this *surah*." The Prophet (SAAS) said, "Your love for this *surah* will make you enter Paradise."

Surah 113 Al-Falaq

Makki or Madani Surah

بِسْمِ اللهِ الرَّحْمٰنِ الرَّحِيْمِ

5 Ayat

Meaning	Words	Meaning	Words
When it is over-spread (ptcl., *madi* III. msc. sing.)	إِذَا وَقَبَ	Say: I seek refuge (*amr* II. msc. sing., *mudari*ᶜ I sing.)	قُلْ أَعُوْذُ
And from (all) evil (prep., noun gen. *mdf.*)	وَمِنْ شَرِّ	With the Lord of (prep., noun gen. *mdf.*)	بِرَبِّ
of the blowers¹ (of magic) (of sorceresses¹) (def. noun fem. pl. *mdfi.*)	النَّفّٰثٰتِ	The day-break (def. noun *mdfi.*)	الْفَلَقِ
In the knots (prep., noun br. pl. gen.)	فِى الْعُقَدِ	From (all) evil (prep., noun gen.)	مِنْ شَرِّ
And from (all) evil (ptcl., prep., noun gen. *mdf.*)	وَمِنْ شَرِّ	That He created (ptcl., *madi* III. msc. sing.)	مَا خَلَقَ
(of) an envier (act. prtc. msc. sing. *mdfi.*)	حَاسِدٍ	And from (all) evil (ptcl., prep., noun gen. *mdf.*)	وَمِنْ شَرِّ
When he envies (ptcl., III. msc. sing.)	إِذَا حَسَدَ	(of) Darkness (act. prtc. msc. sing. *mdfi.*)	غَاسِقٍ

¹ In pre-Islamic Arabia, witchcraft and sorcery were prevalent. They used to tie knots in a cord and blow on them, muttering over them magical formulae in order to injure their victims. As well as indicating women it has been said that this word indicates 'group' (الْجَمَاعَة) or even 'selves' (نُفُوْس or أَنْفُس, singular نَفْس) but the most correct is the first position because the cause of the revelation was the magic of the daughters of the Jew Labid ibn al-Aᶜsam.

Root Words of Surah 113

أَعُوْذُ   I seek protection, refuge, عَاذَ * he took or sought refuge (especially with Allah).

الْفَلَقِ   The daybreak, فَلَقَ * he caused to come forth, he split.

غَاسِقٍ   Darkness, غَسَقَ * it was very dark (the night).

وَقَبَ   * He (it) entered, overspread (as darkness), it was eclipsed.

النَّفّٰثٰتِ   The women who blow (kind of incantation), نَفَثَ * he blew.

الْعُقَدِ   The knots, عَقَدَ * he tied in a knot, عَقْدٌ (pl. عُقُوْدٌ) a compact.

حَاسِدٍ   One who envies, حَسَدَ * he envied, envy.

Translation of Surah 113 Al-Falaq (The Rising Dawn)

(1.) Say: "I seek refuge with the Sustainer of the rising dawn,

(2.) From the evil of what He has created,

(3.) And from the evil of the black darkness whenever it is thick,

(4.) And from the evil of women who blow in knots (in magic),

(5.) And from the evil of the envious when he envies."

Explanatory Notes for Surah 113

The families of Quraysh whose members had accepted Islam, were burning with rage from within against the Prophet Muhammad (SAAS). They were holding secret consultations to kill him quietly; magic and charms were being worked on him so as to cause his death or make him fall ill, or become mad; *shaytans* from among the men and jinn spread on every side so as to whisper one or another evil into the hearts of the people against him and against the Qur'an brought by him. There were many people who were burning with jealousy against him; they could not tolerate that a man from another family or clan should flourish and be prominent. Such may have been the conditions when *Surah Al-Falaq* and *An-Nas* were revealed. Collectively they are called *Al-Mu{c}awwadhatayn*.

The term *al-falaq* ('The dawn' or 'the rising dawn') is often used figuratively to describe 'the emergence of the truth after (a period of) uncertainty' (*Taj al-{c}Arus*): hence, the appellation 'Sustainer of the rising dawn' implies that Allah is the source of all cognition of truth, and that one's 'seeking refuge' with Him is synonymous with striving after truth.

Rabbu'l-falaq 'the Lord of the rising dawn', implies that seeking refuge with Him would mean: "I seek refuge with the Lord Who brings out the bright daylight from the darkness of night so that He may likewise bring well-being for me from all kinds of physical and psychic dangers."

"I seek refuge with Him from the evil of what He has created."

A few things in this sentence deserve consideration; that the creation of evil has not been attributed to Allah but the creation of creatures has been attributed to Allah and of evil to the creatures. That is, it has not been said: "I seek refuge from the evils that Allah has created" but that "I seek refuge from the evil of the things He has created." This shows that Allah has not created any creature for the sake of evil, but all His work is for the sake of good and a special purpose. However, from the qualities that He has created in the creatures to fulfil the purpose of their creation, sometimes evil appears from some kinds of creatures and in most cases with His refuge we can protect ourselves from every evil of every creature, whether we are aware of it or not. Moreover, this contains the prayer for refuge not only from the evils of the world but also from every evil of the Hereafter.

The word *sharr* (evil) is used for loss, injury, trouble and affliction as well as for the means which cause losses, injuries and afflictions; for example, hunger, disease, injury in accident or war, being burnt by fire, being stung or bitten by a scorpion or snake, being involved in the grief of children's death and similar other evils which are evils in the first sense, for they are by themselves troubles and afflictions.

Seeking refuge from evil contains two other meanings also: First, that man is praying to Allah to protect him from the evil that has already taken place; second, that man is praying to Allah to protect him from the evil that has not yet taken place.

The word *ghasiq* in the verse literally means dark and *waqab* means to enter or to overspread. Prayer has been taught to seek refuge in particular from the evil of the darkness of night, for most crimes and acts of wickedness are committed at night, harmful animals also come out at night.

The word *{c}uqad* (in *naffathat fil-{c}uqad*) means a knot that is tied on a string or piece of thread. *Nafatha* means 'he blew'. Blowing upon knots, according to most, rather all, commentators implies magic, for the magicians usually tie knots on a string or thread and blow upon them as they do so. Thus, the *ayah* can be paraphrased: "I seek refuge with the Lord of rising dawn from the evil of magicians, (whether male or female)." This meaning is also supported by the traditions which show that when magic was worked on the Prophet Muhammad (SAAS), Jibril (AS) had come and taught him to recite the *Mu'awwidhatayn* (*Surah* 113 and 114), and in the *Mu'awwidhatayn* this is the only sentence which relates directly to magic.

About magic one should know that in it since help is sought of the shaytans and evil spirits or stars to influence the other person evilly, it has been called *kufr* (unbelief) in the Qur'an: *"Sulayman was not involved in kufr but the shaytans who taught magic to the people."* (Qur'an *Al-Baqarah*: 102).

Hasad means that a person should feel unhappy at the better fortune, superiority or good quality that Allah has granted to another, and wishes that it should be taken away from the other person and given to him, or at least the other should be deprived of it. However, *hasad* does not mean that a person should wish that he too should be blessed with the bounty that the other one has been blessed with. Here, Allah's refuge has been sought from the evil of the ennvious one when he feels envious, and takes a practical step with word or deed to satisfy his heart. For until he takes a practical step, his being unhappy may by itself be bad but it is not an evil for the other person so that he may seek refuge from it. When such an evil appears from an envious person the best thing would be to seek Allah's refuge from it.

Surah 114 An-Nas

Makki or Madani Surah *6 Ayat*

بِسْمِ اللهِ الرَّحْمٰنِ الرَّحِيْمِ

Surah 114 An-Nas

Meaning	Words	Meaning	Words
(of) the sneaking (Devil)[1] (intensive noun *mdfi.*)	الْخَنَّاسِ	Say: I seek refuge (*amr* II. msc. sing., *mudari*ᶜ I. sing.)	قُلْ أَعُوذُ
The one (rel. pro. msc. sing.)	الَّذِيْ	With the Lord of (prep., noun gen. *mdf.*)	بِرَبِّ
Who whispers[1], makes evil suggestions (*mudari*ᶜ III. msc. sing. quad. vrb. root)	يُوَسْوِسُ	The people, mankind (def. coll. noun *mdfi.*)	النَّاسِ
In the breasts of (prep., noun br. pl. *mdf.*)	فِيْ صُدُوْرِ	The King of mankind (noun sing. gen. *mdf.*, def. coll. noun *mdfi.*)	مَلِكِ النَّاسِ
The people, mankind (def. coll. noun *mdfi.*)	النَّاسِ	The God, Deity of mankind (noun sing. gen. *mdf.*, def. coll. noun *mdfi.*)	إِلٰهِ النَّاسِ
Of[2] (prep.)	مِنَ	From (all) evil (prep., noun gen. *mdf.*)	مِنْ شَرِّ
The Jinn (def. noun gen.)	الْجِنَّةِ	(of) Whispering, evil suggestions (def. vrb. n. quad. vrb. root *mdfi.*)	الْوَسْوَاسِ
And (of) the people, mankind (ptcl., def. coll. noun gen.)	وَالنَّاسِ		

[1] The verb خَنَسَ means 'he remained behind', 'he receded'. It is used epithetically for the Devil as he hides when Allah is mentioned.

[2] مِنْ 'of' here is in explanation that 'the slinking whisperer' is of Jinn and men.

Root Words of Surah 114

مَلِك — King, مَلَكَ * he possessed.

إِلٰه — Deity, a god, أَلَهَ * he adored.

الْوَسْوَاس — The whisperer, Shaytan, وَسْوَسَ * he made evil suggestions, whispered evil (quad. vrb.).

الْخَنَّاس — The Shaytan (because he hides himself at the name of Allah), خَنَسَ * he remained behind, hid away.

Translation of Surah 114 An-Nas (Mankind)

(1.) Say, "I seek refuge in the Lord of mankind,

(2.) The Master of mankind,

(3.) The god of mankind,

(4.) From the evil of the slinking whisperer,

(5.) The one who whispers in the breasts of men,

(6.) Of either jinn or mankind."

Explanatory Notes for Surah 114

In this *surah*, the particular mention of mankind brings man closer to Allah's protection and care. Allah (SWT), instructs His Messenger (SAAS) and his followers to recognise His attributes and seek His protection against this sneaking evil which locates itself within their hearts. For they cannot rid themselves of such an evil which creeps into their hearts surreptitiously and imperceptibly without the aid of Allah, the Lord, the Sovereign, the Deity.

The nature of this evil-importing medium is identified in the text first as "slinking whisperer" or "elusive tempter". Its function in outlines is to "whisper in the breasts of men". Then its origin is specified as "from among jinn and mankind".

The style adopted here is quite significant because it draws one's attention fully to the identity of this sneaking whisperer after describing its nature in order to show the process by which that evil is insinuated, so that one is alerted to watch and confront it. For when one is given the full picture one knows that this sneaking whisperer operates secretly. One also realises that it is jinn as well as human, for human beings are not exceptions to spreading evil while unseen.

We do not know how the jinn perform this whispering, but we certainly find its repercussions in the behaviour of individuals as well as in human life generally. We know for sure that the battle between Adam (man) and Iblis (Shaytan, a Jinn) is a very old one. War between the two was declared by Shaytan out of the evil inherent in him, his conceit and his envy and resentment of man. He was given Divine permission to carry out this battle for some purpose which Allah alone comprehends. But, significantly, man has not been left alone, dispossessed of the necessary means of protection. He has been provided with the power of faith – "*Iman*", (that is, conscious belief in and knowledge of Allah and His attributes through conviction and sincere devotion). Meditation and seeking refuge in Allah are among the most effective weapons. When man neglects these means of security and defence, he indeed has only himself to blame.

Ibn ʿAbbas (RA), related that the Messenger of Allah (ﷺ), had said, "Shaytan besieges the individual's heart; he retreats whenever one conscientiously remembers Allah, but insinuates his evil whenever one is unthoughtful of Him."

As for humans we know a great deal of their curious ways of whispering and prompting, and some types like the following are more devilish than the Devil:

A bad companion who injects evil into his comrade's heart and mind while he is unaware, as he is thought to be trustworthy; the ruler's counsellor or advisor who "whispers" to him and turns him into a destructive tyrant; an unscrupulous slanderer who fabricates and decorates tales and makes them sound factual and convincing; a hustler of immoral business and dealings who tries to get through to people by exploiting their sensual, unhealthy desires; a hundred other "whisperers" who lay various traps inconspicuously utilising people's different weak points which they detect and look for. Remembrance of Allah (SWT) is the only protection against these evil powers.

دُعائے ماثورہ

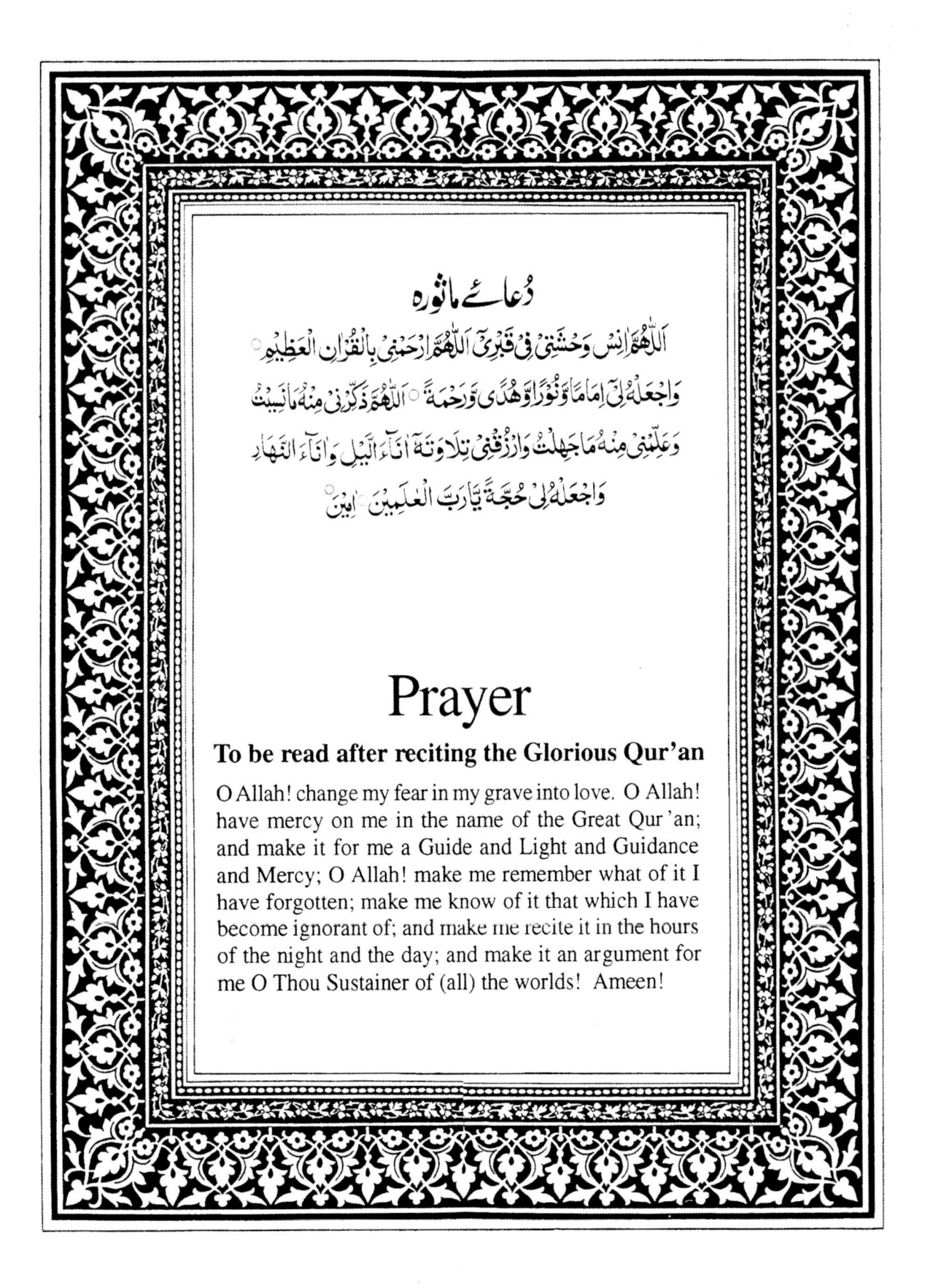

اَللّٰهُمَّ اٰنِسْ وَحْشَتِیْ فِیْ قَبْرِیْ ۞ اَللّٰهُمَّ ارْحَمْنِیْ بِالْقُرْاٰنِ الْعَظِیْمِ ۞ وَاجْعَلْهُ لِیْ اِمَامًا وَّنُوْرًا وَّهُدًی وَّرَحْمَةً ۞ اَللّٰهُمَّ ذَکِّرْنِیْ مِنْهُ مَا نَسِیْتُ وَعَلِّمْنِیْ مِنْهُ مَا جَهِلْتُ وَارْزُقْنِیْ تِلَاوَتَهٗ اٰنَاءَ الَّیْلِ وَاٰنَاءَ النَّهَارِ وَاجْعَلْهُ لِیْ حُجَّةً یَّا رَبَّ الْعٰلَمِیْنَ ۞ اٰمِیْن

Prayer

To be read after reciting the Glorious Qur'an

O Allah! change my fear in my grave into love. O Allah! have mercy on me in the name of the Great Qur'an; and make it for me a Guide and Light and Guidance and Mercy; O Allah! make me remember what of it I have forgotten; make me know of it that which I have become ignorant of; and make me recite it in the hours of the night and the day; and make it an argument for me O Thou Sustainer of (all) the worlds! Ameen!

AL-AZHAR
ISLAMIC RESEARCH ACADEMY
GENERAL DEPARTMENT
For Research, Writting & Translation

بسم الله الرحمن الرحيم

الأزهر
مجمع البحوث الإسلامية
الإدارة العامة
للبحوث والتأليف والترجمة

March 3rd, 1993

Ta-Ha Publishers Ltd.,

Assalamu Alaykum Wa Rahmatullah

BOOK REVIEW

THE QUR'AN Translation & Study (Juz'a 1, 2 &3)
by Dr. Jamal-un-Nisa bint Rafai

With reference to the letter submitted regarding this department's review of the book titled:

THE QUR'AN Translation & Study (Juz'a 1,2 & 3)
by Dr. Jamal-un-Nisa bint Rafai

We convey to you that the above mentioned book has been reviewed as requested. We have the pleasure to declare that this department has no objection as to put the book in circulation or introduced for republication at your expenses. It has been confirmed that this book is free from anything that contradicts the teachings of Islam.

(FATHALLA YASIN GAZAR)
DIRECTOR GENERAL
GENERAL DEPARTMENT OF RESEARCH WRITING
AND TRANSLATION, AL-AZHAR, CAIRO.